SIMPSON

IMPRINT IN HUMANITIES

The humanities endowment
by Sharon Hanley Simpson and
Barclay Simpson honors
MURIEL CARTER HANLEY
whose intellect and sensitivity
have enriched the many lives
that she has touched.

the Art of Eating

COOKBOOK

ESSENTIAL RECIPES

FROM THE

FIRST  25 YEARS

EDWARD BEHR

with JAMES MACGUIRE

 University of California Press   *Berkeley Los Angeles London*

The publisher gratefully acknowledges the generous support of the Simpson Humanities Endowment Fund of the University of California Press Foundation, which was established by a major gift from Barclay and Sharon Simpson.

University of California Press, one of the most distinguished university presses in the United States, enriches lives around the world by advancing scholarship in the humanities, social sciences, and natural sciences. Its activities are supported by the UC Press Foundation and by philanthropic contributions from individuals and institutions. For more information, visit www.ucpress.edu.

University of California Press
Berkeley and Los Angeles, California

University of California Press, Ltd.
London, England

Designer: Lia Tjandra
Illustrator: George Bates
Copyeditor: Clancy Drake
Indexer: Amy E. Novick
Compositor: BookMatters, Berkeley
Printer and binder: Sheridan Books, Inc.
Text: Scala Pro and Scala Sans Pro
Display: Benton Gothic

Library of Congress Cataloging-in-Publication Data

Behr, Edward, 1951–
    The art of eating cookbook : essential recipes from the first 25 years /
Edward Behr ; with James MacGuire.
        p.   cm.
    Includes index.
    ISBN 978-0-520-27029-9 (alk. paper)
    1. Cooking.   2. Cookbooks.   I. Title.
    TX724.B44   2011
    641.5—dc23   2011018973

Printed in the United States of America

20   19   18   17   16   15   14   13   12   11
10   9   8   7   6   5   4   3   2   1

The paper used in this publication meets the minimum requirements of ANSI/
NISO Z39.48–1992 (R 1997) (*Permanence of Paper*).

For Max and Zane

CONTENTS

SOUP

PASTA AND POLENTA

CHEESE, EGGS, AND SALADS

VEGETABLES

FISH, SEAFOOD, AND SNAILS

POULTRY AND RABBIT

MEAT

DESSERT

hese recipes, nearly all from the pages of the magazine, celebrate 25 years of *The Art of Eating*. As I began to collect them, I realized that I'd been working toward a cook's and eater's canon of dishes—a mere partial list so far and surely a permanent work-in-progress—with a good amount of wandering down side paths. To show what's here and suggest the point of view, all the recipes are listed in the table of contents. With few exceptions, they are traditional, ratified by generations of eaters. Often in my writing, I've focused on a traditional dish: tasting it at its place of origin, tracing it back through time, trying to understand the logic behind the place, the ingredients, and the method—getting at the fundamental taste.

Even when overlooked by fashion, the best traditional food remains particularly delicious. Great chefs, no matter how modern their cooking, look to tradition for strength and learning. Like many of them, I'm grounded in the cooking of France and Italy. Classical French cuisine is well known for its firm technical structure, and France, the largest country in western Europe, offers enormous geographic variety and a wealth of regional dishes. Italy, its disparate parts having been united in a single country only 150 years ago, is even more culturally diverse, and some of the food is perhaps even older. The few recipes here from other countries are also traditional and, I believe, linked in sensibility to the rest.

Not that a traditional dish can be reduced to a single definitive version. It's often pointed out that tradition is a moving target. "Traditional food?" I've been asked. "What period of time are you talking about?" To me what matters is that a dish came into being before life was dominated by machines, electricity, and rapid communication, before time was so much equated with money — that it came about when people lived closer to nature and found more of their daily pleasure in eating. I've tried to question each part of each recipe — ingredients, quantities, techniques — adding anything that might be missing, taking away what might be superfluous. And I haven't been opposed to putting in something completely fresh. More than capturing tradition, my aim is to provide something delicious to eat.

Besides, tastes change. It's almost impossible for food not to reflect its own time. Today we often favor reduced cooking times, and we tend to avoid obvious fat. (Despite a recent reaction in favor of it, few of us eat fat the way people once did.) We are more aware of and open to the foods of many cultures, and this subtly affects the ways we cook even the dishes we consider utterly fixed.

These recipes reflect the scope of the magazine, providing both common and unusual tastes, both easy and demanding preparations. There are recipes suited to a beginner and others for experienced cooks; a few call for uncommon ingredients, such as pigs' tongues or a large bed of scented roses. Who, I've been asked, is the audience for this collection? My answer is: anyone who loves food — loves the comfort of the familiar, the stimulus of variety, the freshness of the unexpected, the most delicious taste. Ease or difficulty in cooking are partly beside the point. You don't have to cook at all, I hope, to enjoy this book. Often the introductions to the recipes are longer than the instructions. This is a book for readers — for *eaters* as much as cooks. Eating, after all, is what the magazine is about.

In preparing the manuscript, I've revised all the text that originally made up each recipe, and sometimes I've re-explored a dish, cooking and thinking about it all over again (and typically making few changes in the end). The writing is mostly my own, though the recipes in the magazine are increasingly contributed by others. Some — including a number of those collected here — come from my friend James MacGuire, an accomplished chef and writer with a clear, probing mind, who is a living encyclopedia of classical French cooking and technique. We've been talking together for years about the details of cooking and eating. He's responsible for most of the recipes in the charcuterie chapter and a good handful of other items; a few things we wrote together.

Some of the dishes obviously express my taste for simplicity — for the most that can be achieved with the least means. Even in the more complicated recipes, the goal is a sort of inevitability that might be called "simplicity in effect." Modern Western cooking began to emerge in France in the 17th century as the cooks of the aristocracy gradually broke with the medieval style, using fewer ingredients, turning from spices to the milder flavors of native herbs, and placing a higher value on produce — sometimes even ending a meal with a plain piece of fruit. They wanted primary ingredients to taste clearly and deliciously of themselves, as chefs commonly still do. I especially appreciate dishes built on just two or a few highly successful complements. Yet for all that I praise simplicity, certain recipes I've included — for charcuterie in particular — are elaborate records of how things "ought" to be made. That's the point: whether through simplicity or extra effort, to show just how good food can taste at its very best.

THREE NOTES
TO THE COOK

Tasting | Apart from a few precise formulas, a recipe is an outline to be filled in by the cook. With experience (and often without), a good cook responds to the situation at hand, adding detail and maybe a point of view. It's important to taste as you go: first the raw materials, then usually more than once during cooking, and again, unless you'll spoil a perfect appearance, at the end. Just before serving, the flavor of a dish may need heightening, often with salt and just as often with a little acidity. A squeeze of lemon juice can make a big difference. Unlike wine or vinegar, a little lemon brightens food without readily marking it with its own taste.

Measuring | Specifying measurements for a US cookbook is frustrating, since the medieval units still dominate while the much easier metric system makes its painfully slow advance. I've tried to be friendly to users of both the US and metric systems. As much as possible, I've suppressed the old avoirdupois ounces, now that supermarkets commonly sell fresh meat and produce in decimal fractions of a pound. Apart from liquids, measuring by weight is more accurate than measuring by volume, and metric units express the ratios clearly, so it's easy to multiply for larger quantities. If you have a precise metric scale, by all means use the metric weights in this book. Beware that the US and metric amounts given here are not back-and-forth equivalents but separate sets, internally consistent and rounded off for easy measuring wherever precision isn't at issue. Precision counts especially in the charcuterie recipes, and with these, because there's a dearth of solid recipes in English, I've tried to meet the needs of both home and professional cooks. But professional exactitude can be off-putting to a home cook, who naturally prefers to add a whole egg, a whole shallot, and so forth, rather than a strictly measured quantity. Where that tension occurs, I ask for your patience.

Olive Oil | Fat, so essential to taste, should be very fresh, almost without exception (two come to mind: a little rancidity is part of the taste of rustic dry-cured hams; and it's often said that for an Alsatian kugelhopf the traditional earthenware mold, never washed, should convey a trace of the flavor of rancid butter). Olive oil, called for frequently in these recipes, should taste especially fresh — free of the least hint of rancidity. The category "extra virgin," well conceived by the International Olive Oil Council, is defined by the presence of good flavors and a level of rancidity so low as to be impossible to taste: less than 0.8 percent rancid fat. Forget anything you've heard about "acidity" in olive oil, unless the phrase was "free acidity," which is a scientific way to say "rancid fat." You can eliminate free acidity with chemicals — that's how refined oil is made — but extra virgin olive oil must be unrefined. You can tell the difference by its nongreasy texture — a lightness on the tongue. These days any producer who wants to make extra virgin oil knows how to do it, and the category is commonplace. But "extra virgin" describes the quality only at bottling, not on the day of purchase, weeks or months later. By then, most extra virgin olive oil has suffered from exposure to heat or light or has surrendered its best qualities to age. For any recipe to specify "extra virgin olive oil" is therefore useless. Instead, I call for "excellent, fresh-tasting" olive oil. When you first open a bottle, or if you haven't used it for some time, taste it. The more aromatic oil loses much of its best flavor in as little as two weeks after being opened.

Oils from different olives raised in different places taste different, depending especially on the variety of olive and the ripeness at harvest. Some oils are sweeter and riper; others have more fresh-fruit flavor and tannic bitterness. Some oils are lighter in body; others are more heavy. But as a rule olive oil should taste clean and fresh. An exception is oil used for frying, especially of meats, where somewhat lesser-quality oil will do, its small defects being hidden by the strong taste of browned meat. But where olive oil is served raw — in salad, for instance, or added to soup or pasta just before serving — the full deliciousness of excellent fresh oil will be obvious.

THREE BREADS AND FOUR THINGS THAT REQUIRE BREAD

SCHIACCIATA

Flat Hearth Bread

BREAD MAKES OTHER FOOD TASTE BETTER. Potatoes, rice, and other starches do the same, but not with the same flavors of fermentation or textural contrasts as bread. It enhances a salad, fresh cheese, or grilled meat as much as it does sauces, strong cheeses, or cured meats. You can eat a lot of very fresh bread, but older bread is good, too, as in the age-old use of a slice in a bowl of soup. A baguette, a grainy "country" loaf, sour rye — all have their place, according to what else is on the table. A meal can be anything you want; it can start and end where you like. It can be a single item, such as a big bowl of soup — a beginning and an ending in one — or it can run on in multiple courses. But, at least in the context of Western cooking, nothing is more important than bread. That so many restaurants in English-speaking countries treat bread as an appetizer is an utter misunderstanding or maybe a giving up in the face of customers who don't "get" bread. This and the two recipes that follow are for unfermented or mildly fermented breads — more ambitious bread baking, with all its complications of flour, leavenings, and ovens, fits better in its own book. But each of the breads here has its attractions of texture and flavor. The four other recipes are for items that especially require bread.

Schiacciata, which literally means "flattened" or "squashed," is a kind of focaccia. Even in places where the dominant bread was big and round, flatbreads were once almost universal too. Forming some of the bread dough into flat rounds was a way to test the oven's heat — in the oldest type of wood-fired oven, *schiacciate* go in first, when the temperature is highest. The interior of this Tuscan-style *schiacciata* makes a sweet contrast with the salty crust, because the dough itself contains no salt. But dough without salt ferments more quickly — often too quickly to gain real flavor. The best solution is probably a sourdough leavening, traditional for Tuscan bread (though rare today), but that requires special knowledge, not to say practice and devotion. And the simple commercial-yeast sponge below provides good flavor.

For easier stretching, water in a proportion of 75 percent of the flour by weight (the baker's way of measuring), as below, works well with American unbleached all-purpose white flour at about 11½ percent protein; softer flour, like that used in Italy, requires less water. The salt sprinkled on top should be fine, not coarse. You need at least a couple of *schiacciate* to feed six or eight hungry people, but a home oven will bake just one at a time, so inevitably the second ferments more than the first. Fortunately, the fast cooking in a hot oven overrides much of the difference, and in this bread a lot of flavor comes from the broad expanse of brown crust.

½ teaspoon (2 gr) instant yeast

3¾ cups (500 gr) unbleached all-purpose flour

1⅝ cups (375 ml) water at about 80° F (27° C)

excellent, fresh-tasting olive oil or melted lard

fine salt

coarse semolina

Mix the yeast with 1 cup (130 gr) of the flour and 1 cup (240 ml) of the water. Cover and leave overnight in a cool spot, cooler than 70° F (21° C). Then combine this sponge with the rest of the flour and water to make a soft dough, mixing it only enough to incorporate the flour fully. Put the dough in a bowl, cover it, and place it in a warm spot, 75° to 80° F (24° to 27° C), to rise for 2 hours. Then lift up one side of the dough and fold it onto the other, pressing lightly so the two adhere, cover again, and leave to rise for another hour.

Half an hour into the second rise, set an oven rack in the top half of the oven and line it with a baking stone or quarry tiles. Heat the oven to 500° F (260° C). When the rising time is up, turn the dough out of its bowl and cut it in half with a dull edge. Flatten each half with an open hand — rolling would press out too many bubbles — and then stretch each half to an even round about 12 inches (30 cm) wide. Onto each pour a spiraling thread of oil or melted lard or brush the top minimally with oil or lard. More generously, sprinkle each with salt. Let the rounds rise for 10 minutes. Sprinkle a peel or open-sided baking sheet lightly with semolina and place one round on it. With your fingers, press a dozen or more dimples into the top of the dough, and slip the loaf quickly and confidently off the peel onto the stone or tiles. Remove when well browned, after about 15 minutes, then promptly bake the other round. Serve warm. *Makes 2 loaves.*

CORN BREAD

MARY RANDOLPH PUBLISHED THIS RECIPE in her fine cookbook *The Virginia Housewife,* in 1824, before chemical baking powders transformed American baking. She counted on eggs for loft, or, as here, yeast. Industrial cornmeal has very little flavor, and most of the interest in corn bread comes from using the best cornmeal you can find. The more freshly ground, the better the flavor; the highest quality tends to come from old milling varieties of corn that are stone-ground. In the South, the color of cornmeal is usually white and, as a rule, white and yellow cornmeals have distinct flavors, the first often being earthier and the second richer. Finely ground meal rises higher. Mary Randolph made muffins with her batter; I bake it in a skillet.

2 cups (300 gr) cornmeal

¼ cup (50 gr) unsalted butter plus more for the pan

scant ¾ teaspoon salt

½ teaspoon (2 gr) instant yeast

2 large eggs

1 cup (240 ml) warm milk

Place the cornmeal in a large bowl and rub the butter into it using your fingers, until the combination loses and then regains the consistency of meal. Add the salt, yeast, and eggs. Stir in enough of the warm milk to make a medium-thick batter (finer meal will absorb more liquid). Cover the bowl and set it in a warm spot, at least 80° (27° C), for about 2 hours, during which time, lacking the gluten of wheat, the batter will rise only slightly, increasing by perhaps one-eighth.

Heat the oven to 450° F (230° C). Butter a black cast-iron frying pan about 10 inches (25 cm) wide and set it, empty, in the oven to heat to almost smoking hot. Remove it, immediately fill it with the batter, and return it to the oven to bake until the corn bread is set, 12 to 15 minutes. Serve promptly. *Serves 4.*

FARINATA

Chickpea Pancake

ONCE A COMMON STREET FOOD, *FARINATA* IS A VAST chickpea pancake, soft and floppy, baked in special heavy copper pans about a yard wide; you eat pieces with your fingers. *Farinata* is mainly Ligurian, but it's made on a long stretch of the Mediterranean coast from Nice, where the name is *socca*, through Liguria, where in dialect it's called *fainâ*, into neighboring Tuscany, where it's *cecina*. You can bake a very good *farinata* in a home oven using a smaller pan, although the transformation of batter to bread is less remarkable than it is in the traditional wood-fired oven, whose physics produce powerful heat. It's important that the chickpea flour taste nutty, and strongly of chickpeas. At some natural food stores, it tastes like green peas; better-quality chickpea flour is sold at some Italian and Indian food shops. Different *farinata* recipes call for different proportions of chickpea flour to water — for different tastes, thicknesses, or ovens. A very hot masonry oven requires a thin batter; thicker batters are for home ovens. Before cooking, you can add some chopped fresh rosemary or thyme, or green onions chopped at the last minute (if they wait half an hour, you'll taste the difference).

2 cups (500 ml) cold water

2¾ cups (300 gr) chickpea flour

½ teaspoon salt

excellent, fresh-tasting olive oil

Whisk together the water, flour, and salt, and let the combination rest for several hours while the flour absorbs the water. Heat the oven to 500° F (260° C). Skim any froth from the batter, which will remain watery. Oil a 12-inch (30-cm) diameter pizza pan with a rim, one heavy enough that it won't easily warp. Pour in 2 tablespoons of oil and enough stirred-up batter to cover the surface less than ¼ inch (6 mm) deep. Stir to partially mix in the oil (if the batter waits before baking, stir again). Bake until golden and dark brown in spots, about 15 minutes. If necessary, finish under a broiler. Repeat with the remaining batter — oiling the pan, stirring the batter, and baking. Eat the *farinata* as soon as it is no longer burning hot. *Makes 2.*

CAPERS IN OLIVE OIL

CAPERS ARE FLOWER BUDS, and those preserved in dry salt have the strongest, clearest floral taste; they're far better than capers in vinegar, which taste mainly of vinegar. (For certain purposes, the vinegar's piquancy is essential and you can't substitute the ones in salt.) Some freshness is important, because capers in salt lose their floral flavor gradually during the year before the next harvest. If the salt surrounding them is yellowish, that's a sign of age. Capers grow wild all around the Mediterranean, but they're especially appreciated in Sicily, where they have countless uses. Most often, they're combined with garlic and cured anchovies. They go equally well with tomatoes, green olives, celery, and herbs, as in the sweet-and-sour eggplant dish Caponata (page 16). They go into pasta sauces and accompany all kinds of meat and fish (see Pesce Spada alla Stemperata, page 159). Some of the best capers come from the growers' co-operative on the Sicilian island of Pantelleria, between Sicily and Tunisia.

The floral taste of capers is underlined by the very best red-wine vinegar, such as you might make at home from the bottle ends of very good wine; that vinegar is also floral in its own way. And olive oil soothes the salt and acidity of both capers and vinegar. Modern oil, made from olives picked earlier and treated more carefully than in the past, stresses fresh-fruit flavor and can recall cherry or vanilla. It goes very well with the vinegar and capers in salt. This simple recipe was told to me by Ebe Veronesi of the Veronesi family oil mill in Lazise sul Garda in northern Italy. The oil from around Lake Garda, on the cool northern fringe of the olive's range, is unusually delicate in flavor and texture, but strong olive oil, such as Tuscan, is also good with capers.

capers in salt

red-wine vinegar

excellent, fresh-tasting olive oil

Rinse the salt thoroughly from the capers and drain them well. Place them in a jar or small bowl, pour vinegar over them to cover, soak for 1 hour, and drain well. Pour olive oil over the capers to cover. To serve, spoon capers onto a piece or slice of bread and fold it around them so they won't roll off.

ANCHOYADE

Anchovy Spread

THIS VARIABLE PROVENÇAL MIXTURE for toasted or grilled slices of bread differs from the Piedmontese *bagna cauda* used for dipping raw vegetables — a sauce now common in Provence — mainly in being thicker and uncooked. Anchoyade can be made thicker still with many more anchovies, and sometimes it includes a little vinegar. I like parsley, which is often omitted, and I prefer the texture that comes from reducing the parsley in a mortar. If you don't have one, a rougher-textured paste can be made by mashing the garlic and anchovies with finely chopped parsley using just the back of a fork. There's no way to measure parsley accurately, and anyway flat-leaf varieties taste stronger — and even beyond that, intensity varies. Here, fortunately, with the other strong flavors, the exact amount of parsley doesn't matter.

4 cloves garlic

4 or more salted anchovies, the filets cleaned of salt, stripped from the bones, and rinsed

2 large handfuls chopped parsley

1 cup excellent, fresh-tasting olive oil

black pepper

Mash the garlic to a paste in a mortar; add and mash the anchovy filets, then the parsley. Mix in the oil. Grind pepper from a mill. Spread the paste on toasted or grilled bread while it is still hot, and eat immediately. *Makes about 1 cup.*

TAPENADE

Olive Spread

THE WORLD HAS SEEN PLENTY OF TAPENADE, but maybe it hasn't been said often enough that *tapeno* in Provençal means "caper," and that the texture of tapenade should be smooth, whether from a mortar or food processor (the earliest recipe we have passes the paste through a sieve). I once thought tapenade—*tapenado* in Provençal—must be an ancient food, but J.-B. Reboul in *La Cuisinière provençale*, which was published in 1899 and is the source of the first recipe, says tapenade was created by the chef Meynier at the Maison Dorée in Marseille. Reboul calls for 200 grams of olive pulp, 100 grams of anchovy filets, 100 grams of tuna, a spoonful of English mustard, and 200 grams of capers, then 200 milliliters of olive oil, a pinch of spices, "not a little pepper," and "one or two little glasses of Cognac"! Richard Olney, in *Lulu's Provençal Table,* his wonderfully collaborative 1994 cookbook about Lulu Peyraud's cooking at home at Domaine Tempier in Bandol, wrote that her tapenade "is the simplest (no tuna, no lemon, no brandy, no mustard) I know—and the best." Which didn't prevent him from giving his own somewhat different recipe in another book. Recipes abound. Mine is influenced by one from the Provençal-speaking chef Guy Gedda. I've made the garlic optional, because it isn't automatic and because raw garlic may appear repetitively elsewhere in a meal. In Provence, capers have a slightly peppery taste and are pickled, but I prefer the ones in salt, even in tapenade, because of their floral taste. Tapenade goes well with many things, including roast lamb or pork and grilled fish (served hot or cold), but the prime use is to coat bread or toast.

2 cloves garlic, *optional*

salt

1½ cups (200 gr) black olives, not wrinkled and intense, and preferably from Provence, pitted

⅔ cup (100 gr) pickled capers or ¾ cup (75 gr) capers in salt, drained if pickled or rinsed if in salt

a dozen salted anchovies, the filets cleaned of salt, stripped from the bones, and rinsed

black pepper

about ½ cup (125 ml) excellent, fresh-tasting olive oil

In a mortar, add the salt and, if you use it, the garlic, and pound it smooth. Add the olives, capers, and anchovies, and reduce them to a soft paste. Last, grind in some pepper and incorporate the olive oil a spoonful at a time. *Or in a food processor,* combine everything but the oil, and reduce it to a paste, pausing several times to scrape down the sides of the bowl. Pour the oil in slowly, pulsing and scraping down as needed to ensure the paste is smooth. Tapenade keeps well in a glass jar in the refrigerator for 2 weeks or more. *Makes about 1½ cups (400 ml).*

CAPONATA

Sweet-and-Sour Eggplant

THIS SICILIAN ACCOMPANIMENT TO BREAD is a way to preserve eggplants. Its elaborate taste recalls the Arab influence on the island's cooking, although there's no clear evidence of where the word or the dish came from. Caponata exists in diverse forms; the kind below sometimes contains unsweetened cocoa powder.

2 to 3 pounds (1 to 1.25 kg) eggplant

2 tablespoons salt

2 celery heads

excellent, fresh-tasting olive oil

2 onions, coarsely chopped

2 ripe red tomatoes, peeled and chopped

3 tablespoons capers preserved in salt, rinsed

1 cup (125 gr) pitted green olives

½ cup (125 ml) good wine vinegar

1½ tablespoons sugar

leaves from a branch of fresh basil, torn or chopped

blanched, slivered, freshly toasted almonds for serving

Slice the unpeeled eggplant into 1-inch cubes, mix with the salt, and leave to drain for about 1 hour in a colander. Meanwhile, remove the outer stalks from the celery heads and trim the hearts to about 5 inches, or 12 cm, then slice them into 1-inch, or 2- to 3-cm, pieces. (Reserve the outer stalks for another use.) Rinse and dry the eggplant and fry it in olive oil, stirring and turning until it is cooked through. Drain on paper towels. Fry the onions in the same pan until they begin to color. Add the tomatoes and sliced celery hearts, and cook together for 10 minutes, until they begin to soften. Add the capers, olives, vinegar, sugar, and basil, and simmer gently for another 10 minutes. Taste for salt. Refrigerate overnight, before serving cool or tepid and sprinkled with almonds. Sealed in a jar, this caponata keeps well for a week or more in the refrigerator. *Makes about 5 cups (a little more than 1 liter) enough for 6 to 8 people.*

CHARCUTERIE

RILLETTES DE TOURS

Salted and Stirred Pork

THIS CHAPTER COVERS MOST OF THE BASIC KINDS OF COOKED CHARCUTERIE, omitting *boudins blancs* and *noirs* but extending even to a traditional use of saltpeter in *cervelas lyonnais* and in a brine for the components of headcheese. Although the charcuterie recipes call for a few rare ingredients and were written partly with a professional in mind, they are fully doable at home. The rillettes are simple (the *rillons* even simpler).

Like most of the preparations in this chapter, this recipe for *rillettes de Tours* comes from my friend James MacGuire, a highly accomplished chef, who says, "The notion that charcutiers use rillettes to rescue the bits of meat that stubbornly cling to pork bones was dispelled for me years ago when I saw the chef Charles Barrier, at his restaurant in Tours, put half a pig into an enormous pot and set it on the stove to simmer." Barrier had learned the process at age thirteen from a charcutier whose nickname for rillettes was *confiture de cochon* — "pig jam" — and not just because rillettes are spread on bread but also because, in the old days, after the long cooking in fat they were put up for later use, like the confits of southwest France.

Essentially, James explains, there are two types of pork rillettes, those of Tours and those of Le Mans. The latter are cooked very slowly for a long time, which leads to a pale color and a fine texture. The Tours version is cooked more quickly, which tends to give slight browning and leave a coarser texture. Using half the pig ensures the proper texture: during the last stage of cooking, as the rillettes are being stirred, the paler, finer-textured muscles are reduced to a paste that binds the chunks and filaments of the darker, more fibrous cuts.

The underlying proportions, whether you start with half a pig or not, are two-thirds lean to one-third fat. Use a cut from the shoulder that combines different colors and textures of lean. A real butcher shop with a friendly butcher is a big help; ask for the fat trimmed from the piece you're buying as well as additional fat trimmings to make up the needed weight. You don't need the exact ratio, as long as there are 13 grams of salt per kilo of meat and fat, exclusive of bone (that's just under 1 teaspoon per pound, or 1.3 percent salt). The bones give more flavor, although they can be hard to come by, so here James calls for spareribs (reckoning, when calculating salt, that they contain 50 percent bone). If you have any extra pork bones, use those, too.

The method is simple. The fat, cut into small pieces, goes into the bottom of the pot, the bones are placed on that, and the lean meat, in large pieces, is placed on the bones. This keeps the lean from burning on the bottom if the fire gets too hot. The whole is simmered for roughly three hours, assuming a tender young pig; an older one might take five or even six hours. Toward the end, a bit of attention is necessary. The meat must be cooked until it is tender and no longer stringy, yet not so long as to become textureless pulp, and the slight browning on the bottom of the pot must not turn dark and bitter (careful attention and low-enough heat will keep it from doing that).

The traditional, palate-cleansing accompaniments to these rillettes are cornichons and a glass of *sec* or *demi-sec* Vouvray, but you can also drink a drier, more everyday wine, such as a puckery Chenin from a lesser appellation. (The wine and pickles don't go together, of course — sip the wine after the rillettes and not the cornichons . . .)

---

1 pound (500 gr) pork fat from outer trimmings

roughly ¾ pound (300 to 400 gr) spareribs in 1 or 2 pieces, and any extra pork bones you may have

2 pounds (1 kg) lean pork shoulder with varied colors and textures of flesh

¼ cup (50 ml) water

1 tablespoon (22 gr) salt

Cut the fat into roughly ½-inch (1-cm) dice, and put the pieces in the bottom of a somewhat large pot with a lid. Place the spareribs and any other pork bones on the fat. Cut the lean pork into roughly 2½-inch (6-cm) squares, and place those on top. Pour in the water.

Cover the pot, bring the contents to a boil, and then lower the heat to maintain a fairly strong simmer. As the cooking continues, with the pot still covered, check at intervals to be sure that nothing has begun to stick and that there is some watery liquid in the bottom. Add a bit of water if necessary.

After about 2 hours, start to check for doneness: cut off a piece of dark lean meat, and a piece of light, place both on a plate, and see whether they will crush with a fork — the light muscles will be done first. (The exception among dark muscles, if you start with half a pig, is the tenderloin, which cooks about as fast as the light.) Toward the end of cooking, usually around 3 hours, confirm the doneness by chewing a small piece of just the dark meat. It is ready when it is yieldingly tender but doesn't promptly turn to mush.

Carefully remove the spareribs to a plate, and if they've left any small bones behind, discard them. When the ribs are cool enough, scrape off their meat but not gristle and add that meat back to the pot.

Now the active phase begins. Keep the lid off, add the salt, and turn the heat to lowish medium. Tip the pot once in a while so you can see the bottom. The goal is to evaporate excess moisture and then with the remaining juices to form a rich brown glaze on the bottom of the pot. Stir regularly to prevent sticking and, if necessary, lower the heat. Once the glaze has formed and the fat is almost transparent (if it's cloudy, there's too much water left), begin stirring with a wooden spatula or spoon, reaching down to the bottom of the pot. As you do, the meat will break into small pieces and fibers, and the remaining moisture will dissolve most of the bottom glaze, providing flavor and color. Mash stubborn pieces of meat as necessary to break them up. There will come a moment when the binding effect of the fine-textured meats will bring the whole together in a mass, with just a little melted fat at the bottom of the pot. The rillettes are ready.

While they are still extremely hot, transfer them with a spoon to immaculate crocks, individual ramekins, or other ceramic or glass containers, regularly stirring the mixture still in the pot to reincorporate melted fat. Level the rillettes in each container with the back of a spoon, and immediately press plastic wrap directly onto the hot surface. Cool and refrigerate.

The rillettes keep well this way for about 5 days. To keep them longer than that — say for up to 1 month, refrigerated, paint the chilled surface with a very thin layer of burning-hot lard (not included in the ingredients above) to seal the surface from air. When the layer of lard sets, paint again if needed to ensure the rillettes are completely sealed. Before you eat them, allow them to warm a little, so they are no longer deeply chilled. *Makes about 2½ pounds (1.2 kg), enough for perhaps 18 to 20 people.*

RILLAUDS D'ANJOU, OR RILLONS DE TOURAINE

Salted and Browned Pork Belly

THE *RILLAUDS* OF ANJOU, JUST LIKE THE *RILLONS* OF TOURAINE, are large cubes of pork belly, salted briefly and then slowly cooked by themselves until brown, which renders much of their fat. The taste isn't hammy but rather porky and meaty. *Rillauds* were once made saltier than they are now and were preserved in their fat, a form of confit. Originally, they were always cooked with the rind on, and even now it may be better to buy a piece of belly with the rind on (in that case it may also come with the bones) and then cut off the rind yourself, because sometimes a butcher cuts away too much fat along with the rind. The belly should be a thick piece well interleaved with both fat and lean. A fattier piece does give more depth of rendered fat and thus better browning, if you cook the *rillauds* in just their own fat, but putting in extra lard submerges them and ensures full, even browning. (Render the lard yourself, or buy it from a butcher shop that renders in-house.) Many French charcutiers help the browning along by adding Arôme Patrelle, a savory caramel coloring akin to Kitchen Bouquet, but you can easily achieve a deep color without that. The key is very slow cooking to achieve full browning and tenderness, but not cooking to the point that the layers of fat and lean come apart. *Rillauds* are an excellent appetizer with bread and either a dry Chenin Blanc or a light red, preferably from Anjou or Touraine.

3 pounds (1.5 kg) fresh (unsalted) pork belly

1½ tablespoons (20 gr) salt

black pepper

1 pound (500 gr) lard, *optional*

Dry the belly with paper towels and cut it into 2-inch (5-cm) cubes. Mix them thoroughly and evenly with the salt and a good amount of freshly ground pepper. Refrigerate the meat overnight or for up to 24 hours. Rinse and dry again. In a wide, heavy pan, such as cast iron, brown the cubes very slowly; on their own they will soon provide a depth of fat, or add the optional lard. Turn once or twice, as needed. Cook until tender — about 3 hours. Take the *rillauds* from the fat with a slotted spoon. Serve them hot, reheating if needed. *Makes about 16 pieces, depending on the thickness of the belly; one piece is a serving.*

MOUSSE DE FOIES

Duck or Chicken Liver Mousse

THE USUAL COMMERCIAL *MOUSSE DE FOIES*, like related preparations of *foie gras,* cuts corners and is a way to use bits of perhaps inferior liver. The luscious texture of the intact liver is lost and no other equally appealing one takes its place. A carefully made *mousse de foies,* in contrast, gains its own particular smooth, melting lusciousness. This recipe is based on one that James MacGuire's close friend the late chef Charles Barrier of Tours once found in an old book. Use very fresh livers, preferably ones that are more café-au-lait in color, called *foies blonds.* They contain more fat and give a more delicate taste. White pepper is purely for appearance; if you don't care, use black—it tastes better. To reduce the chance of overcooking, poach the mousse in a single large ceramic mold, such as a soufflé dish, although you can use individual ramekins (not too large because of the richness). Serve with thin slices of toasted "country" bread, still warm, for guests to spread the mousse on and make their own *tartines.* Barrier would accompany this with a rich but not too sweet Chenin Blanc from the Loire.

2 cups (500 ml) heavy cream

1 cup (200 gr) unsalted butter in 1-inch (2-cm) pieces, at cool room temperature

1 cup (200 gr) rendered duck fat, at cool room temperature

1 pound (500 gr) duck or chicken livers, trimmed of nervy bits before weighing

6 yolks from large eggs

3 tablespoons (50 ml) Cognac or Armagnac

continued

Heat the oven to 325° F (165° C). Choose a 4- to 5-cup (about 1-lt) mold that's 3 to 4 inches (8 to 10 cm) tall (the shape doesn't matter), so the mixture will be about 2 inches (5 cm) deep and the sides will rise another inch (2 to 3 cm) or so above that, allowing for a water bath of about the same height as the mixture. To serve as a bain-marie, choose an oven pan large enough to hold the mold, and boil enough water to fill it, to be ready when the time comes.

Boil the cream and keep it hot. Purée the butter and duck fat in a food processor. Then, with the machine running, add the livers 1 or 2 at a time, followed by the egg yolks 1 at a time. Stop and scrape down the sides of the bowl with a spatula. With the machine again run-

1 tablespoon (20 gr) salt

½ teaspoon (2 gr) freshly ground white pepper

ning, and taking care not to splatter and burn yourself, gradually pour in the hot cream.

Strain the mixture into a large bowl. Add the brandy, salt, and pepper, and whisk thoroughly to dissolve the salt. Pour into the mold, and place it in the oven pan. Place the pan on the oven rack and pour boiling water around the mold to come just a little higher than the mousse mixture inside. Cover the bain-marie with aluminum foil, and bake approximately 45 minutes to 1 hour to an interior temperature of about 165° F (72° to 75°C). The top of the mixture should be convex but without cracks; the former liquid should now be delicately resilient. (If the mousse is baked too long, the small amount of air in it will cause it to rise like a soufflé, with disastrous results.) Remove the mold from the oven.

Promptly cover the cooked mousse with plastic wrap, pressing it lightly onto the whole surface so as to eliminate air (this is simpler than the classic tactic of pouring aspic onto the cooled mousse). Cool, then refrigerate to chill completely before serving; the mousse will keep in this way for up to 4 days. To serve, scrape off and discard the mottled surface from the amount to be served, and with a tablespoon dipped in very hot water, form egg-shaped portions. The exposed surface of the remaining mousse will gradually turn gray; that part, too, is best scraped off just before serving. *Makes about 3 pounds (1.5 kg), enough to serve 20 as a first course.*

PÂTÉ DE CAMPAGNE

Country Pâté

THIS RECIPE FOR A *PÂTÉ DE CAMPAGNE* in the manner of the Chalosse area of the department of the Landes in southwest France comes from Jean-Claude Frentz and appears in his *Livre du compagnon charcutier-traiteur*. It's the simplest of country pâtés to make, because the meats are ground, mixed cold with the other ingredients, and baked immediately. For most country pâtés, the cubed meats are cured beforehand for 24 to 48 hours with nitrate or nitrite, salt, and sugar, and then above all the fats are poached and mixed into the other ingredients while still warm, giving the finished pâté a yielding, almost spreadable texture. This one, by contrast, is firm, suitable for eating with a knife and fork.

It's important to find pork jowls, because during cooking their fat becomes tender yet doesn't liquefy, which would diminish yield and, worse, lead to a dry pâté. A good butcher shop — try one of the new wave of shops that buy directly from farms and offer skilled cutting — can find you those jowls, as well as pork liver and shoulder, and will probably also weigh and grind them for you. If so, make the pâté in short order: ground meats go off quickly. (For more detail on grinding meat, see page 36.)

The shape of the pâté can be round, oval, or rectangular; the top can be fairly flat or generously mounded. Before baking, you can cover the top with caul, the lacy fat that surrounds a pig's stomach, which helps to protect the pâté and keep it moist. Alternatively, cover the top with thin slices of barding fat, making a solid layer, tucked in around the edges. A browned top is attractive, but a covering of aluminum foil during cooking reduces drying and slows the penetration of heat, making it less likely that the pâté will overcook. Once out of the oven, pâtés are often gently weighted to press out air bubbles in the mass, which would otherwise gradually turn gray. To press, cut a piece of heavy cardboard to fit inside the vessel on top of the foil and then add canned goods or other objects totaling about a pound (500 gr). If you make terrines often, you can cut a wooden board to fit inside your container and use it each time.

As the finished pâté chills in the refrigerator, the flavors compose themselves; the taste is better on the second or third day. Accompany slices of pâté with bread, of course, and with cornichons or *pruneaux à l'aigre-doux,* "sweet-and-sour prunes." To make those, combine ½ pound (250 gr) of pitted prunes, preferably from the famous growing area around Agen, with ⅔ cup (150 ml) of red wine, ½ cup (100 gr) of sugar, and ⅓ cup (70 ml) of red-wine vinegar; bring to a boil, cool, and refrigerate — they're best made a few days ahead.

½ cup (60 gr) finely chopped onion

1½ tablespoons (15 gr) lard or a mild-tasting oil (20 ml)

⅔ pound (300 gr) lean pork from the shoulder

⅞ pound (375 gr) fresh pork jowl without rind

¾ pound (335 gr) fresh pork liver, trimmed of the nervy bits

caul fat to cover the loaf, *optional*

1 large egg

1 teaspoon (7 gr) finely chopped fresh garlic

4 teaspoons (20 ml) Armagnac

1 tablespoon (20 gr) salt

1 teaspoon (2.5 gr) ground black pepper

Cook the onion gently in the fat, covered, without coloring, until translucent. Refrigerate until cold. Cut the lean pork, jowl, and liver into rough 1-inch (2- to 3-cm) cubes, spread them out on a baking sheet, and refrigerate until very cold, 1 hour or more. Meanwhile, if you are using caul fat, rinse it well in tepid water and leave it soaking.

Combine the onion and cubed pork in a bowl with the egg, garlic, and Armagnac; sprinkle with salt and pepper. Pass the meat just once through the coarse holes (¼ to 1/16 inch, or about 7 mm, in diameter) of a sharp meat grinder. Mix thoroughly with your hands and continue to blend for a few minutes, until the texture, although remaining loose, becomes sticky and slightly elastic. Put it into a 6- to 8-cup (1.5- to 1.75-lt) terrine, preferably ceramic or ovenproof glass — the shape doesn't matter as long as the container holds the right amount and is at least 3 inches (8 cm) deep. Pat the mixture firmly into place to eliminate air pockets.

If you use caul fat, squeeze it gently to eliminate the soaking water, and place it over the terrine with the excess hanging over the sides. Trim with scissors so as to leave an inch or two (3 to 5 cm) all around. Then carefully tuck that border down between the pâté mixture and the sides of the terrine until it is taut. Cover the top of the container with two layers of aluminum foil.

Bake at 300° F (150° C) for roughly 1 hour, taking the dish from the oven when a thermometer shows the center of the pâté has reached about 165° F (72° to 75°C) or when a metal skewer inserted for half a minute and then quickly placed on your bottom lip feels almost burning hot. Uncover and cool to room temperature, then cover with plastic wrap and refrigerate overnight. *Makes about 2 pounds (a little less than 1 kg), enough to serve perhaps 12 people.*

A BRINE FOR SMALL ITEMS

FIRST A WORD ABOUT THE CUT OF PORK called in France *échine*, which must be the least known cut of any pig—and yet the best for boneless chops, a roast, a braise, and certain charcuterie. Certainly, it's the only part of a supermarket pig with any real flavor and marbling. Known in the United States as the "rib end of the pork loin" or the "blade loin roast," it is the marbled, tender shoulder end of the loin and should include the first four or five ribs and none of the shoulder blade. Its flavor comes from fat and from being part of the exercised shoulder, although it remains tender. For those who only know smoked ham, a brined *échine*, with its pigginess, will be a revelation. Besides going into Fromage de Tête (page 31) or Jambon Persillé (page 34), it can be poached on its own and served with lentils or sauerkraut or even as a sort of cold boiled ham.

The French call the brining or dry-salting of small items *"la petite salaison."* You also hear *"demi-sel,"* which implies a milder cure than the dry, salty ones of old. *Petit salé* refers specifically to three cuts—two forms of sparerib plus the *quasi,* the small piece around the aitch bone (where the loin meets the ham)—cuts that charcutiers sell raw or cooked (either one is served cooked, usually with lentils). The following brine will also cure tongues for headcheese (next recipe) or a belly, which, once brined, can be hung to dry overnight and then smoked, if you're equipped for that. Brined hocks, feet, and even ears all have their uses. The thing to remember is that this is an immersion brine for pieces of meat no more than 3 inches (8 cm) thick. Professionals inject brine into larger pieces, especially hams, before immersing them, so the cure penetrates quickly. Prompt curing plays it safe microbiologically and ensures that the outer parts of a ham aren't too salty by the time the cure reaches the center.

This brine combines nitrate and nitrite, giving the complex flavors that result from the first plus the safety of the second. The amount of salt is moderate, so refrigeration and the freshest ingredients are a must. In the past, brines were stronger and were reused, with further additions of salt and saltpeter, and when a new brine was made, some of the previous was added as a "starter." But those tactics give a more aggressive salty taste and less control and consistency, and they're less safe. In contrast to some American recipes that call for large amounts of sugar, a matter of taste, this traditional French one doesn't, and it contains no spices—not that they're bad, but they cover the delicate flavors of the brined pork. Saltpeter, or potassium nitrate, is important to the flavor of certain cured meats. In the United States, during the 1970s health controversy over nitrates and nitrites (they produce nitrosamines, which can be harmful in food cooked to high temperatures), saltpeter was largely eliminated from brined products and replaced with sodium nitrite. The combined amount of added nitrate and nitrite is now limited to 200 parts per million in ham and 150 in bacon. The motivation may have had less to do with health and more with the fact that the nitrite cure is faster and arguably more surefire, because nitrite almost immediately fixes the meat's rosy color and ensures its safety. Around the same time the Americans began to convert to nitrite, the French did, too, but French artisans continued doing things the old way in large enough numbers that charcuterie books from the eighties include both the saltpeter method and the nitrite one, and they are clear that the former gives more complex flavor. It was already known that a lactic fermentation transforms the nitrate into nitrite, but the reasons for a difference in flavor remained speculative until early in the 21st century, when it was found that enzyme activity breaks down amino acids and forms compounds that in turn are the precursors of various flavor compounds. The European Union nonetheless banned saltpeter from cooked charcuterie, although the British and others fought for and won exceptions for a number of their traditional products. Surprisingly little reaction came from France, however, whose charcutiers seemed to feel that the extra time and trouble of the saltpeter cure weren't worth it.

It's important that the saltpeter be food grade. It appears that US pharmacies no longer sell it, and unfortunately we haven't found a mail-order source that sells both potassium nitrate and sodium nitrite, the latter of which is mixed with salt and sold as Prague Powder No. 1 or Insta-cure No. 1, and colored an eerie pink so as not to be confused with regular salt. Two sources are Post Apple Scientific in North East, Pennsylvania, and the Sausage Source in Hillsboro, New Hampshire. An alternative to a classic stoneware crock to hold the brine is a high-quality, food-grade acrylic "flour bucket" with lid from King Arthur Flour in Norwich, Vermont.

Metric measurements are off-putting to those unused to them, but they're easier and precision is so important here that it's essential to use them.

3 lt cold water

450 gr plain salt without additives

40 gr Prague Powder No. 1 or Instacure No. 1

30 gr sugar

9 gr saltpeter (potassium nitrate)

Mix all the ingredients, having carefully weighed the dry ones, in a nonreactive, nonmetal container, such as one made of stoneware or food-grade plastic, making sure the dry ingredients are completely dissolved. Cover and refrigerate.

Add completely cold pieces of meat, belly, tongues, and so on to the completely cold brine, and top them with a ceramic plate smaller than the diameter of the container, so they remain submerged. They must float in plenty of brine—too much meat will mean not enough cure to go around. Refrigerate.

The pieces will be fully brined in 5 to 7 days. (After that the meats will keep in the brine a little beyond a week, but this brine is not strong enough for real preservation.) Before cooking, soak them overnight in cold water in the refrigerator to reduce the amount of salt. Do not reuse the brine. *Makes a little more than 3 liters, enough to brine 2 kilos of meat.*

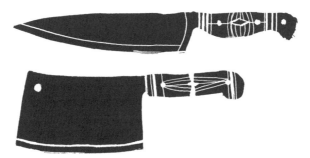

FROMAGE DE TÊTE

Headcheese

LIKE SO MUCH OTHER CHARCUTERIE, the varied forms of headcheese surely originate in the need to make quick use of spare parts at pig-slaughtering time. The basics for headcheese are that whole heads, extra skin, and feet are boiled up, and the highly gelatinous bouillon sets to a firm consistency that temporarily protects and preserves the contents. The cuts in question impart the rich porky flavors and textures that are essential to headcheese. James, whose recipe this is, notes that in France, certain kinds of headcheese, differing from region to region, are called *fromage de tête* while others are called *hure,* literally "head." In technical books, *hure* contains less *gelée* than *fromage de tête,* and a third preparation, *museau,* consists of compact layers of cooked pig's head with hardly any *gelée* at all, more or less the same as *tête roulée.* (Excellent with both *museau* and *tête roulée,* with their large quantity of rind, are a mustard vinaigrette with chopped parsley and paper-thin slices of onion, the latter two items, especially the onion, cut at the last minute.) The execution of any of these depends on who's making them. *Fromage de tête* is the specialty of Gilles Verot in Paris—he once won the Jean Carmet trophy for the best in France—who also makes *hure pistaché.* His *fromage* contains head, but his *hure* is filled with only tongues and garnished with pistachios. Even so, its soul lies in the long-simmered *jus* and *gelées* that form its base.

Your own version will depend on the ingredients you can find and the amount of *gelée* you incorporate. It's common anywhere in France to throw in extra tongues for meatier texture; otherwise, the headcheese is dominated by skin and other gelatinous components. Because a pig's head is not easy to find and you may not want to deal with one, the recipe that follows is based on *hure,* but half a pig's head could replace the feet or hock. The important thing, for genuine flavor and a toothsome but melting *gelée,* is to put in some combination of head, tongues, hocks, feet. Once the meats are done, home recipes call for simply cooling them in the cooking liquid in a mold. Charcutiers further cook the mixture inside the mold, as below, which improves keeping and makes the headcheese easier to slice. Brining the pork beforehand, as called for in the recipe, yields the best flavor and texture, but it's not absolutely essential.

5 whole fresh pork tongues (about 2 pounds or 1 kg before brining)

1 meaty pork hock (about 2 pounds or 1 kg before brining) or 3 pig's feet plus ¾ pound (350 gr) pork shoulder, preferably *échine*

more pork rinds, if available

about 3 quarts (3 lt) Brine for Small Items (page 28)

2 onions (about 300 gr), quartered

1 carrot (75 gr)

½ stalk celery (75 gr)

1 small bay leaf

1 or 2 branches fresh thyme

1 clove

a dozen parsley stems

1½ to 3 envelopes (10 to 20 gr) Knox powdered gelatin (each envelope contains 7 gr), as needed

¼ cup (50 ml) white wine

salt

1 shallot, finely chopped, making about 3 tablespoons (30 gr)

½ small clove garlic, finely chopped (for the record, if you multiply to make larger amounts, the metric measure is 1.3 gr)

black pepper

Put the tongues, hock, or other meats (the rind, too, if you already have it, as a way of keeping it) in the brine in the refrigerator for 5 to 7 days (see page 29). Before you start the headcheese, soak the brined meats overnight in cold water in the refrigerator to reduce the saltiness, and drain.

Choose a pot that will snugly fit the brined meats, onions, carrots, celery, bay leaf, thyme, clove, and parsley; and add them. Pour in cold water just to cover and put a plate on top to keep the meats submerged. Bring to a boil and immediately reduce the temperature to the gentlest simmer, so that the cooking liquid will not turn cloudy. Simmer 2½ to 3 hours, until the meats are tender but not mushy. Cool, cover, and refrigerate the full pot overnight.

The next day, first notice whether the *jus* has set firmly or delicately. Then put the pot over low heat to melt the cooking liquid. Take the pot off the burner and remove the meats. Trim the tongues of their rind and gristle, and retrieve the meat from the hock, setting aside the skin and discarding the bones. The yield should be around ¾ pound (325 gr) of tongue meat and ½ pound (225 gr) of hock or a similar total (about 1¼ pounds, 550 gr) from the feet and shoulder meat.

Strain the cooking liquid, and skim the grease from the surface. Measure out 2 cups (450 ml) of the liquid, and set the rest aside for another purpose (such as to make a sauce for a future pork roast). It's unlikely (unless you started with a gelatinous broth or used a high proportion of head and feet to water) that the refrigerated cooking liquid was quite firm enough, but if it was fairly well set, whisk just 10 grams of powdered gelatin into ½ cup (125 ml) of the warm cooking liquid, and add it back to the rest along with the wine. If the cooking liquid was barely set, 20 grams of gelatin might be necessary. After whisking in the gelatin, take the precaution of pouring a few drops of the liquid onto a plate and refrigerating it for 5 to 10 minutes to confirm that it sets firmly enough to peel off the plate easily and yet remains tender enough to melt on the tongue. Taste the *gelée* and add salt as needed, remembering that cold preparations call for higher seasoning.

To the meats, add the shallot, garlic, and a few grinds of black pepper, and mix. Pour the meats into a mold of appropriate size, approximately 1 liter—an ovenproof glass loaf pan has the advantage that you can see what's going on inside—and pour in the desired amount of *gelée* (⅔ cup or 150 ml will hold things together; twice that is typical). If you want, top the whole with a layer of cooked rind placed skin side up (you can choose to eat it or not), and then, to improve keeping and slicing, cover well with parchment and set a small nonreactive roasting pan on top to prevent the contents from floating above the sides of the loaf pan. Place the whole thing in a 350° F (175° C) oven for approximately 20 minutes, until a thermometer registers 160° F (70° C), or until, when you insert a skewer for half a minute and then quickly place it on your bottom lip, it feels almost burning hot. Cool without removing the parchment and roasting pan. Then remove roasting pan and refrigerate. *Serves perhaps 8 to 10.*

JAMBON PERSILLÉ

Parsleyed Ham

ORIGINALLY AN EASTER DISH, THIS IS BURGUNDY'S FAVORITE and best-known charcuterie item, and it's still popular at Easter, when it contains hard-cooked eggs. The green of parsley contrasts appealingly with the pink meat and white fat, all bound by a little jelly, which makes this a relative of headcheese. Unlike some charcuterie, *jambon persillé* is not especially salty or rich: it's served in thick slices because you can eat a lot of it. In North America, the difficulty in making it may be in finding a lightly cured ham that has been neither smoked nor cooked and has the skin on. (If you're feeling ambitious, you can make your own using the brine on page 28.) Should the ham you find be too salty to eat in a large portion, then soak it for a day, changing the water several times. Keys to success are avoiding overcooking or undercooking the meat and making sure the garlic flavor isn't pronounced. If the cooking liquid never boils after the meat is added, it will be transparent enough without having to be clarified with beaten egg white, which removes flavor along with suspended particles. The parsley adds an important balancing taste of freshness. Whenever you use parsley, chop it no more than half an hour in advance, because after it's cut it steadily loses flavor. In one of *jambon persillé*'s few variations, a little fresh tarragon is mixed with the parsley. Serve the ham with bread and Aligoté wine, from Burgundy's second white grape after Chardonnay. That's the advice of the charcutier Christian Sabatier of the Halles de Dijon, whose outstanding *jambon persillé* first inspired me to write about it.

BROTH

1 bottle (750 ml) white wine, such as Aligoté

3 cups (750 ml) water

fresh or dried thyme, savory, oregano

2 bay leaves

branches of fresh parsley

continued

In a large pot, bring all the ingredients for the broth to a boil. Then put in the meats with enough additional water to cover them by about an inch (2 or 3 cm). Bring the pot to a simmer, adjusting the heat so the liquid maintains a steady, very low bubble. Cook the ham until the meat is very tender and the skin and the feet have released their gelatin — about 3 hours. Remove the ham, discard the vegetables, and strain the liquid through a rinsed and wrung-out smooth kitchen towel.

1 dozen whole black peppercorns

2 whole cloves

2 cloves garlic

1 onion, halved

1 carrot, cut in sections

4½ pounds (2 kg) mild, brined ham (*demi-sel*) or pork shoulder or a combination, neither smoked nor sweet, or *échine* cured in the brine for small items (page 28)

2 pig's feet (in a pinch, use calf's feet)

salt

2 cloves garlic, very finely chopped

1 cup (45 gr) finely chopped parsley

½ cup (100 ml) white-wine vinegar

black pepper

Skim all the fat from the surface of this stock. Boil until it is reduced by half, and taste for salt, adding some if needed. Remove the skin from the ham, in one piece as much as possible, and reserve it. Separate the meat into pieces along its natural divisions using your fingers and a knife, leaving all the fat in place but discarding gristle and bones.

Combine the garlic and parsley with the vinegar and grind in black pepper. Pour a quarter of the stock into a gallon (4-lt) bowl, sprinkle generously with the parsley mixture, and arrange a layer of meat, placing the pieces all in the same direction so they can later be sliced neatly across the grain. Cover with more parsley, and continue to add layers, moistening each well with stock, and finish with more stock up to the level of the meat. Arrange the reserved skin on top faceup. Press lightly with a weighted plate, and chill overnight. Parsleyed ham is best eaten right away; it will keep no more than a week in the refrigerator. Don't unmold it, but cut it in the bowl across the grain into slices ¾ inch (2 cm) thick. *Serves 15 or more as a first course.*

SAUCISSES DE TOULOUSE

Fresh Sausages

WHEN YOU MAKE YOUR OWN FRESH SAUSAGE, you control the quality of the meat, the grind, the proportion of fat and all the rest, so you end up with a quality and, if you like, with kinds that you don't normally find in a store. Some of the most delicious sausages are straightforward and simple, with few added flavors, such as these *saucisses de Toulouse* and the *saucisses au vin blanc* for raw oysters that follow. This recipe for *Toulouse* is also the basic one for sausage meat, *chair à saucisses,* traditionally used by French housewives to stuff tomatoes or peppers or poultry, and with various additions it can serve as a model for other fresh sausages, including lamb or beef merguez.

The flavorful cut used for making sausage as a rule is the shoulder, which happens to be relatively inexpensive. The lower part is called the picnic in the United States, and the upper part is the butt or Boston butt and often sold boneless. For the necessary additional fat, fresh fatback is good but hard to find. Easiest is to call ahead and ask a good butcher to set aside the outer fat trimmed from pork loins and chops. Don't worry too much when it comes to the proportion of fat to lean. For larger quantities, the amounts of all the ingredients can be multiplied.

If you grind the meat yourself, be sure your device pushes it efficiently past a sharp, clean-cutting blade. If the cutting is poor and the meat takes too long to get through, then the fat warms and softens and the sinews separate from the lean in long, tough strings, ruining the texture of the cooked sausage. For small quantities, an alternative to a grinder is rhythmic chopping with a matched pair of 10- or 12-inch (25- or 30-cm) chef's knives—not modern light ones but old-fashioned Sabatiers. This doesn't require a heroic effort, doesn't warm the meat, and goes surprisingly quickly, and afterward the cleanup is much easier, aside from flung bits of meat.

Chilling is key. When the fat remains hard and intact during grinding and stuffing, lean will adhere to lean and the texture of the cooked sausage will be more homogeneous. If the materials warm, the fat will smear and coat the tiny pieces of lean, which, after cooking, leaves you with dry ball bearings of meat in grease. Before you grind and again before you stuff, the meat must be deeply chilled—just above freezing is ideal.

If you own a good sausage stuffer and are familiar with its use, we suggest putting the mixture into natural hog casings, which are traditional for most fresh sausages. The size, roughly 1½ inches (4 cm) in diameter, allows the meat to cook through without drying out. (Rinse the insides by slipping one end of the length of casing over the kitchen tap and letting the water run through it.) If you don't have a stuffer, however, don't run out and buy one, not only because of the expense, but also because some machines are immensely frustrating to use. They churn the mixture, warming the fat and ruining the texture; especially guilty are meat grinders with an interior screw and stuffing horn attachment and certain plunger-type stuffers. Instead of wrestling with one of those, make *crépinettes*. Wrap patties of the mixture in caul fat, called *crépine* in French. It's worth seeking that out rather than cooking bare patties, because the caul, like casings, both protects the surface and adds a hint of the earthy aroma of an andouillette. Like a stuffed sausage, *crépinettes* can be either grilled or sautéed.

If you sauté, once the sausages or *crépinettes* are out of the pan, you can pour off all but a thin layer of fat, add a good amount of chopped shallots, and cook them gently. You can then deglaze with white or red wine, assuming the pan is nonreactive—otherwise, deglaze with water—and pour the flavorful liquid over the sausages (you can skip the shallots if you don't have them). Besides the array of possible starch accompaniments (potatoes, polenta, lentils, various dried beans) and salad (not least the creamy heart of frisée chicory), a good and sometimes overlooked accompaniment is cooked greens. Because of the fat, sausage goes easily with many wines, white and red. And because of the fat and salt, the wine's primary job is to be refreshing, thus somewhat low in alcohol.

2 pounds (1 kg) boneless pork shoulder, about 80 percent lean and 20 percent fat, which means some additional fat, such as outer trimmings saved by a butcher

2¼ teaspoons (16 gr) salt

½ teaspoon (1.5 gr) finely ground black pepper

a few gratings (0.5 gr) nutmeg

½ clove (2 or 3 gr) garlic, very finely chopped, *optional*

at least 5 feet (1.5 meters) of hog casings, well rinsed outside and in, or several pieces of caul fat

If a butcher grinds the meat, make certain that it remains coarse—that it is passed through coarse holes, ¼ to 5/16 inch (about 7 mm) in diameter, only once. *If you grind the meat yourself,* trim any tough silverskin and connections, cut both lean and fat into rough 1-inch (2-cm) cubes, and mix them together. Spread them on a metal sheet or pan and chill them, uncovered, in the coldest part of the refrigerator for an hour and then put them in the freezer for a final 5 minutes. Pass the deeply chilled meat through the grinder once, using a grinding plate with ¼- to 5/16-inch (about 7 mm) holes. Spread the ground meat on a metal baking sheet or roasting pan and place it, uncovered, in the coldest part of the refrigerator for at least 30 minutes, followed by 5 minutes in the freezer.

Mix together the salt, pepper, and nutmeg, making sure there are no clumps, and, using your hands, combine these thoroughly with the deeply chilled meat. Sprinkle on the garlic and mix again. Continue to knead the meat for a few minutes until it gains body and becomes sticky. (If you are working a day ahead, refrigerate the meat overnight at this point.) If the mixture is still quite cold, go on to the next step. Otherwise, again spread the ground meat on the sheet or pan and chill it for another 30 minutes, followed by 5 minutes in the freezer.

If you are equipped and have experience, stuff the mixture into casings. *Otherwise,* make *crépinettes.* Rinse the caul fat well in room-temperature water, and then let it soak for about 10 minutes. In the meantime, divide the sausage mixture into 8 mounds; roll them into balls. Gently squeeze the excess soaking water from the caul fat and spread the pieces out on a work surface. Place the balls of sausage at intervals, so there is enough caul around each one to wrap it up. Use scissors to cut the caul, and pull it up around the ball so the edges overlap and form a sack (it's fine to patch). Gently flatten each *crépinette,* and turn it over so the seams are on the bottom.

The sausage meat, whether unstuffed, stuffed, or in *crépinettes,* will keep in the refrigerator for several days. If you've stuffed it into casings a day ahead, leave the sausages uncovered overnight in the refrigerator so the surface dries, which helps with both keeping and browning.

If you've twisted the sausages into links, cut them apart before cooking. Prick each sausage in 2 or 3 places so it won't burst open in cooking. Now and then, even pricked, a sausage, cooked too fast with too much heat, will burst. If just-stuffed sausages wait overnight, they tend to explode less, and their flavor deepens. (Probably they explode more if cooked immediately because the stuffing is then very firmly packed — nobody likes a limp sausage. Later the casing gradually stretches and the contents set.) Grill them over hot coals, place them under a broiler, or sauté them. If you sauté, you can reduce the chance of overcooking by finishing the sausages in a slow oven. They're done when they have shrunk at least slightly and, when pricked to the center with a knife or skewer, the juices run clear at a point, after anywhere from 12 to 25 minutes, depending on the heat you use. *Serves 4.*

Variation: **SAUCISSES AU VIN BLANC** (*White-Wine Sausages for Raw Oysters*)

These slightly peppery *saucisses au vin blanc* go very well with raw oysters, providing a contrast not only of flavor but of cold with hot, raw with cooked. The two go very well with a rich, dry white Bordeaux, but the sausages probably originate farther north in the oyster-producing Charente-Maritime, where the people proudly drink their own more modest wine. You eat an oyster, take a bite of sausage and then one of bread, swallow some wine, eat another oyster, etc. Once, the oysters would have been *plates*, meaning the stronger-flavored European species, now only a tiny minority of the oysters cultivated in France.

To make *saucisses au vin blanc*, prepare and grind the meat as for *saucisses de Toulouse*. Mix in the seasonings using the same methods, increasing the pepper to ¾ teaspoon (2 gr) and adding ¼ to ⅜ cup (50 to 75 ml) of white wine and, if you like, a large handful of chopped parsley. Peppercorns vary in freshness and potency, and if you doubt the degree of pepperiness—it shouldn't distract too much from the oysters—fry a spoonful of the mixture and taste before you make the sausages or *crépinettes*. Fill casings as for the *Toulouse*, or divide the meat into two dozen small mounds and wrap them in caul fat. *Serves 4 as a main course, assuming a dozen oysters per person.*

CERVELAS LYONNAIS

Lightly Cured Sausage

THE *CERVELAS LYONNAIS* IS A WIDE SAUSAGE OF SUCCULENCE AND DELICACY (although somewhat changed by EU rules eliminating saltpeter), and the truffled, pistachioed version baked in brioche is one of the truly great French regional specialties. The *cervelas* has ancient origins, coming into France long ago from Italy, where it once contained pig's brains (*cervello* is brain in Italian). The particular *cervellata* of Milan, composed of pork fat, beef kidney fat, Parmesan, salt, and spices, including saffron (and once used to flavor *risotto alla milanese*), became commercially extinct after the Second World War. But in the south of Italy, various meaty and more or less wide sausages by that name survive. In France, too, the *cervelas* takes different forms: the spiced and smoked one of Strasbourg is considerably different from this one of Lyon, which is less complicated to make and is cured for only a short time and sold raw, then poached by the buyer and served in thick slices. In the same broad category are the northern Italian *cotechino* with its large component of coarsely ground skin and, mainly from the province of Parma, the *mariola,* which is like *cotechino* but sometimes aged. From the Franche-Comté of France come the *saucisses de Montbéliard* and *de Morteau* and the large *Jésus de Morteau,* all as a rule smoked, and from the Dauphiné but typical of Lyon comes the *sabodet* (composed half of cooked head and skin). In Lyon, especially for the year-end holidays, the most luxurious *cervelas* contain not only pistachios but also black truffles (*Tuber melanosporum,* not to be confused with lesser kinds). Thin cross sections of truffle are dexterously slipped between the sausage mixture and the casing, so they appear just under the surface. It's easier, though, and tastes better if you chop the truffles very fine and put them into the mix at the same time as the final flavorings (white wine, brandy, and so on).

Credit for this recipe goes to James. Before you begin, be forewarned that *cervelas* is a cured sausage. You need curing salt and, optionally, saltpeter, which preserve the sausage and create its characteristic pink color and texture; you also need equipment for stuffing beef casings (which are wider than hog casings) and a warm spot in which to hang the *cervelas* for a short time to cure. James opts for an 80:20 proportion of lean to fat, but you can use 75:25, and more fat than that was common in the past. The process is the same as for *saucisses de Toulouse* through the seasoning and mixing. The *cervelas* are then aged for 48 hours in the refrigerator to begin the curing and after that hung in a warm place for 24 hours to complete it. Beef casings are too wide for sautéing or grilling—the outside of the sausages would burn before the inside was done—but they're ideal for the cured, unaged, poached *cervelas lyonnais*. Making them takes about three days from mixing through hanging. The amount of salt is not enough for drying but larger than that for fresh sausage, again because the *cervelas* are not grilled or fried but only poached. Serve them in thick slices with steamed potatoes or with another classic complement, *pommes à l'huile:* boil potatoes in their skins, peel and slice them, pour a little white wine on the still-hot potatoes, dress them with a mustardy vinaigrette, and add finely cut chives and thinly sliced shallots.

With apologies to those unused to the metric system, this is one of two recipes with only metric measures, because of the precision needed when using curing salts. For further accuracy the curing salt is premixed with regular salt. (The French version of cure no. 1 dilutes the nitrite by an extra tenfold.) James also gives the option of adding a minute amount of saltpeter for a more traditional tang and texture (see page 29 for sources of food-grade saltpeter). The cures one buys containing nitrate are mixed with salt so that, if someone puts in too much, the taste will in theory be so salty that no one will eat it. There's no particular danger in the tiny amount of saltpeter here, but you do have to weigh it accurately. Professionals make ten or a hundred kilos of the cure mixture to have on hand, so problems of measuring minute amounts don't come up. Here, to ensure no one adds too much, we first dilute the nitrite and nitrate by mixing them with salt and then add them, although that means you'll have leftover amounts for future use.

To make the nitrate-salt cure: Thoroughly mix 90 grams of salt and 10 grams of Prague Powder No. 1 or Instacure No.1, making sure there are no clumps. This is enough for a number of batches of *cervelas;* it keeps well in an airtight container, but must be thoroughly remixed before each use.

To make the optional saltpeter-salt mixture: Thoroughly mix 90 grams of salt and 10 grams of saltpeter, making sure there are no clumps. This, too, is enough for a number of batches of *cervelas* and keeps well in an airtight container, but it must be thoroughly remixed before each use.

---

800 gr lean pork from the shoulder

200 gr pork fat, including that trimmed from the shoulder

12 gr nitrate-salt cure (see note above)

continued

Trim any tough silverskin and connections from the pork lean and fat, slice them into rough 1-inch (2- to 3-cm) cubes, and mix them together. Spread them on a metal sheet or pan, and chill them, uncovered, in the coldest part of the refrigerator for an hour, unless the meat has remained very cold while you were cut-

11 *or* 13 gr salt

1.8 gr saltpeter-salt mixture (see note above), *optional*

3 gr sugar

1 gr freshly grated nutmeg

4 gr ground black pepper

35 ml white wine

15 ml Cognac or Armagnac

60 gr peeled pistachios, *optional*

30 to 50 gr black truffles (*T. melanosporum*), the larger amount if you can afford it, *optional*

about 3 feet (1 meter) beef casings, middles, 2¼ to 2½ inches (about 60 mm) in diameter

ting it, and then put it in the freezer for a final 5 minutes. Pass the deeply chilled meat through the grinder once, using a grinding plate with ¼- to 5/16-inch (about 7-mm) holes, and then spread the meat on a large metal sheet or pan. Place it uncovered in the refrigerator for 30 minutes, followed by 5 minutes in the freezer.

In a small bowl, thoroughly combine the 12 grams of nitrate-salt cure with 13 grams of salt, or, if you are using saltpeter, combine the 12 grams of nitrate-salt cure with 11 grams of salt and the 1.8 grams of saltpeter-salt mixture. Add and mix in the sugar, nutmeg, and pepper, again making sure there are no clumps.

Put the chilled meat into a large bowl. Sprinkle the small bowl's cure-salt-spice mixture onto the meat, and add the wine, brandy, pistachios, and truffles. Mix thoroughly, using your hands, continuing until the curing mixture has melted in and the meat gains a sticky, slightly elastic body, which may take 3 to 4 minutes. Cover and refrigerate for about 48 hours, while the meat cures. When you take the mixture from the refrigerator, feel to see if it is quite cold. If it is, go on to the next step. Otherwise, again spread the ground meat on a metal sheet or pan, and chill it for 5 to 10 minutes in the freezer.

When you are ready to make the sausages, rinse the casings thoroughly inside and out by slipping one end of the length of casing over the kitchen tap and letting the water run through it. Cut the casings into 12-inch (30-cm) lengths, and with a short piece of butcher's string firmly tie off one end with a secure knot. (In Lyon, they often turn the casing inside out, tie it off, and then turn it back around, which hides the closure on the inside.) Stuff the meat into the casings, maintaining enough pressure to keep the sausages very firm. Tie off the open end with another knot—it's a good idea to have one person hold the end tightly closed while another does the tying. Leave enough extra string to make a loop from which to suspend the sausages.

Hang them for 24 hours in a warm place, at 75° to 85° F (24° to 30° C), such as near a warm furnace, suspended from a pipe. To protect from drafts and excess drying, form a tent around the whole using plastic, such as an unscented plastic garbage bag, avoiding contact between the plastic and the sausages themselves. As they ferment, the sausages will first turn bright red, then a deeper burgundy color. They're ready when they've settled back to a reddish-pink, the casings have dried slightly (becoming almost parchmentlike), and the meat inside has firmed (it no longer has the yielding texture of freshly ground meat). Refrigerate and use within 5 days.

Place the sausages in cold water, bring the water temperature gradually to 175° F (80° C) over medium-low heat, and then, adjusting the heat as needed to hold the temperature, poach for about 40 to 60 minutes (at this temperature they won't overcook), being sure to reach an internal temperature of 162° to 167° F (72° to 75° C). *Makes 2 or 3 sausages, enough to serve 6 as a first course or 4 as a main course.*

SOUP

ASPARAGUS SOUP

UNLESS YOU HAVE PERFECTLY FRESH ASPARAGUS, peel it to bring the taste closer to just-picked. (For more thoughts on peeling, see page 108.) I prefer that a soup have its own inherent consistency rather than one thickened with added starch. Some soups, such as this purée, are slightly thick all by themselves. And unlike a sauce, a soup doesn't have to cling to anything, but only fill a spoon. Instead of olive oil, you can use butter (and then, if you like, add a cup of rich cream at the end). This asparagus soup can also be served cold with a little extra salt and a slice of lemon for squeezing beside each bowl; if you add the lemon juice in the kitchen, the acidity will quickly turn the color olive drab.

---

2 pounds (1 kg) asparagus spears

2 shallots, sliced thickly

2 or more tablespoons excellent, fresh-tasting olive oil, not too bitter

salt and black pepper

Break off and discard the tough bottom stems of the asparagus spears and, unless the asparagus was just picked, peel it. Boil the asparagus and shallots together in plenty of lightly salted water until they are completely tender, anywhere from 2 to 7 or more minutes, depending on the thickness and freshness of the spears, the heat of the stove, and the quantity of boiling water. Drain, reserving several cups of the cooking liquid. If you want to use the tips of the spears for garnish, cut them off and set them aside.

Purée the asparagus and shallots in a food mill, food processor, or blender, adding olive oil to taste and thinning with a little of the cooking liquid if it's needed to help a machine form a smooth purée. Don't let the purée cool, but promptly transfer it to a pan over a medium flame. Add more cooking liquid to thin the purée to soup consistency. Taste and season with salt and pepper. Heat to a boil and serve promptly in hot bowls. Garnish with the asparagus tips, if you saved them. *Serves 4 to 6.*

SOUPE AUX CHOUX À L'HUILE DE NOIX

Spring Cabbage Soup with Walnut Oil

A QUICK CABBAGE SOUP USUALLY GETS MUCH OF ITS FLAVOR from cured pork, such as smoked sausage. This one instead gains flavor from walnut oil. The closest I have to an old, primary source for this recipe is a 1954 cookbook in Roger Lallemand's regional series, *La Cuisine de Chez Nous* — the very first volume, about the former French province of the Bourbonnais in central France. Lallemand, a chef, wasn't from the Bourbonnais, but his restaurant was located there. The first of the book's two cabbage soups is a basic *soupe aux choux,* or *potée bourbonnaise,* made with cured pork and vegetables, including the "mandatory cabbage and potatoes." Lallemand wrote, "The soup is very often served with slices of rye bread, toasted or not." More uncommon is his *soupe aux choux à l'huile de noix,* a quick vegetarian soup that doesn't taste at all watery, as some of the old everyday soups do. Be certain the walnut oil comes from a good mill and that it has passed quickly through the retail pipeline — in short, that it isn't the least bit rancid. (The Leblanc brand, from Burgundy, has a marked toasted flavor that goes well with the toasted bread.) Borrowing an idea from Lallemand's companion recipe, I like this soup with rye bread (no seeds). Here's my rendering, with a little more detail than the original and some extra walnut oil. Hazelnut oil is good too.

2 small spring Savoy cabbages, if possible, or other cabbage, thinly sliced to make about 1 pound (500 gr)

2 tablespoons walnut oil plus more for serving

2 or 3 potatoes (about 1½ pounds or 700 gr), either floury or waxy, peeled and thinly sliced

a dozen or so thin slices of seedless sour rye bread or "country" bread, preferably *pain au levain*

salt and black pepper

In a large pot over medium heat, cook the sliced cabbage in 2 tablespoons of walnut oil, stirring now and then, until the cabbage wilts and some of it begins to color. Add the potatoes together with 1 quart (1 lt) of cold water and let the soup simmer. Meanwhile, toast the bread. When the potatoes are done and the cabbage has just begun to fall apart — after about 15 minutes — season with salt and pepper. Distribute the slices of bread among 4 heated bowls and ladle the soup over, or place the slices in the bottom of a heated tureen, pour the soup over, and serve at the table. Optionally, pour a little more oil on top. *Serves 4 as a filling first course.*

CARROT SOUP

THIS BASIC SOUP RELIES FOR THICKENING ONLY ON THE PURÉED CARROTS THEMSELVES. Like so many other vegetables, the carrots in regular supermarkets these days tend to taste old and to have picked up off-flavors. During summer when the roots first reach a good size, just-picked carrots—particularly a variety such as Nantes—have an especially fresh, light taste. Eaten during the winter—assuming careful storage—some carrots have a much richer flavor. Either kind suits soup. Chervil, with its fine leaflets and light anise flavor, goes very well with carrots. It's the most delicate of the herbs commonly used in flavoring, and it is perhaps the most important of the four components of fines herbes (the others being parsley, chives, and tarragon). Yet these days it is among the least-appreciated herbs, which may explain why fines herbes are now so seldom used. (When used as garnish in restaurants in France, it's almost invariably old and tastes like refrigerator—nothing like its wonderful flavor when fresh.) If you don't have chervil, use a few tiny leaflets of fresh carrot top, if you have those, or skip the garnish altogether. Serve with croûtons, if you like.

2 pounds (1 kg) carrots, peeled and sliced

1 onion, sliced

3 cups (750 ml) water

2 cups (500 ml) chicken broth or stock

salt and black pepper

½- to ¾-inch (1- to 2-cm) cubes of 1- or 2-day-old white bread, *optional*

unsalted butter, *optional*

½ cup (125 ml) heavy cream

leaflets plucked from fresh chervil for garnish

Boil the carrots and onion in the water until they are soft, about 10 minutes. Drain them, reserving the cooking liquid, and purée them, using a blender, food mill, or food processor and adding a bit of the cooking liquid as necessary. Combine the purée, cooking liquid, and broth, heat to a boil, and season with salt and pepper. If you'd like to serve the soup with croûtons, make them while the soup is heating by sautéing the cubes of bread in butter, until golden on all sides. When they are done, take them from the pan and keep them hot. Add the cream to the soup, bring it to a boil, and put the soup into a heated tureen or directly into heated individual bowls. Garnish generously with chervil. If you use croûtons, pass them at the table so they keep all their crunch. *Serves 4 to 6.*

CARROT AND TOMATO SOUP

HOMAGE TO THE LATE-SUMMER VEGETABLE GARDEN, the carrot-tomato combination is excellent, with sweetness coming from one and sweetness plus acidity coming from the other. They need be only in rough balance. Using onion plus shallot in place of meat gives a rich flavor. As with most soups, you can stir in some rich cream, sweet or ripe, at the end of cooking or add a spoonful of crème fraîche to each bowl. If you add cream, use butter, not oil, to cook the vegetables.

1 pound (500 gr) ripe red tomatoes

1 onion, chopped

2 shallots, chopped

1 tablespoon excellent, fresh-tasting olive oil (not too bitter) or unsalted butter

½ pound (250 gr) carrots, peeled and sliced in rounds

½ cup (125 ml) water

2 branches parsley

salt and black pepper

chives, sliced very finely crosswise

crème fraîche for garnish, *optional*

Peel and chop the tomatoes, saving all the seed-filled juice. Cook them in their own liquid, nothing more, until they soften, just a few minutes, then pass them with their juice through a strainer to eliminate the seeds and any coarse flesh.

In a large saucepan over medium heat, cook the onion and shallots in the oil until translucent. Raise the heat, add the carrots, and sauté for several minutes to color them lightly. Add the strained tomato and the water and bring to a boil. Add the parsley and simmer, covered, until the vegetables are tender. Cool for 5 minutes so that the liquid doesn't burst out of the food processor when you turn it on, and fish out the parsley. Purée the soup in a food mill, blender, or food processor, season with salt and pepper, and reheat it in its pot. Put the thick soup into a heated tureen or heated individual bowls, sprinkling the top generously with chives and, if you like, passing crème fraîche at the table. *Serves 4 as a small first course or 2 to 3 as a larger course.*

SOUPE DE CHÂTAIGNES

Chestnut Soup

ONCE, WHEREVER CHESTNUT TREES GREW, the nuts were important food for the poor, and yet their taste is luxurious. This chestnut soup, one of my very favorite soups, presents its main ingredient beautifully. It happens to be French, although chestnut soups are made in many places. Chestnuts can be had only during the end-of-the-year season, of course, and the flavor of the soup depends on their quality—the best, when hot, have an aroma of honey—and on the clear flavor of the chicken stock. Along with that, milk is a light, traditional addition that respects chestnut flavor, but for years I've instead added cream, as below. Make your stock with a generous quantity of leeks, or reboil it with leeks before adding it to this soup.

If you don't have homemade stock, don't resort to canned, whose taste of can permeates anything to which it's added. Instead, make a different chestnut soup, such as this one from the Limousin, also very good: cook the chestnuts in water together with the typical winter soup vegetables (onion, leek, carrot, turnip, potato), put everything through a food mill (a blender or processor risks making too fine a purée), and then add butter, milk, and cream.

The drawback to chestnuts is the peeling, which, depending on the batch, can be tiresome. Some cookbooks say chestnuts can require an hour or more of cooking after peeling, which may be true of some kinds, but overcooking the chestnuts or the soup at any point will send the chestnut aroma into the air—lost forever.

1⅛ pounds (530 gr) chestnuts in the husk

milk

2 cups (500 ml) chicken stock

1½ to 2 cups (350 to 500 ml) cream, *optional*

salt

spoonfuls of crème fraîche for garnish, *optional*

With a sharp knife, cut an X through the husk on the rounded side of each chestnut. Place the nuts in boiling water, cook for 8 minutes, and take the pan from the heat. Remove 4 or 5 at a time from the water, squeeze to loosen the husk and the skin, and peel them. The skin will slip easily from some and cling to others. If necessary, use the point of a paring knife to loosen tightly adhering bits. As the nuts cool, the skin clings more stubbornly: return those nuts to the hot water to reheat. If any chestnut looks doubtful, smell it, and if you still aren't certain, taste it; discard any without a clear chestnut flavor.

Place the peeled nuts in a large saucepan, and add enough milk to cover — about 2 cups (500 ml). Cook very gently, without a lid, until the chestnuts are completely soft, about 20 minutes. Purée the hot nuts and milk in a food processor or blender, or pass them through the fine screen of a food mill. For a perfectly smooth texture, pass the purée through a fine strainer. To prevent a skin from forming, cover until it's time to serve. (The purée can be made a day ahead and refrigerated.)

Shortly before serving, combine the purée with the stock and bring them to a boil over medium heat, stirring now and then. Add enough additional milk, or use cream, to arrive at a runny but not watery consistency. Season with salt. Immediately before serving, reheat the soup briefly without boiling (to preserve the aroma) and ladle into hot bowls. Garnish the all-milk version, if you like, with spoonfuls of crème fraîche. *Serves 4 to 6.*

MARYLAND CRAB SOUP

THE BLUE CRAB, *CALLINECTES SAPIDUS* — whose name means "savory beautiful swimmer" — is found all along the Atlantic Coast of North and South America and has been introduced elsewhere. It naturally proliferated in the vast, shallow, biologically rich Chesapeake Bay, embraced by the state of Maryland and now badly damaged by pollution. From the early days of settlement, the cooks employed in Maryland homes, as throughout the South, were African American. They contributed certain ingredients and tastes, not least the heat of red pepper, and the cooks in wealthier homes used many French techniques.

Closely related to this Maryland crab soup is Charleston's she-crab soup, prepared in winter when the female crabs are filled with roe. It was made famous by William Deas, an early 20th-century African American chef, whose recipe appears in the classic *Two Hundred Years of Charleston Cooking,* first published in 1930: he calls for she-crabs, milk, cream, onion, sherry, a little Worcestershire sauce, and a trace of flour thickening. By contrast, the typical Maryland crab soup of the 19th century appears to have contained cream and red pepper, with sherry a more recent and now reflexive addition. Still more recent is the use of Old Bay seasoning, which has become nearly omnipresent and is to me irrelevant to the taste of almost anything.

The recipe that follows comes from *Fifty Years in a Maryland Kitchen,* written by Mrs. B.C. Howard and published in Baltimore in 1873. Of her four recipes for crab soup, this one calls for neither sherry, celery (another common crab flavoring), nor pork (still another one). The flavor is very light if you don't use the mustard-colored crab fat, which is also called the mustard, tomalley, or liver (and is really the hepatopancreas), located beneath the top shell. If the crabs come from certain polluted waters, it may not be safe to eat. The taste of blue crab is to me richer than that of some other species, which can be sweet and delicate to a fault. You could surely use other species of crab, although as a lover of blue crab, I find that hard to imagine. As a point of reference, it takes at least twenty blue crabs to yield a pound of picked crabmeat. If you pick your own for this recipe, the meat and fat of five large blue crabs should suffice; if you buy already-picked lump crabmeat, you'll need a larger quantity to make up for not having the fat. The crabmeat should of course be impeccably fresh.

5 large steamed or boiled blue crabs
or ½ pound (225 gr) fresh jumbo lump
crabmeat

1 teaspoon unsalted butter

1 quart (1 lt) milk

nutmeg

ground mace

salt and black pepper

cayenne pepper

½ cup (125 ml) cream

If you are picking your own crabs, remove the meat in as large flakes as you can and pull out the fat as well, keeping it separate. When the crabmeat has all been picked, feel it methodically but gently, breaking it as little as possible, and discard any bits of shell. Combine the crab fat with the butter, using the back of a fork to produce an even consistency.

In a pot, heat the fat-and-butter mixture (or just butter if you have no crab fat), milk, and crabmeat to the lowest simmer. Add the merest hints of nutmeg and mace, and then season with salt and black and cayenne pepper—just a trace of heat is typical in Maryland. Add the cream and continue to cook at the lowest simmer for no more than 10 minutes. *Serves 6.*

POTAGE BILLY BY

Cream of Mussel Soup

ACCORDING TO THE 1962 COOKBOOK *Chez Maxim's: Secrets and Recipes from the World's Most Famous Restaurant,* presented by the Countess of Toulouse-Lautrec, the variously spelled soup Billy By originated at the restaurant Ciro's in Deauville in 1925. William Brand (Billy B.) wanted to spare his well-off American friends from having to eat mussels from the shell in the French way, using the fingers and an empty shell as tongs, and so he had the restaurant serve just the broth, no meats at all, in the form of a cream soup. Louis Barthe, who was cooking at Ciro's at the time, told that story, and he brought the soup to Paris when he became chef at Maxim's. The cookbook's version, typically for its time, calls for fish stock. But mussels should taste of mussels, not fish — they have plenty of flavor by themselves. James and I skip the fish stock, using just the broth from a well-flavored *marinière,* and add the mussel meats. The soup can be served either hot or cold. Closely related and more common on French menus is *soupe aux moules,* which is often flavored with saffron or curry, and either of those or bulb fennel could be added to Billy By at the same time as the celery below. For advice on buying mussels, see page 140.

1 large onion or 2 shallots, chopped

1 stalk celery, chopped

3 or 4 branches fresh parsley

⅓ bay leaf

¼ teaspoon dried thyme, or 3 or 4 branches fresh

1½ cups (350 ml) white wine

2 pounds (1 kg) mussels, cleaned

2 cups (500 ml) heavy cream

black pepper

a lemon, for juice

Choose a heavy pot wide enough that the mussels will form a single layer, or cook them in two pots or in batches. Cook the onion, celery, parsley, bay, and thyme gently in the wine for a few minutes, until the onion and celery are soft. Raise the heat to high, add the mussels, and cover tightly. The mussels will open in 2 to 8 minutes, depending on their size, the intensity of heat, and the quantity in relation to the width of the pot. After about 2 minutes, stir to redistribute the mussels. When half have opened, to avoid overcooking, start removing the open ones with tongs or a slotted spoon. Discard any that remain shut after 8 minutes.

Remove the cooked mussels from their shells, and strain the broth through a cloth-lined strainer — if there's no grit in the broth, a fine-mesh metal strainer without a cloth will do. Bring the broth to a boil, add the cream, and bring again to a boil, stirring. Grind in pepper and add lemon juice to taste, perhaps 2 teaspoons. Add the mussels to the boiling liquid and allow them just long enough to heat through, no more than half a minute. Serve promptly in hot bowls or, in warm weather, chill the soup and serve it in chilled bowls. *Serves 4.*

CHICKEN, SAUSAGE, AND OYSTER GUMBO

THE DEPTH OF FLAVOR IN SLOWLY COOKED CAJUN DISHES comes partly from a Cajun brown roux, which is cooked very dark, almost burnt, so that most of the flour's thickening power has been fried out of it. The roux gives a little body, but mainly it gives a mysteriously delicious, muddy richness, which sets this gumbo apart from the French and Italian dishes in this book. Cajun gumbos are essentially soups, although some people like theirs thicker than others; two more characteristics of gumbos are that the central ingredients tend to come in large pieces, and that they are served with at least a little rice. It used to be that the meat or fish used was determined by whatever was readily available at that season or moment, including game. If you omit the sausage and oysters below, you have a plain chicken gumbo. Filé, the powdered leaves of sassafras originally used by the Choctaw Indians, is itself a powerful thickener. Add it only after the cooking is done: if it boils, it becomes stringy and unpleasant. And if you use filé, be certain it's fresh — green in color and spicy in aroma. Cajuns often mix English into their French and call gumbo by an English name; in French this would be *gombo de poule aux huîtres et aux saucisses boucanés*.

¾ cup (175 ml) lard or good cooking oil plus more for browning the chicken

1 cup (135 gr) all-purpose flour

one 4- to 5-pound (2-kg) chicken

2 large onions, chopped

4 quarts (4 lt) cold water

1 pound (450 gr) Cajun andouille or other spicy smoked sausage, cut in ¼-inch (6-mm) slices

continued

To make the roux, combine the lard or oil and the flour in a large, heavy pot and cook slowly over low to medium heat, stirring from time to time and adjusting the heat to avoid burning—if the roux does burn, start again. Cook it to a deep brown, roughly 45 minutes, stirring almost continuously toward the end. Remove the roux from the pot and set aside; you will have about 1 cup (250 ml).

Cut the chicken into 8 pieces: 4 sections of breast roughly equal in size (including the wings attached to 2 of them) plus 2 thighs and 2 drumsticks. Brown the chicken pieces well in fat and remove them from

¼ teaspoon ground red pepper

½ cup (25 gr) finely chopped parsley

1 small green bell pepper, chopped

green onion tops, cut crosswise in ⅜-inch (1-cm) slices (1 cup or 90 gr in all)

2 or 3 cloves garlic, chopped, *optional*

3 dozen oysters, shucked, with their juices

salt

filé powder, *optional*

cooked long-grain rice, to serve

the pot. Add the roux and onions to the pot and stir over medium heat until the onions are translucent. Add the water all at once and bring it to a simmer, stirring from time to time to dissolve the roux. Add the browned chicken, andouille, and red pepper; simmer slowly for 1 hour, stirring from time to time. Carefully skim the fat from the surface. Add the parsley, bell pepper, green onions, and garlic, and simmer for another ½ hour. Carefully skim the fat again. Add the oysters and cook for another 5 minutes. Taste for salt and thin with water if necessary. Optionally, add filé to taste just before serving — don't cook the gumbo after that — or let each person add filé at the table. Put some rice in each bowl and ladle the gumbo over it. *Serves 8.*

Variation: **SEAFOOD GUMBO**

To make this into a seafood gumbo, halve the amounts of fat and flour used to make the roux, so that you end up with ½ cup (125 ml) of it. Leave out the chicken and reduce the amount of water to 2 quarts (2 lt); add 1 pound (500 gr) of raw shrimp and, optionally, several blue crabs cut up, together with just ¼ pound (125 gr) of sliced andouille, the green onion tops, bell pepper, parsley, and red pepper. Cook for 30 minutes, add 3 dozen shelled oysters, and cook for 5 minutes more. (For seafood dishes, the roux is often made somewhat lighter in color, which leaves more thickening power; in that case, add less of it.)

POTÉE JURASSIENNE

Soup and "Boiled" Meats

A *POTÉE* IS A COUNTRY DISH OF VEGETABLES, especially cabbage and potatoes, with sausage or another form of cured pork, and often some fresh meat. It's a basic everyday French soup — it's more soup than braise. Once, it was cooked in earthenware. The *potée* becomes *jurassienne* only when some of the meat or sausage is smoked, such as the *saucisse de Morteau* from the Jura Mountains in the former province of Franche-Comté on the border with Switzerland. The choice of vegetables and the proportions are matters of season and taste. Pierre Dupin, in his 1927 *Les Secrets de la cuisine comtoise,* warns: "Above all no onion!" But he concedes that "a clove of garlic will be tolerated." He's otherwise a purist who allows no flavoring, not even salt, beyond that coming from the meats. But if you like you can perfectly well include an onion or other vegetables, and it certainly won't hurt to add a bouquet of herbs (parsley, celery, thyme, bay). Shell beans, the kind that are meant to be shelled before cooking, can be picked as soon as they form and eaten at any stage of maturity and moisture up to completely dried, which is the way most of us eat them. The *potée* is served in two courses. First, the liquid is ladled as a soup over stale bread, preferably sourdough; these days probably most people would like it toasted. Afterward, the meats are served with the very soft — mostly overcooked — vegetables, which act as a kind of condiment. The wine in the glass might be a rich traditional *sous-voile* white from the Jura or one of the region's excellent light reds, such as one from native Poulsard grapes.

½ pound (250 gr) dried shell beans, or fresh, shelled ones in season (about half the weight is lost in shelling)

1 pound (500-gr) smoked bacon in one piece

a 1-pound (500 gr) or larger *saucisse de Morteau,* or another smoked sausage

1 pound (500 gr) beef, lamb, or mutton or a meaty lamb or mutton bone

continued

Soak the beans, if dried, overnight, and drain them. If the bacon is very smoky, place it in a pan of cold water, bring to a boil, and immediately remove the bacon and discard the water. Prick the sausage in several places so it doesn't break open in cooking. Cut the meat into large pieces along the divisions between the muscles. In a large pot of cold water, bring the sausage, bacon, and meat or meaty bone to a simmer. Skim any impurities that rise to the top. Add the carrots, turnips, and shell beans; in another 30 minutes add the cabbage;

4 to 6 carrots (about 400 gr), peeled and sliced in rounds

4 to 6 summer turnips or 1 winter turnip (about 500 gr altogether), peeled and quartered or sliced

1 cabbage (about 3 pounds or 1.3 kg), outer leaves trimmed, quartered

6 waxy potatoes (about 2¼ pounds or 1 kg), peeled and cut in large pieces

salt and black pepper

slices of stale bread, preferably sourdough

and in another 45 minutes add the potatoes. When the potatoes and shell beans are soft, grind in pepper; taste and season, if needed, with salt.

Remove the vegetables to a hot platter and the meats to a cutting board. Slice the latter and arrange them alongside the vegetables, keeping all covered and hot. If you like, toast the bread. Serve the cooking liquid as soup over the bread in hot soup plates. As a second course, in the same plates, serve the meats over the vegetables. *Serves 6.*

PURÉE DE PETITS POIS

Green Pea Soup

SOUPS OF FRESH, SWEET GREEN PEAS, cooked nearly like Petits Pois à la Laitue (page 126) but puréed and called *purées,* are very Parisian. Variations are made by adding one or two other ingredients: lettuce, chervil, cream, butter, croûtons, mint. Much better than starchy old peas in their pods are good frozen ones. Instead of thinning the purée to make soup, you can drain the peas and reduce their cooking liquid nearly to a glaze before adding it and butter to the thick purée. This goes well with braised meats served separately from the braising liquid or with it, if it has been reduced to a sauce. Shelling peas is tedious, but if you have either the patience, children to do the work, or an efficient home pea sheller (I've seen one), by all means increase the amounts.

3 pounds (1.5 kg) peas in their pods to yield at least 1½ cups (175 gr) shelled peas — more mature pods may yield twice that amount

1 flavorful new butterhead lettuce, such as Tennis Ball

a dozen stems of parsley

a thick slice of 1- or 2-day-old white bread cut into ½- to ¾-inch (1- to 2-cm) cubes

2 tablespoons (30 gr) unsalted butter

½ cup (125 ml) heavy cream

salt

fresh chervil leaves for garnish, torn into individual leaflets, *optional*

Shell the peas. Discard the coarse outer leaves of the lettuce and wash the head carefully, making certain it is free of grit; slice the head in half vertically, through the stem. Simmer the lettuce and peas with the parsley, uncovered, in just enough unsalted water to cover, until the peas are soft, roughly 15 minutes. Remove the pot from the heat and transfer the lettuce halves to a bowl. When they are cool enough to handle, squeeze the liquid from them back into the pot and discard them. Drain the peas, saving all the cooking liquid; boil to reduce it to about 1 cup (250 ml). Meanwhile, push the peas through a fine sieve with a plastic spatula. Put this paste and the reduced liquid in a small pan.

Sauté the cubes of bread in the butter, turning until they are golden on all sides. As you do so, bring the soup to a boil. Add the cream and heat briefly without boiling. Season with salt and serve in heated bowls garnished with tiny leaflets of chervil and the croûtons. *Serves 2 modestly.*

SOUPE À L'OIGNON

Onion Soup

SOME OF THE MOST RICHLY FLAVORED SOUPS OF ALL are onion. Some are purposefully pale, but deep flavor comes from gradual browning. Although many recipes call for sweet onions, any basic onion is excellent. More onions bring both more flavor and more sugar, the fuller flavor balancing the sweetness. Often there's a little flour thickening, unidentifiable amidst the falling apart, sometimes sieved, onion. The cheese of bistro-style French onion soup sits on a slice of stale baguette, but in any soup a slice of sourdough retains more substance; the soup here contains two layers of bread. The liquid can be anything from water to white chicken stock to rich dark beef stock, but with this quantity of bread, I like light stock or a stock-water combination. For adding to onion soup, no cheese beats Gruyère, whether Swiss or French (the latter being Gruyère de Comté, or Comté). Choose a youngish cheese that will melt readily.

1 pound (500 gr) onions, finely sliced

¼ cup (50 gr) unsalted butter

1½ quarts (1½ lt) boiling water, broth, or stock

salt and black pepper

8 or 12 thin (less than ½ inch or 1 cm) slices of "country" bread, preferably sourdough

¼ pound (125 gr) Gruyère, grated

In a large, heavy, covered pot, cook the onions slowly in the butter until they are thoroughly soft, 30 minutes or more (older onions are drier and remain firmer than new ones). Raise the heat and brown the onions lightly, stirring now and then to avoid the least burning and bitterness, another 30 minutes or more. Add the boiling liquid, stir, and bring to a slow bubble and cook, partially covered, for 10 minutes. Taste and season with salt and pepper, remembering that the cheese will add more salt. Take the pot off the heat.

Heat the oven to 450° F (230° C). Fill a wide oven-proof vessel with half the bread, sprinkle that with half the cheese, and then add the rest of the bread in another layer. Pour the soup over, if necessary adding just enough water to float the bread, and sprinkle the rest of the cheese on top. Put the vessel in the oven and cook until it bubbles not just at the edges but throughout and the top browns, about 15 minutes. If the color isn't deep enough, finish the soup for a minute or two under the broiler, watching it carefully. *Serves 4 to 6, depending on what follows.*

CLEAR TOMATO SOUP

THIS MINIMALIST COMBINATION RELIES OF COURSE ON THE QUALITY of the tomatoes and stock, and possibly even of the salt. It's not a consommé—it's not as concentrated, nor is it clarified with egg white. As a point of comparison, classic *consommé madrilène* contains celery-flavored chicken stock with tomato added during clarification, plus a little red pepper in honor of Spain; the garnish is a tiny dice of raw tomato and cooked red pepper, or nothing at all if served cold. The soup here doesn't achieve as much finesse, but it's hugely more refined than a soup clouded with tomato pulp. It's a great soup: the sort of thing—a plain clear liquid—that no one I know ever serves at home and that, in this age of either rustic or showy professional food, doesn't appear in restaurants either. Use stock made from bones and meat that have been browned very little or not at all, and use a tomato at the height of the season.

1 extra-large ripe summer tomato (about 1 pound or 500 gr)

1 quart (1 lt) light, clear chicken or veal stock

salt

Chop the tomato and put it with all its peel, seeds, and juice in a pot together with the stock. Let this simmer gently for about 15 minutes, then strain it in a colander lined with a smooth kitchen towel without using pressure that might force through any hint of tomato pulp. Taste and season the soup as needed with salt, and serve it, very hot and ungarnished, in cups. *Serves 4.*

SOUPE AUX CERISES

Cherry Soup

THIS CHERRY SOUP FROM THE FRANCHE-COMTÉ IN EASTERN FRANCE is not, as it may sound, a dessert, but a first course. The food that follows, writes Pierre Dupin in *Les Secrets de la cuisine comtoise* (1927), must be heightened in taste, such as a main course of game and then strong cheese. Pitting cherries, especially without some sort of cherry pitter, is a lot of trouble; I leave the pits in place. Although Kirsch originated in Germany, it has been made in the Franche-Comté for at least three hundred years. The croûtons here are not the usual cubes, but whole slices of bread.

6 slices of white or near-white bread, preferably sourdough

5 tablespoons (75 g) unsalted butter

2 pounds (900 gr) sour cherries or 5 ounces (150 gr) dried cherries

1 tablespoon all-purpose flour

1 tablespoon sugar or more as needed

1 tablespoon Kirsch or more as needed

Fry the slices of bread in 4 tablespoons (60 gr) of the butter until they are colored on both sides. Place them in hot bowls or a hot soup tureen and hold in a warm place.

If you like, pit the cherries. Melt the remaining 1 tablespoon (15 gr) of butter in a large pot over a medium-low flame and add the flour, stirring and cooking for a minute without browning, to make a roux. Add the cherries and then enough water to cover; add 1 tablespoon of sugar and the Kirsch. Bring the whole to a boil, and as soon as the cherries are tender, taste and, as needed, add more sugar and perhaps Kirsch.

Promptly serve the boiling soup, ladling it over the croûtons in the hot bowls or tureen. If the cherries aren't pitted, let everyone know. *Serves 6.*

WINTER SQUASH SOUP WITH VIN JAUNE

I'VE LOST TRACK OF THE ORIGINS OF THIS SOUP, which might have been my own innovation. It uses *vin jaune*, the unusual, very dry white wine from the Jura region of eastern France, which has an oxidized taste from being aged, like sherry, *sous-voile*, "under a veil" of protective yeast. The wine's flavors, which partly recall those of sherry, flatter the nutty side of winter squash. Instead of *vin jaune*, you can use another similarly treated but less expensive Jura white wine.

Winter squash comes in different shades of flavor and degrees of sweetness, from somewhat bland conventional butternut to sweet Delicata to handsome, ribbed Rouge Vif d'Étampes to giant, hard Blue Hubbard (in New England, some people split this with an ax or by dropping it on a granite step), and many more. Probably any variety would work in this soup, but one with character is better. Depending on the kind, you'll lose roughly a third of the weight to peeling and seeding. If you have a little extra cooked squash, save it to thicken another winter soup; if you have a lot, spread it the next day in a shallow oven dish, top it with thin slices of butter, and bake it in a hot oven until the surface starts to brown.

1 winter squash (at least 3 pounds or 1.4 kg)

1 small onion, finely chopped

½ tablespoon (10 gr) unsalted butter

about 2 cups (500 ml) chicken or veal stock

salt and black pepper

½ cup (125 ml) *vin jaune*

Peel, halve, and seed the squash, and cut the flesh into pieces 1 to 2 inches (2 to 5 cm) across. Put the cut-up squash in a pot and add enough water just to cover the bottom. Cover and cook slowly, stirring now and then — with slow-enough cooking, no more water is needed — until the squash is soft enough to be stirred easily into a rough purée, 20 to 25 minutes. Measure out 3 cups (750 ml) of cooked squash and set it aside. Save any remaining squash for another use.

In a large saucepan, cook the onion slowly in the butter, stirring several times, until it is translucent but not colored. Add and stir together the stock and the 3 cups of cooked squash, and heat through. Season the soup with salt and grind in pepper. Optionally, use a food mill or food processor to give a fine, even consistency. Just before serving, add the wine and bring the soup momentarily to a boil. Pour it into a heated tureen or ladle directly into heated individual bowls. *Serves 4 as a first course.*

BREAD AND ZUCCHINI SOUP

THIS SUMMER SOUP IS ADAPTED from the cookbook *La Cucina del Piemonte* by Giovanni Goria, published in 1990, where it is given the dialect name *supa ed cosòt.* It's a hot soup that employs bread, making something substantial and yet light from vegetables and mere broth into a main course. Like many soups, sauces, and stews—and not only Italian ones—this starts with cooking chopped onions slowly in fat. Gentle cooking transforms the onions' complicated sulfur compounds, giving a much fuller, deeper flavor than quick browning does. Usually other aromatic vegetables are also present to give a base of flavor, especially carrots and celery. The mixture is called *soffritto* in Italian, *mirepoix* in French. Italians don't generally make rich, concentrated stock; they use broth left from something else, such as "boiled" meat. Here, use broth or stock mixed with water so it remains in the background of the fresh vegetable taste. *Zucchini* is the general Italian word for summer squash, not just the green kind, though for the soup green is my first choice if it comes from a flavorful variety, such as Costata Romanesco.

leaves from a small branch of sage

leaves from a small branch of rosemary

1 onion, finely chopped

1 clove garlic, finely chopped

2 ounces (50 gr) cured pork back fat (*lardo*) or pancetta, finely chopped

excellent, fresh-tasting olive oil

3 large (1 kg) ripe red summer tomatoes, peeled, seeded, and chopped

1 pound (500 gr) small zucchini, sliced in rounds

1 quart (1 lt) hot meat broth or diluted stock

4 slices 1- or 2-day-old "country" bread, preferably sourdough, cut in small pieces (enough to fill a 3-cup or 750-ml measure)

salt and black pepper

Parmigiano-Reggiano cheese for serving

Finely chop the sage and rosemary together. In a large nonreactive pan over medium-low heat, combine the herbs, onion, garlic, and fat and cook this *soffritto* gently in a little olive oil until the onion is translucent. Add the tomatoes and continue to cook for another 10 minutes.

In a separate frying pan, cook the zucchini in a little olive oil until half tender. Transfer the zucchini to the large pot containing the *soffritto* and add the hot broth and bread; cook until the zucchini is tender, a few more minutes. Season with salt and pepper. Serve in a heated tureen or heated bowls, pouring, if you like (and as Goria suggests), a little fresh olive oil on top and passing the cheese at the table. *Serves 4 as a main course.*

PASTA AND POLENTA

PICI

Eggless Tuscan Pasta

TUSCAN FOOD IS STRAIGHTFORWARD, RUSTIC, AND FRUGAL. In contrast with most northern Italian pasta, in which egg is mixed with soft wheat flour (not durum), *pici* (sometimes called *pinci*) are eggless. They're mixed with water and hand-rolled in a shape like fat spaghetti. In his authoritative *La Cucina toscana*, published in 1995, Giovanni Parenti says, "An egg is rarely tolerated, and only for color." *Pici* are a food of the poor that has become food of the affluent because of the hand labor required. Conveying the making of a *picio* in words isn't easy — it almost requires a lesson in person — but *pici* are a point of reference, a reminder of fundamentals. Originally, they were often served with little more than olive oil, Parenti says, but sometimes there was a *ragù* of fresh sausage containing plenty of tomato and onion and some dried or fresh mushrooms. And in fact *pici* go well with many sauces that are thick enough to adhere to the narrow strands. The grating cheese in Tuscany always used to be the region's own, made from ewe's milk, though today it's nearly always Parmigiano or another cow's-milk cheese. If you don't have relatively low-protein Italian tipo 00 flour, mix unbleached all-purpose flour 2:1 with unbleached pastry flour. Best is a flour (or flour mixture) with about 9 percent protein.

3¾ cups (500 g) soft flour plus more as needed

about ⅔ cup (150 ml) water

excellent, fresh-tasting olive oil

Mound the flour on the counter and make a well in the center. Add enough water, initially by stirring with a fork, to make a soft dough, sprinkling on more flour or water as needed. Knead by hand for a few minutes, until the dough is smooth and no longer sticky. Lightly coat the surface of the ball of dough with olive oil, wrap it in plastic, and let it rest for 1 hour.

Take a quarter of the dough and roll it out ⅛ inch (3 mm) thick. With a sharp knife, cut off a piece about ½ inch (1 cm) wide by 8 to 10 inches (20 to 25 cm) long. On a wooden surface, roll the dough back and forth with one hand to form a fat spaghettilike shape, as narrow and even as you can, of variable length up to 18 inches (50 cm); use the hand that is not rolling to feed the length of dough to the other one. As each piece is done, sprinkle it lightly with flour and set it aside. Boil as you would any fresh pasta, draining the *pici* before they are quite done, because they will soften further in any sauce. *Makes a little over 1 pound (600 gr), enough to serve 4.*

PUCCIA

Polenta with Cabbage and Pork

PUCCIA, FROM PIEDMONT IN NORTHERN ITALY, IS IN ORIGIN a poor person's one-dish meal. Eat it hot in soup plates, or chill it in an oiled pan and then slice it and fry it slowly in olive oil. Polenta, like any cornmeal porridge, gains full flavor only after an hour or more of cooking. The corn, if possible, should come from an old milling variety, such as *ottofile* from Piedmont; the ears should have been fully ripened in the field and the dry kernels should be freshly ground. Polenta meal comes both coarse and fine; I prefer the coarse. A usual ratio of water to meal is 6:1, by weight, but with *puccia* the head of cabbage contributes a lot of water, and the quantities below account for that.

1 pound (500 gr) boneless fatty pork shoulder, cut in 1-inch (2- to 3-cm) cubes

1 head cabbage (about 3 pounds or 1.3 kg), outer leaves discarded, cored and thinly sliced

1 onion, chopped

1 stalk celery, chopped

1 carrot, peeled and chopped

2 quarts (2 lt) water

salt

3 cups (440 gr) coarse polenta meal or 3⅓ cups (500 gr) fine polenta meal

strong Piedmont cow's-milk cheese (Raschera, Castelmagno, Bra Duro, or Parmigiano-Reggiano)

black pepper

Simmer the meat and vegetables together in 2 quarts lightly salted water for about 10 minutes. Very slowly, sprinkle in the cornmeal so as to avoid lumps. Over very low heat, continue to cook, stirring from time to time, until the pork is utterly tender, at least 1 hour. Add enough cheese — grated or sliced, depending on the kind — to give a marked taste and season with salt and pepper. *Serves 6 to 8.*

RAGÙ BOLOGNESE

Bologna-Style Rich Meat Sauce

EVEN AROUND BOLOGNA, BASIC *RAGÙ* HAS INFINITE VARIATIONS: this is one. The historic region of Emilia, of which Bologna is the largest city, loves its fats, and the cuts of meat called for below are fatty. Rather than being ground fine like hamburger, the meats should be coarsely ground. You can request this from a butcher or do it yourself by hand with a single sharp knife — or, rhythmically, with a matched pair of chef's knives, one in each hand, and a heavy cutting board. The milk contributes sweetness and a softening richness to *ragù*. It's excellent over homemade egg pasta, such as the tagliatelle of its home region, with, of course, Parmigiano-Reggiano. Or choose another pasta shape, such as penne, that will capture some of the sauce in every bite. Buy no more of the cheese than you will use within a few weeks, and preferably from a newly opened wheel whose aroma hasn't begun to diminish. Because grating the cheese at the table gives maximum freshness, I often pass it wrapped in a napkin together with a grater. Lynne Rossetto Kasper's fine cookbook *The Splendid Table* (1992), about the food of Emilia-Romagna, explores the origins and variations of *ragù* and suggests that it tastes best within two hours of cooking, which seems to me true. Among its other uses, *ragù* is also an ingredient of lasagna, and it goes beautifully with polenta.

1 onion, finely chopped

1 carrot, finely chopped

1 stalk celery, finely chopped

2 tablespoons lard, excellent, fresh-tasting olive oil, or a mixture of olive oil and butter

¾ pound (350 gr) beef or veal chuck or skirt steak, ground

¾ pound (350 gr) pork shoulder or veal chuck, ground

continued

In a large heavy pan, cook the onion, carrot, and celery in the fat over low heat, stirring, until the vegetables are translucent but not brown. Add the beef, pork, and ham, and cook, stirring now and then, until the meats are no longer red but not yet brown. Add the wine and cook, still over low heat, until it has almost evaporated. Add the tomatoes, stock, and milk. Cover and cook, adjusting the heat carefully so that only a few bubbles appear and the liquid slowly concentrates. After 3 to 4 hours, scarcely any liquid should remain. If you cook the *ragù* very slowly with only barely active bubbles, there will be no danger of sticking or burning; not all

½ pound (250 gr) dry-cured ham, such as prosciutto di Parma, sliced and finely chopped

¾ cup (175 ml) red or white wine

½ cup (125 ml) diced fresh or canned tomatoes

1 cup (250 ml) rich stock or water

1 cup (250 ml) milk

salt and black pepper

1½ pounds (700 gr) dried tagliatelle or penne, or 2¼ pounds (1 kg) fresh pasta

stoves lend themselves to such low heat, so check now and then and add a spoonful of milk or water if needed. Season with salt and pepper. Cook the pasta and drain it and, just before serving, mix the *ragù* with the pasta. *Serves 6.*

PESTO TRAPANESE

Raw Tomato-Basil Pesto

OTHER PASTA SAUCES ARE AS GOOD, BUT NONE IS BETTER. This creamy pesto from the city of Trapani in westernmost Sicily is partly like the famous pesto from Genoa, but the Sicilian one contains no cheese, adds tomatoes, and uses almonds in place of walnuts or pine nuts. Both kinds are served raw over hot pasta, which in Trapani, ideally, is homemade *busiate* (long corkscrews), though other shapes are often used, such as *bucatini* (long, narrow, hollow tubes) and even spaghetti. The proportions of ingredients for *pesto trapanese* vary considerably from cook to cook. It's more important that the tomatoes be delicious and not gorged with water from too much rain or irrigation. The sauce is not beautiful to look at, its color being more or less muddy depending on the ratio of basil to tomato. In Sicily, the honored variety of basil, *basilico siciliano*, has tiny leaves and, from the Sicilian perspective, a more intense perfume than the Genovese variety, which I know well from growing it for years. The essential point about basil, at least the Genovese kind, is that it is vastly superior — much more strongly and distinctively perfumed, the leaves paler and more tender — if it is grown in part shade. Full sun produces tougher, darker green leaves that the Genovese consider "minty."

To peel almonds, put them in boiling water for half a minute, remove them with a slotted spoon, and then pop them out of their skins and dry them. Prepare the tomatoes by scoring an X in the blossom end and putting them into the same pot of boiling water for 30 to 45 seconds; then cut out the core of each and pull off the skin. (You can pull off the skin of an extremely ripe tomato almost as easily without any blanching at all.) Slice the tomato in half; with your little finger, scoop out the seeds and gel and discard them. Compared with a food processor, a mortar produces a superior texture — more uneven and slippery. If you have one with a capacity of at least a quart (a liter), use it. Giuseppe Coria, the great recorder of Sicilian recipes, wrote, "Let the sauce rest for as long as it takes to cook the pasta."

about ¼ cup (35 gr) peeled almonds

2 to 4 cloves garlic

1 teaspoon salt

½ to 1 cup (15 to 30 gr) basil leaves

½ cup (125 ml) excellent, fresh-tasting olive oil

4 to 6 ripe red summer tomatoes (about 2 pounds or 900 gr total), peeled, seeded, and coarsely chopped

black pepper

1½ pounds (700 gr) dried pasta

In a large mortar, mash the almonds to a paste with the pestle and remove them. Put in the garlic and the salt, and reduce those to a paste; then add the basil and reduce it. Return the almonds to the mortar, add the olive oil, and turn with the pestle until the whole becomes creamy. Add the tomatoes little by little, mashing each time so as to retain the emulsion.

Or, if you are using a food processor, reduce the almonds, garlic, salt, and olive oil to as smooth a paste as possible. Only then — to avoid a brown color, an utter purée, and a loss of flavor — add the basil and pulse several times, and then add the tomatoes and pulse several times, and don't pulse again.

With either method, taste the sauce and season it with salt if needed and grind in pepper. Cook the pasta and drain it well, then mix it immediately and thoroughly with the room-temperature raw sauce in a large warm bowl, and serve it in warm individual bowls. Because you can't serve the sauce chilled and you can't heat it, use it within about 2 hours (the flavor is good for several hours — left overnight in the refrigerator, it largely deteriorates). *Serves 6.*

SALSA DI NOCI

Walnut Sauce

CLOSE KIN TO THE FAMILIAR BASIL PESTO, *SALSA DI NOCI* also comes from the Italian Riviera and was originally always made in a mortar. Other versions of it include butter, ricotta, Parmigiano, bread crumbs, or smaller proportions of green herb than are called for here. Sometimes there's no cream; sometimes there's no garlic. Occasionally, I've used walnut oil for part of the olive oil. Parsley varies in intensity, and in any case it's impossible to measure precisely — for this recipe, compress the leaves moderately in the measure and in the future use more or less, according to your taste. Add too little parsley and the sauce needs Parmigiano at the table; add enough parsley and the cheese would only distract; the amount specified below normally puts the taste in the right range. Typically, *salsa di noci* goes on tagliatelle, ravioli, or *pansoti* (fat shapes stuffed with greens). With pasta stuffed with greens, use only a little parsley in the sauce, chopped and stirred in at the end. This sauce also goes on fish, like similar French sauces, which are sometimes made with skinned walnuts. *Salsa di noci* with pasta is a good first course but, to me, is too rich for a large serving.

1 cup (100 gr) walnut pieces

1 clove garlic

¼ teaspoon salt

¾ cup (35 gr) flat-leafed parsley leaves, washed and well-dried

½ cup (125 ml) excellent, fresh-tasting olive oil

½ cup (125 ml) heavy cream

salt and black pepper

1 pound (500 gr) dried pasta or 1½ pounds (750 gr) fresh tagliatelle, ravioli, or *pansoti*

Reduce the walnuts to a paste in a mortar or food processor. Add the garlic, salt, and parsley and again make a paste, scraping down the sides. Add the oil and stir with the pestle or process again to form an emulsion. Add the cream, mixing briefly, taste, and season with salt and pepper. Cook the pasta and drain it, then mix the room-temperature sauce with the hot pasta (heating the sauce directly causes it to break). *Serves 6 to 8 as a first course.*

CHEESE, EGGS, AND SALADS

FRESH CHEESE

JUST-MADE CHEESE IS PRIMORDIAL FOOD, AND YET — at least in North America — few people have tasted it; they don't know the delicate texture and relatively simple, clean, satisfying lactic flavors. Making fresh cheese may sound intimidating, but after a few times it can become routine. The taste and timing of fresh cheese, like aged cheese, are affected by tiny variables in every element of the process: milk, temperature, culture, acidity, rennet, and equipment. Consistent results come from control and experience: you have to jump in and try, and make adjustments the next time.

Milk is turned into a solid — into tender curd — by the addition of rennet and lactic bacteria. The latter convert the milk's sugar into lactic acid. Strong-enough acidity will, all by itself, set a curd — though a weak one, from which more than the usual amounts of protein and calcium will run off with the whey. For firmer curd, cheesemakers commonly add a little rennet, which will also set curd all by itself. At the risk of oversimplification, there are two ways to set curd: warmer, faster, and firmer, from more rennet; and cooler, slower, and more tender, from more acidity. For fresh cheese, the cooler, slower process, relying on acidity and just a little rennet, is best.

Good raw milk — clean but with benign contamination from lactic bacteria — will sour on its own and clabber overnight. In the United States, you generally have to get raw milk directly from a farm — about half the states allow on-the-farm sales of raw milk — and you must be certain it is clean and safe. But these days, dairy operations are so hygienic that raw milk is almost always too clean to clabber itself, without enough microlife to do the work. Even some of the most traditional European makers add starter cultures. Pasteurized milk, its organisms having been killed off by heat, always requires an added starter.

All else being equal, raw-milk cheese tastes better. That's because of the original difference in flavor (raw milk is faintly floral; pasteurized tastes of caramel), the more diverse microflora (even if the population is small), and the unaltered protein, which gives superior texture (raw-milk curd is firmer and easier to work with). Ideally, you begin with ultra-fresh raw milk, still warm from the cow's udder. (Since animals are milked twice a day, cheese often used to be made twice a day too.) But if you don't use the milk promptly, refrigeration is essential. And if you don't have raw milk, you can still make good fresh cheese from pasteurized milk —

provided it has been heated no higher than 172° F (78° C) — but you have to add some kind of bacterial culture that will create acidity.

I like fresh cheese with no more than moderate acidity. Strong acidity hides a lot of the dairy taste, and too much acidity gives an almost metallic taste. Moderate acidity not only allows the pleasure of more dairy flavor but allows more tenderness.

When I was experimenting with fresh cheese for this book, wrestling in purist fashion with raw milk, Randolph Hodgson of Neal's Yard Dairy in London, who has enormous knowledge of cheesemaking, suggested that I set a cup of raw milk on my kitchen counter and see whether it would sour overnight. If it did, I should wait and see whether it would form curd within thirty hours. Then I would know something about the qualities of the milk, and, if needed I could try rennet and starters. In fact, my cup of raw milk took thirty hours to sour and fifty hours to set curd. Happily, it tasted delicious. I used that cup of curd to seed a fresh batch of raw milk, and used the whey from that to seed another batch, just as cheesemakers often used to do — although with steady recycling of whey, the wrong microbes can take over. With my good results, I was lucky. Cheese is protected by acidity, and when it takes thirty hours for acidity to develop, then distasteful and even dangerous microbes can multiply.

How best to proceed safely and reliably at home? Adding yogurt with live bacteria isn't great, because those bacteria work at higher temperatures. Adding cultured buttermilk gives a strong buttery taste that has little to do with the real taste of fresh cheese. And adding a little store-bought fresh cheese is unreliable or worse, because by the time cheese is made, it has become so acidic that the beneficial lactic bacteria are dying. The best option is a freeze-dried powdered cheese culture, which keeps a long time if sealed from moisture and stored in the freezer.

The traditional molds for small fresh cheeses are tightly woven baskets or glazed earthenware pots pierced with holes. Modern plastic molds are made in different sizes and shapes associated with different European cheeses. For fresh cheese, I like the molds intended for the small rounds of Saint-Marcellin. Breaking up the curd before you transfer it to the molds speeds the work of filling them, and the whey drains faster. But if instead you carefully ladle the curd into the molds, breaking it very little, the cheese will be more moist and delicate.

As to the milk, cow's milk gives more neutral-tasting fresh cheese; goat's milk tends to make cheese that's sharper in acidity — though not especially goaty if the bucks were kept separate from the does; and ewe's milk, with its higher proportion of fat and other solids, gives richer, creamier cheese. The milk can be either whole or skim, but the more fat there is, the more tender the cheese; you can increase the fat by adding 1 to 2 cups (250 to 500 ml) of heavy cream to the recipe below — combine it with the whole milk at the beginning of the method. Rennet, too, comes in different kinds—animal and microbial, tablet and liquid—and in different strengths. I use US liquid veal rennet at 1:15,000 strength; you can use a proportionate amount of other rennet, and the required amounts of both rennet and culture can vary: experiment if your first effort isn't entirely successful. Ingredient quantities in the recipe that follows can be doubled or tripled.

Rennet, cultures, cheesecloth, and molds are available from New England Cheesemaking Supply and from Dairy Connection. For more information about making fresh cheese, see Jean-Claude Le Jaouen's *La Fabrication du fromage de chèvre fermier* (translated into English as *The Fabrication of Farmstead Goat Cheese*) and *American Farmstead Cheese* by Paul Kindstedt.

Serve fresh cheese plain; with salt and pepper; with olive oil and salt and pepper; with all these plus a mixture of herbs including, optionally, garlic—or use it to make Cervelle de Canut (page 84). You can serve it with sliced bulb fennel or roasted bell peppers marinated in garlic and olive oil. It can be a first course or the center of a light meal. You can cook with it, using it in place of ricotta or baking a cheesecake with it. For dessert, pour rich cream over it (see Crémets d'Anjou, page 249) or eat it with fruit or sugar or honey.

2 quarts (2 lt) whole milk

6 drops liquid rennet (see note above)

1/16 teaspoon freeze-dried mesophilic cheese culture

1½ teaspoons salt

Pour the milk into a stainless steel pot. If it has a thick bottom (preferably one that wraps at least partway up the sides), you can warm the milk directly over a very low flame, stirring now and then. If the bottom of the pot is thin or you're wary of overheating, set the pot in a larger one half-filled with water, and place the pair of pots over medium-low heat. Raise the temperature of the milk to 90° F (35° C), measuring with a cook's thermometer or judging in relation to body temperature.

Take the warmed milk from the heat; add the rennet and starter culture, stirring to mix them evenly throughout the milk. Cover the pot and set it in a warm place, about 75° to 85° F (24° to 29° C). In roughly 8 hours—depending on all the variables of milk, rennet, starter, temperature—a soft curd will have formed. Tip the pot to see whether the tender curd pulls away from the side. The first time you use a particular culture and rennet, you may have to wait less or more time; if longer, probably no more than a few extra hours, but if curd has not formed in 24 hours, then discard the milk and begin again, using more culture or rennet or both. The curd is firm enough to use when it shrinks away on its own from the sides of the pot and is covered with a ¼-inch (1-cm) layer of whey. If the curd seems weak, so that too much may slip through the holes of a mold, then drain it in a nonreactive colander lined with cheesecloth that has been rinsed and wrung out. Otherwise, you can ladle the curd directly into 6 small cheese molds (with a total capacity of at least 6 cups or 1.5 lt).

Set the cheesecloth-lined colander over a wide pot, or set the cheese molds on a stainless-steel rack in a stainless-steel roasting pan (if you don't have a rack, just use the pan and empty the whey often). With unhomogenized (including raw) cow's milk, some cream is likely to rise and form a thin layer on top; if that troubles you, stir it in—this will also break the curd. Better is to just ladle the curd gently into the colander or molds, breaking it as little as possible. All the curd may not fit in the molds, but the whey will immediately start to flow and the curd to sink; wait 5 to 10 minutes and add the rest of the curd to the molds. If you use a colander, bring together the corners of the cheesecloth, tie them with a length of string, and make a loop at one end. Use that to hang the bag (from a knob on a kitchen cabinet or your kitchen sink faucet, or improvise something else), with the pot beneath to catch the whey. After an hour or two, mix the cheese in the cloth to hasten the draining (the single large shape drains more slowly than small ones). If you don't have a use for the whey—it's a good replacement for milk in rich baked goods, and an excellent garden fertilizer and food for pigs—discard it.

After about 3 hours of draining, carefully test whether the cheese in the molds is firm enough to hold together by tipping one partly out of its mold. When it holds together sufficiently, gently turn each mold upside down, letting the cheese fall into your hand. Replace it in its mold with the other side up. With the cheese in the cheesecloth, after 3 hours of draining, turn the cheese into a bowl, mix it with the salt, and tie it again in the cheesecloth to continue to drain. After about 3 more hours, lightly salt the tops of the cheeses in the molds, turn again, and lightly salt the other side. After 2 more hours, turn the large cheese or the small ones out onto a platter.

You can eat fresh cheese immediately at its peak of freshness, when it tastes its very best—partly because it hasn't yet been chilled. After that, keep it in the refrigerator, covered to protect it from off-flavors; it will remain in good condition, continuing to release whey, for 2 to 3 days, or a little longer, depending partly on the amount of salt. *Makes about ¾ pound (300 gr) of fresh cheese.*

CERVELLE DE CANUT

Fresh Cheese Beaten with Herbs

CERVELLE DE CANUT, "BRAIN OF A SILK WORKER," is an essential Lyonnais food, named for the city's silk weavers, who were at their peak in the 19th century and were said to live on it. It combines well-beaten *fromage blanc,* or fresh cheese, with chopped herbs, the imperative flavors coming from chives and black pepper. The mixture is also called *le claqueret,* from *claquer,* which means "to bang," as in the course of beating. Fresh cheese is unripened and is in principle new-made, but far more common in the United States are unripened white cheeses that have been extruded into plastic like sausage into casings. Loosely speaking, these cheeses are fresh, and, if only because their mediocrity is largely hidden by the other ingredients, they're appropriate for *cervelle de canut,* of which there are many versions. Out of choice or economy, restaurants often reduce the herbs to just chives; cream or crème fraîche is commonly substituted for olive oil; I call for less garlic and vinegar than some (compared with the past, we're less used to vinegar, and sourness in general); and whether vinegar is needed at all depends on your taste and the acidity of the cheese. Ewe's milk isn't produced in the area around Lyon, but you could substitute a ewe's-milk cheese, with a richer result. Today in the city's restaurants, *cervelle de canut* is commonly served as an alternative to or an addition to the course of aged cheeses, but it's a more logical opening to a meal. It's best eaten on the day it's made, with bread, of course.

1 pound (500 gr) well-drained fresh cow's-milk or goat's-milk cheese

1 shallot, finely chopped

1 clove garlic, very finely chopped or mashed to a paste

⅜ cup (20 gr) finely chopped flat-leaf parsley

⅜ cup (20 gr) finely chopped chervil, *optional*

⅜ cup (20 gr) finely sliced chives

4 tablespoons (60 ml) excellent, fresh-tasting olive oil

2 tablespoons white wine vinegar, *optional*

up to ½ cup (125 ml) dry white wine

salt and black pepper

Beat the cheese until it's smooth and mix in the shallot, garlic, and green herbs. Mix in the olive oil and vinegar, and then enough white wine so that the mixture spreads easily at cool room temperature. Taste and season with salt, if needed, and grind in a generous amount of black pepper. If the *cervelle de canut* will wait for several hours, refrigerate it, but serve it cool, not chilled. *Serves 6 to 8 as a first course.*

FOCACCIA COL FORMAGGIO DI RECCO

Cheese Focaccia

THE LIGURIAN SEASIDE RESORT TOWN OF RECCO SPECIALIZES in this cheese focaccia, which, unlike the usual kind, contains no yeast. Instead, two layers of flour-and-water dough are stretched pasta-thin and used to enclose fresh cheese. You eat the focaccia hot from the oven with a knife and fork. The melted, liquidy cheese mixes with the crust and softens it, so it becomes like pasta, with the cheese acting as a tart sauce. Instead of Stracchino or Crescenza, now used in Recco in place of the disappeared local fresh cheese, you can use fresh, moist cow's-milk or ewe's-milk cheese (heat tends to bring out the goatiness in goat's-milk cheese). The dough must be soft and have the same consistency throughout, so that it stretches easily and evenly. If you have it, Italian tipo oo flour is ideal; otherwise, use all-purpose flour or, as in the recipe for Pici (page 70), a combination of all-purpose and pastry flour to approximate the roughly 9 percent protein of tipo oo. (You can't reproduce a flour by just blending to get the protein right, but you do at least get the protein.) Although it requires more skill, you will get better results from forming the focaccia on a peel and then sliding it onto a hot baking stone in the oven, rather than forming and baking it in a pan.

2¼ cups (300 gr) unbleached all-purpose flour

1 cup (225 ml) water

coarse semolina

1 pound (500 gr) Stracchino or Crescenza cheese

excellent, fresh-tasting olive oil

salt

Pile the flour on a work surface and make a well in the center. Add the water and, with just one hand, gradually combine the two; as they come together use two hands and then knead for a few minutes to make a smooth, soft, elastic, nonsticky, and easily pliable dough. Let it rest, covered, for at least 1 hour.

Heat the oven to 500° F (260° C), or, if you have a wood-fired oven or a high-temperature commercial one, heat it to about 700° F (375° C). Divide the dough into 4 pieces. Working on a flour-dusted surface, roll out one of them to a thin sheet. Dust a 12-inch (30-cm) diameter shallow metal pizza pan or a baking sheet with coarse semolina. Stretch the sheet of dough carefully, using the backs of your hands, to the thinness of the thinnest pasta. It should be wide enough to extend well past the edges of the round pan.

Distribute half the cheese in tablespoon-sized pieces over the dough. Roll and stretch a second sheet of dough, and cover the first. Press lightly between the pieces of cheese to expel air. Cut away the extra dough to leave a half-inch (1-cm) border all around, and fold the edges in, pressing to seal them. Poke several holes near the center of the focaccia, pour a little olive oil around the center, give the top a bare sprinkling of salt, and bake it in the hot oven. The focaccia is done when it is golden all over and darker brown in spots—about 15 minutes in a conventional oven and 7 to 8 minutes in a hotter wood-fired or commercial oven. Repeat to make a second focaccia. Eat them hot. *Serves 4.*

GOUGÈRE

Gruyère Puff Pastry

THE SAVORY *GOUGÈRE*, ITS CRUNCHY OUTSIDE CONTRASTING with the tender inside, is made in various parts of France, but it is associated especially with Burgundy. It probably descends from the *gouiere,* a cheese-flavored cake to which references survive from the early 1300s. Instead of being made as a large ring, the *gougère* is now more often formed in *petits choux,* little balls, to go with apéritifs. In theory, the *gougère* flatters wine and, as usual with cheese, the flattery occurs much more often with white wines than reds. The dough is *pâte à choux,* the same as for cream puffs, which is raised miraculously by eggs alone, though the addition of cheese weighs down the *gougère* a little. The cheese is Gruyère, much of which is insipid; be sure to taste when you buy and choose a well-flavored one.

Someone who read the manuscript for this cookbook pointed out that it's far easier to combine the eggs with the rest of the dough by machine than by hand, which is true. But I sold my KitchenAid years ago because it did so few things well in proportion to the space it occupied on my counter. I tried and similarly got rid of several competing mixers, keeping only my tough old Cuisinart, which I use now and then and which would surely work here. But machines get in the way of the sensuality of cooking, and it's the senses that teach us how to cook. And while beating the eggs into the dough in the pan takes time and effort, so does cleaning a machine. I opt for the direct handwork.

⅞ cup (200 ml) water

¼ cup (60 gr) unsalted butter

¼ teaspoon salt

1⅛ cups (150 gr) unbleached all-purpose flour

4 large eggs

3 ounces (85 g) Gruyère, coarsely grated, plus more for the top

either milk or one egg yolk for glaze, *optional*

Bring the water, butter, and salt to a boil in a saucepan. Remove the pan from the heat and add the flour all at once, stirring vigorously with a wooden spoon until the dough detaches from the sides of the pan and forms a mass. Return the pan to medium heat and cook the dough, flattening it against the bottom of the pan and turning it over repeatedly for 1 to 2 minutes, until a subtle haze of butter appears on the surface of the dough and a thin film of dough cooks to the bottom of the pan—don't let it color. Cool the pan for several minutes off the heat. Add the 4 eggs, one at a time, incorporating each fully before adding the next. Stir in the 3 ounces of cheese.

To make *gougère* in a ring, heat the oven to 375° F (190° C). Butter a baking sheet and, using a pair of tablespoons, arrange mounds of the dough to form a continuous 8-inch (20-cm) ring with a 2- to 3-inch (5- to 7-cm) opening in the center. Smooth the top of the ring with the back of a wet spoon, and brush with milk or with a glaze of the egg yolk beaten with 1 teaspoon of water.

To make the *gougère* in *petits choux*, heat the oven to 400° F (200° C). Butter a baking sheet and on it set small mounds far enough apart to allow them to triple in size without touching. Don't smooth their tops, but do brush them with milk or the egg yolk–water glaze.

Distribute the remaining grated cheese over the surface of the *gougère*. Bake until deep golden, about 50 minutes for the ring and 25 for the *petits choux* at their higher temperature (with these, start checking after as little as 15 minutes). If the *gougère* isn't fully cooked and crisp, it may collapse. Cool the ring briefly on a rack, so the bottom doesn't soften from its own moisture, and serve warm. The small balls are best eaten as soon as they're cool enough to safely put in your mouth. *Serves about 6 to 8 before a meal or as the opening to it.*

Variation: **CHEESE FRITTERS**

The dough for these, compared with the one for *gougère,* is lighter in flour and heavier in cheese, but the hot oil causes the fritters to swell fully and hold their shape. I make them with sharp Cheddar, but you could use Gruyère or another full-flavored cheese. In an ideal world, the olive oil for deep-frying would always be the freshest and best, but that would turn deep-fried food into a rare luxury. You can use another kind of oil, preferably unrefined.

Make the dough just as for the *gougère,* decreasing the flour to 1 cup (125 gr) and increasing the grated cheese to 6 ounces (150 gr). In a high-sided pot or a special deep-fryer, heat 1½ inches (4 cm) of good olive oil or another good, light oil at 365° F (185° C). (If you don't have a thermometer, scoop up a rounded teaspoonful of the dough and drop it in to see whether it swells and browns in about 3 minutes, turned about midway.) Scoop rounded teaspoonfuls of the dough into the oil without crowding the pot and fry to a deep golden color, turning each ball once. Drain the fritters on paper towels and serve hot (you can hold them for a short time in a warm oven). *Makes about 20 fritters, enough for about 6 to 8 people as the opening to a meal.*

CHEESE SOUFFLÉ WITH TOMATO SAUCE

I USE FLAVORFUL GRUYÈRE OR STRONG CHEDDAR IN THIS SOUFFLÉ, though other cheeses can also be good. I've always found soufflés easy to make, which makes me suspect the feared collapse is more a part of lore than common experience. A slower oven (about 350° F or 175° C) produces a lower, sturdier soufflé; a faster oven (400° F or 200° C) produces a lighter, more vulnerable one. Too much cooking dries a soufflé, but there's no one right degree of doneness. For me and many others, the ideal is a slightly flowing center that, as you break into and serve it, is still cooking from the residual heat. You can beat the egg whites in any clean bowl (fat getting in the way of foam), but the classic and best bowl is, at least for sensual reasons, made of unlined copper. A trace of the metal, Harold McGee explains in *On Food and Cooking*, bonds with elements in the whites to keep the foam strong once it has formed and prevent it from turning grainy and losing volume as you incorporate it. Just before each use, the copper must be cleaned with salt and either half a lemon or a vinegar-drenched paper towel; rubbing removes tarnish (actual verdigris is toxic), and the fresh shiny surface ensures the chemical reaction. Adding a little acid to the whites, through a different chemical effect, accomplishes the same thing. Still, you can create a useful if weaker egg-white foam without adding either copper or acid. The tomato sauce that accompanies the soufflé is very easily made and extremely good.

TOMATO SAUCE

1 shallot, finely chopped

2 teaspoons excellent, fresh-tasting olive oil or unsalted butter

3 large ripe, red tomatoes (together weighing at least 2 pounds or 1 kg), peeled, seeded, and chopped

salt

To make the sauce: Cook the shallot gently in the oil until translucent, about 5 minutes. Add the tomatoes and cook the combination gently until the vegetables are completely tender. Pass the sauce through a coarse strainer or the fine holes of a food mill and season with salt.

To make the soufflé: Butter and flour a 2-quart (2-lt) soufflé mold. Over medium heat, melt the 3 tablespoons (40 gr) of butter in a saucepan and cook the flour in the melted butter for 1 minute (to diminish the raw taste of the flour, it's always said). To this roux, add

SOUFFLÉ

3 tablespoons (40 gr) unsalted butter plus more for the mold

¼ cup (35 gr) all-purpose flour plus more for the mold

1¼ cups (300 ml) cold milk

6 eggs, separated

¼ pound (110 gr) grated aged Cheddar or Gruyère

salt

ground hot red pepper or pepper sauce

ground black pepper

nutmeg

¾ teaspoon cream of tartar, if you use a noncopper bowl

the milk all at once, and immediately whisk the combination smooth. Stirring continuously, bring the sauce to a bubble over medium heat. Take the pan from the stove. Stir in the egg yolks, then add the grated cheese and stir only enough to mix. Season well with salt and red and black peppers, remembering that, once the dish is baked, the taste will be diluted by air; add a trace of grated nutmeg. Transfer the mixture to a large bowl.

Heat the oven to 400° F (200° C). If you have a large unlined copper bowl, rub it with vinegar and salt, rinse and dry it with a clean towel, and beat the egg whites in it until they just form stiff peaks. For a noncopper bowl, add the cream of tartar to the whites and beat them. When the foam is stiff enough, it will cling to the bowl; before and after, it will slip, and it's better to beat too little than too much. Fold the beaten whites by thirds into the cheese mixture, and fill the mold. Bake for about 30 minutes until, if you jostle the soufflé slightly, it quivers in a way that suggests the outside is set but not yet the center (this becomes clearer with experience). Wait a few more minutes only if you prefer the soufflé fully set. Bring it immediately to the table and pass the sauce. *Serves 3 or 4 as a main course.*

WELSH RABBIT

THE MOST TRADITIONAL WELSH RABBIT —the alternative name "rarebit" surely came later as a gesture toward the uninitiated —contains very few ingredients, and certainly no adulterating flour or egg that would make the emulsion more durable. Here I've merely tried to quantify the way Welsh rabbit was prepared by my grandfather, who came from an English farming family about fifty miles from the Somerset village of Cheddar. (I've come up with amounts, but I continue to measure by eye.) Everything depends on having good, strong cheese, aged but not too old, or you'll have a grainy, oily consistency rather than a smooth one. In a different way, too much beer also prevents the rabbit from coming together. The Worcestershire sauce gives a more aged taste to the cheese, and if the cheese is really flavorful (yet not too old to melt well), you could reduce the amount of Worcestershire or do without. I believe the brand makes a difference, like the brand of mustard, but I admit that I skip the mustard myself, making the dish even simpler. Welsh rabbit is quickly made, and it must be eaten as soon as it is done. Any further cooking, like reheating, risks rendering the fat from the cheese, and, taken from the heat, the rabbit soon sets —hot plates are essential.

8 slices of white "country" bread

1 pound (500 gr) aged Cheddar

½ teaspoon dry Colman's English mustard

1 teaspoon Lea and Perrins Worcestershire sauce

scant ½ cup (110 ml) ale (not dark)

Heat the plates and toast the bread. Meanwhile, cut the cheese into pieces and melt it slowly in a wide frying pan. When the cheese is nearly all melted, add the mustard, Worcestershire sauce, and ale. Stir actively and continuously over high heat until the cheese and ale form a homogeneous sauce. Spoon it, bubbling hot, over the toast on the hot plates; serve and eat it immediately. *Makes 4 moderate-sized portions.*

FONDUE FRANCHE-COMTOISE

Cheese Fondue

FONDUE REQUIRES THE STANDARD EQUIPMENT: an enameled cast-iron or glazed ceramic pot to put over a flame, a stand to hold it with a burner below, and long-handled forks. It's usually said that the difference between a Franc-Comtois fondue and a Swiss one is that the latter contains Kirsch. Present-day Franc-Comtois purists take a minimalist approach, their only complication being to add two or three different ages of Comté cheese: young for smooth consistency, older for the dominant flavor, and a little of the truly old for its different aromatic range. Often fondue contains flour to keep the consistency more stable over the flame, especially if it cooks too hard or long—the sort of practice that may have originated in restaurants. Ideally, the wine for both the pot and the glass is a traditionally made *sous-voile* Jura white (Chardonnay, Savagnin, or a blend). Fondue is mainly a winter dish.

a large loaf of white or near-white "country" bread, preferably sourdough

2 cups (500 ml) white wine plus more as needed

1 clove garlic, finely chopped

2½ pounds (1.2 kg) Comté with the hard part next to the rind, coarsely grated or sliced in thin strips

salt

Cut the bread into large dice, up to ¾ inch (2 cm). In a pan on the stove, boil the wine with the garlic until the liquid is reduced by half. Strain into a fondue pot and discard the garlic. Place the fondue pot on the stove over low heat, add the cheese, and stir it continuously with a wooden spoon or spatula until smooth. Add more wine as needed to achieve the consistency of rich but pourable cream. Taste and, if necessary, add salt. Carry the hot pot to the table and place it on the stand over the flame of the burner, so the fondue continues to bubble gently. *Serves 6.*

PEPPER AND POTATO FRITTATA

THE COMBINATION MAY SOUND BORING, BUT IT ISN'T. I learned it from Lucy DiNapoli, whose mother came from Catania, Sicily. I cook the frittata in a heavy, well-seasoned 10-inch (25-cm) cast-iron frying pan, with a lid borrowed from another pot. It's good hot or cool, or, leftover, in a sandwich with crusty Italian bread.

1 potato, quartered and sliced in ¼-inch (5-mm) pieces

excellent, fresh-tasting olive oil

1 green bell pepper, sliced

1 onion, sliced

1 clove garlic, very finely chopped

6 large eggs

salt and black pepper

In the pan you'll use for the frittata, cook the potato slices over medium-low heat in plenty of oil until they are brown and cooked through, less than 5 minutes per side. Drain them on a paper towel. Meanwhile, in a separate pan, cook the pepper, onion, and garlic together in 2 tablespoons of oil until soft (the pepper will be khaki colored).

Mix the pepper, onion, and garlic with the potatoes and adjust the heat to medium-high. Immediately, beat the eggs with salt and pepper and pour them over the vegetables. Reduce the heat to very low and cook, covered, until the eggs are almost set, 10 to 15 minutes. Remove the cover and place a plate over the pan and carefully invert the frittata onto the plate, then slip the frittata back into the pan just long enough to set the other side fully. Alternatively, if the handle of the pan will withstand the heat, finish the top of the frittata under the broiler. *Serves 4 as a first course, 2 as a main course.*

ŒUFS EN MEURETTE

Poached Eggs in Red-Wine Sauce

THESE BURGUNDIAN POACHED EGGS ARE COLORED MAHOGANY by the *meurette* sauce, whose key ingredients are red wine and onions. The *meurette* goes back at least five hundred years; it was originally a sauce for fish, and the name used by itself still means a red-wine fish stew, also called a *matelote*. Not just eggs, but chicken, veal, and brains are sometimes cooked *en meurette*. The eggs for poaching should be very fresh, from hens that have lived outdoors eating plants whose carotene colors the yolks a deep orange. This is a home recipe, lightly thickened with *beurre manié;* if the sauce is barely cooked after it's added, there won't be a floury taste. Chefs make the sauce in advance, adding stock or demi-glace to give body and smoothness, and they poach the eggs in a separate red-wine court bouillon. The stock or demi-glace takes the edge from the wine. Chefs also add the ritual Burgundian garnish of lardons (small sticks of salt pork or smoked bacon), mushrooms, and tiny whole onions; at home, too, the fat of the sautéed lardons usefully counters the sharpness of the wine. They're always blanched in advance to take away a little salt, give back some water, and render some fat that would later end up in the sauce.

Rather than using one egg per person, serve two or three to make the dish the center of a meal. (In gourmand Burgundy, I was once served three *œufs en meurette,* plus two other courses, before the main course.) For the meal to be fully Burgundian, the wine in the sauce and at the table should of course be Burgundy.

6 tablespoons (90 gr) soft unsalted butter plus more as needed

2 tablespoons all-purpose flour

3 onions, chopped, or a combination of onions and leeks

3 carrots, peeled and chopped

continued

Make the *beurre manié* by kneading 3 tablespoons (45 g) of the butter with the flour; set aside. Cook the onions and carrots gently in 2 tablespoons (30 g) of the butter in a wide, nonreactive pot until the onions have softened but not colored, about 10 minutes. Add the liquid, 2 of the garlic cloves, and the bay, thyme, parsley, cloves, and nutmeg. Turn the heat to high and boil until reduced by half, roughly 1 hour. Strain the

2 bottles (1.5 lt) red wine or 1 bottle
(750 ml) red wine plus an equal
amount of broth or stock

3 cloves garlic

1 bay leaf

several branches fresh thyme or
½ teaspoon dried thyme

half a dozen branches flat-leaf parsley

2 whole cloves

a hint of freshly grated nutmeg

5 ounces (150 gr) lean salt pork or
pancetta

8 slices good white bread

clarified butter, *optional*

8 large eggs

salt and black pepper

liquid into a shallow, nonreactive frying pan, about 9 inches (23 cm) across.

Cut the salt pork or pancetta across the grain into ¼-by-¼-inch (6-by-6-mm) lengths, for lardons. Put the lardons into a pan of cold water, bring them to a boil, strain, and rinse in cold water. Sauté them in the remaining 1 tablespoon (15 g) of butter until the edges just begin to crisp; drain them on a paper towel and keep them warm. Fry the slices of bread slowly in clarified butter (or toast and butter them). Rub these croûtons with the remaining clove of garlic and distribute them among 4 warm soup plates; keep warm.

Heat the *meurette* in the frying pan until it steadily but barely bubbles. (To make neat, cohesive poached eggs, it helps to break each first into its own small dish.) Slip the eggs into the liquid close to the surface. Cook them just until the whites are set—test them with a finger—about 5 minutes. The yolks will still be liquid. Remove each egg with a slotted spoon, trimming any loose white, and place it on a croûton. Over medium heat, little by little, whisk just enough *beurre manié* into the bubbling liquid to make it slightly thick. Grind in pepper and season only lightly with salt, since the lardons will add more. Strain the sauce over the eggs and garnish with the sautéed lardons. *Serves 4.*

SCRAMBLED EGGS WITH ASPARAGUS

THESE ARE FRENCH-STYLE *ŒUFS BROUILLÉS*, COOKED SLOWLY with constant stirring to achieve the sensual consistency of smooth custard with only a few soft curds; the eggs are flowing yet thick enough to eat with a fork. The combination with asparagus is classic (and even better if you can include morels, first cooked gently in butter). Croûtons, cut from a white loaf, fried in butter, and scattered on top, give a crisp contrast, although their too-frequent use is a bore and I don't call for them here. I peel asparagus for almost every purpose, and I almost always use unsalted butter. Excellent salted butter, if you can find it, will do equally well for most uses, though it can be very salty. (Salt speeds rancidity, and most salted butter in North America has a rancid edge. Besides, better cream tends to go into unsalted butter, where defects show more clearly.) You can cook the eggs directly over a low flame, with constant stirring, if you have a wide pan with a thick bottom that will heat evenly, but you will almost certainly need the help of a heat diffuser. Safer is a bain-marie. Richard Olney, an impeccable cook whose recipes are models of clarity, called for adding most of the cut-up butter at the end to stop the cooking and prevent the butter from turning to oil. With the eggs, he drank a glass of *premier cru* Chablis.

½ pound (250 gr) asparagus spears, peeled

½ cup (125 gr) unsalted butter, diced

12 large eggs

salt and black pepper

Cut the asparagus into ¼-inch (5-mm) slices, leaving the tips whole. Cook the asparagus, tips included, in 1 tablespoon (15 gr) of the butter over medium-low heat, stirring now and then, until tender, about 12 minutes. Set the asparagus aside, leaving it in the pan to stay warm.

Choose a somewhat high-sided pan or a metal bowl that can be placed in a bain-marie—a larger pan full of water kept just below a boil. Break the eggs into a bowl and whisk them well with salt and a grinding of pepper. Melt 2 tablespoons (30 gr) of the butter in the pan set directly over very low heat or in the bowl set in the bain-marie, and pour in the eggs. Begin to stir, preferably with a wooden spatula whose square edge makes it easy to cover the whole cooking surface of the pan set directly over low heat or in the bowl. Stir occasionally, but don't let curds begin to form. It can take 30 minutes or more to achieve a thick custard. Remove the eggs from the heat just before they reach the ideal consistency, because they'll continue to cook from the residual heat. Add the rest of the butter while stirring, still moving the spatula across the whole bottom of the pan, and then mix in the asparagus. Serve the eggs on warm plates. *Serves 4.*

SALADE FRISÉE

STANDARD FRENCH BISTRO FARE INCLUDES AN OFTEN-SUBSTANTIAL first-course salad based on *chicorée frisée,* curly chicory, also known confusingly and more correctly as curly endive (the species is *Cichorium endivia* var. *crispum*). Large and small variations on this salad are nearly endless. The usual cured pork can be omitted, but the crunch of croûtons—or at least toast—and the piquancy of garlic are essential. Sometimes the egg is left out, though it soothes the bitter greens. The egg can be poached, boiled to *mollet* (so it has a thickened but still flowing yolk), or cooked harder than that. A poached egg with a fully flowing yolk gives the salad the most luscious texture. In place of a single poached egg, you can use two *mollet* ones (being drier, their effect doesn't go as far), quartered or sliced. Or chop a single hard-cooked egg and incorporate it directly into the dressing; the disintegrating yolk will mix evenly and thicken the dressing, so it will need to be thinned with a little water. Instead of chicory, you can use blanched cultivated dandelion, arugula, or a combination of various strong or hot greens. An old form of the salad is dressed by rinsing with vinegar the (nonreactive) pan used to fry the pork. A good basic vinaigrette for most purposes is composed of one part of vinegar to four to six parts of excellent olive oil, with enough salt and pepper to heighten the taste of the greens and, if you like, some mustard to make a more lasting emulsion—mustard is delicious and belongs in this full-flavored salad, although it hides the best flavors of really good olive oil. Rather than frying the croûtons, you can dry them on a sheet pan in the oven; or toast a large slice of "country" bread, rub both sides well with garlic, and cut it into ¾- to 1-inch (2-cm) squares. For the lardons, you can substitute *rillauds* (page 23), slices of grilled sausage, finely diced ham, and so forth.

2 ounces (50 gr) lean salt pork or pancetta without rind

1 tablespoon (15 gr) unsalted butter

1- or 2-day-old "country" bread cut into ½- to ¾-inch (2-cm) cubes, enough to make roughly 2 cups (or fill a 500-ml measure), for croûtons

1 medium to large head curly chicory

red-wine vinegar

salt and black pepper

excellent, fresh-tasting olive oil

1 clove garlic, very finely chopped

Dijon mustard with some bite, from a fresh jar

1 very fresh egg for poaching or 2 eggs for boiling (a less fresh egg peels more easily)

Slice the pork against the grain into ¼-by-¼-inch (6-by-6-mm) lardons. Put the lardons into a pan of cold water, bring them to a boil, then strain and rinse in cold water. Sauté them in the butter until the edges just begin to crisp; drain on a paper towel and keep warm.

Tear the chicory leaves into pieces, discarding the coarse green tips, and put them into an extra-large salad bowl. Mix a vinaigrette of vinegar, salt and pepper, and olive oil, adding the garlic and enough mustard to give some heat, and thinning the emulsion, if needed, with water to the consistency of heavy cream. Sauté the lardons and croûtons in 2 tablespoons of olive oil, turning to color them evenly. Remove the pan from the heat.

Meanwhile, if the egg is to be poached, bring a small, shallow pan of water to a boil and remove it from the heat. Gently break the egg into the water, cover the pan, and poach until the white is just set, about 3 minutes. Or boil 2 eggs to *mollet* — 6 minutes for large eggs — and peel and quarter them. Set the well-drained poached egg, or the sliced *mollet* eggs, atop the greens along with the croûtons and lardons. Dress with the vinaigrette and mix thoroughly. *Serves 2.*

INSALATA DI ARANCE

Orange Salad

ORANGE SALADS, WHICH CAN OPEN OR CLOSE A MEAL, are typical of both Sicily and Spain. The oranges should be slightly tart, to play the role normally played by vinegar. The oil for this salad should taste especially fresh and, in my view, strongly of fruit in the modern style. The salad is good as a minimal combination—oranges, oil, salt, and pepper—or you can add one or more of the garnishes below. Whenever onions are served raw, cut them at the last minute, because cutting sets off a complex sequence of changes in the sulfur compounds, which soon become unpleasant.

4 large eating oranges (or enough smaller ones to serve 4 people)

⅓ cup (80 ml) excellent, fresh-tasting olive oil

salt and black pepper

black olives, *optional*

thin slices of bulb fennel, *optional*

thin slices of onion, *optional*

Peel the oranges using a very sharp knife (a 10-inch or 25-cm chef's knife is efficient) so as to cut cleanly and avoid pressing out juice. First cut a disk from the top and bottom of each fruit to reveal a flat circle of flesh; then, following the arc of the fruit, cut wide strips from top to bottom, each time cutting down to the flesh. Afterward trim any remaining white pith. Slice the peeled oranges crosswise into rounds about ¼ inch thick (a generous ½ cm). Remove any seeds. Vigorously stir together the oil, a good pinch of salt, and finely ground pepper, and pour this dressing over the orange slices. Allow the salt to dissolve for about 15 minutes before serving. Optionally, add any combination of the olives, fennel, and onion. *Serves 4.*

LETTUCE SALAD WITH ROQUEFORT AND WALNUTS

WHEN I SERVE A LETTUCE SALAD, I ALMOST ALWAYS put it between the main course and cheese, if any. There's no compelling reason why (that's simply what my parents did), but in the case of this salad, serving it after the main course makes sense, and then no separate cheese course is needed. The interest in this salad is partly textural. The best butterhead lettuces, also called Boston (though that may strictly describe just one variety, also known as Tennis Ball), have a velvety tenderness that underlines the creaminess of the blue cheese, while the endive provides a contrasting, refreshing crunch. In place of Roquefort, which in stores is sometimes past peak, you can use another blue cheese, but choose a softer, sweeter kind and not a drier, nutty one.

3 ounces (85 gr) Roquefort cheese

½ to ¾ cup (120 to 180 ml) heavy cream

meats from 4 or 5 walnuts, very finely chopped

1 tablespoon finely cut fresh chives

black pepper

1 tablespoon white-wine or cider vinegar

salt

velvety butterhead lettuce

Belgian endive, in crosswise slices, or mâche

Mash the cheese roughly with a fork, and combine it with ½ cup (120 ml) of cream, the walnuts, chives, and freshly ground pepper. Just before serving, add the vinegar and thin as needed with additional cream. Taste and add salt, if needed. Toss the greens with the dressing — not all may be needed, depending on the greens and their quantity. *Serves 4 to 6.*

BEET SALAD WITH ANCHOVIES

THIS SALAD APPEARS IN THE BILINGUAL *VIEILLES RECETTES DE CUISINE PROVENÇALE,* or *Vieii Receto de cousino prouvençalo,* by C. Chanot-Bullier, about the food of Provence. Still in print, it was originally self-published in 1966, but with its old-fashioned scarcity of measurements and limited instructions, it seems decades older. What make it special are its combinations of flavors and clear presentation of tradition, which make it one of the best cookbooks ever written. The author called this salad, in Provençal, *lei bleto-rabo de Gardano,* after a town (Gardanne in French) near Marseille. The beet-anchovy alliance is one of the simplest and best, with the sweet beet, garlic, cured fish, and vinaigrette all vying pleasantly with one another. Usually red-wine vinegar has more flavor and is best for a vinaigrette, but here the difference is mostly lost among the other strong flavors, and any good wine vinegar will do.

2 or more salted anchovies

1 pound (500 gr) beets, cooked tender, cooled, and peeled

2 or more cloves garlic, peeled and halved

wine vinegar

excellent, fresh-tasting olive oil

salt and pepper

Clean the salt from the anchovies, strip the filets from the bones, and rinse them. Cut the beets into small dice. Slice the anchovy filets into bits, and add them to the beets along with the garlic. Make a vinaigrette with the vinegar, oil, salt, and pepper, and dress the beets with it. Mix well and taste for salt (the sweet beets will stand a lot). *Serves 4.*

VEGETABLES

ASPERGES, SAUCE MALTAISE

Asparagus with Blood-Orange Hollandaise

THE BEGINNING OF ASPARAGUS SEASON HAPPILY OVERLAPS the end of citrus season. Traditionally, the sole purpose of *sauce maltaise*—hollandaise with fresh blood-orange juice—is to accompany asparagus, and there's nothing better. (It also goes well with poached or grilled non-oily fish.) Even more than regular hollandaise, *sauce maltaise* proves the lightness of butter. As to the mechanics of making it, boiling the vinegar briefly beforehand takes away the rawness that characterizes even the best vinegar. Using clarified butter eliminates the 15 percent or so of water in most butter, along with the rest of the nonfat components, making a much thicker but less dairy-tasting sauce. Unclarified butter, as in the recipe that follows, gives the desirable dairy flavor but a thinner result. If that's unacceptable, boil the orange juice to reduce its quantity by half. In the version below, the hollandaise, an emulsion of butter in egg yolk, is made by first whisking the egg yolks to create a sabayon, some of whose air remains to lighten the final sauce.

Blood oranges, like regular ones, vary in acidity. A regular orange gives the same flavor, but a dark blood orange makes a wonderfully garish pink sauce in contrast with the yellow-green peeled asparagus. I use pieces of zest because they're easier to make than grated zest, and they won't pass through or clog the strainer. Leaving grated zest in the sauce gives a coarse texture that in my view is at odds with the nature of *sauce maltaise*, which is one of the great refined sauces. As with so many classical French preparations with geographical names, this one wasn't borrowed from another cuisine. *Orange maltaise,* in French, is simply an old way to say blood orange, because long ago the fruit came from Malta.

Peeling green asparagus is worth the trouble. (White asparagus, with its more fibrous stems, must be peeled—and unless it's extremely fresh, it has a cardboardy flavor.) Peeling removes any stringiness from green asparagus, along with any hidden grit, and peeling eliminates much of the crude taste of old, store-bought green asparagus. (The spears you pick from your own garden and cook promptly are almost a different vegetable.) Besides, it's nearly impossible to boil asparagus properly without peeling it, since the tips cook faster and start to fall apart at about the moment the unpeeled stems are fully cooked. Because much of the flavor resides in the skin, peeled asparagus tastes more delicate. The catch is that peeling just-cut asparagus takes away almost too much flavor, and pencil-diameter spears can't be peeled.

As to drink, the old view was that wine and asparagus don't go together, but especially with butter, as in this case, many successful matches exist with white wine. I like a concentrated dry Loire Chenin Blanc. A more aggressive, though not new, idea is a dry Alsatian Muscat, hard to find these days (most producers now leave at least a little sugar in the wine).

2 to 3 pounds (1.25 kg) asparagus, tough ends broken off and the stalks peeled

1 tablespoon lemon juice, white-wine vinegar, or cider vinegar, plus more if needed

yolks from 3 large eggs

2 square inches (5 cm square) orange zest (no bitter pith) in 1 or 2 pieces

1 cup plus 2 tablespoons (250 gr) unsalted butter, cold, cut in roughly ½-inch (1-cm) cubes

a blood orange for juice

a lemon, for juice, *optional*

salt

Bring at least 2 gallons (8 lt) of well-salted water to a boil. If the asparagus spears vary much in thickness, you can separate them by size and tie them in bundles about 2½ inches (7 cm) across. Slip them into the pot and watch closely, because asparagus quickly becomes overcooked. Just-picked thin spears are done in as little as 2 minutes, the fattest in no more than 5. Older spears take longer. With experience, you can tell the doneness by the way the spears droop; otherwise, check with a fork or a taste. Drain them well and wrap them in a towel to keep them hot and absorb further moisture.

In a small nonreactive saucepan, boil the tablespoon of lemon juice or vinegar with 2 tablespoons of water for a few moments to reduce the quantity by half. Take the pan from the heat, wait a minute for it to cool, then whisk in the egg yolks. Place this pan in another, larger one containing hot *but not boiling* water, and continue to whisk as the mixture foams and slightly thickens — be sure to take the pan from the heat before the egg begins to curdle. Add the orange zest. Add the cubes of butter several at a time, whisking to form an emulsion. Return the pot to the hot water for more warmth, as needed, to melt the butter but not curdle the egg.

Whisk in orange juice, little by little, to taste, without adding so much that the saucelike consistency is lost. If the orange juice happens not to be very acidic, squeeze in some lemon juice. Taste and season with salt. Pass the sauce through a fine strainer. Reheating risks curdling, so if the sauce won't be served immediately, hold it in a warm place — such as over warm water, covered — for no more than half an hour. Whisk again before serving over the well-drained asparagus, hot or tepid, on warm plates. *Makes enough sauce for 2 to 3 pounds of trimmed asparagus, which may serve 4 to 6 people, the amount of asparagus anyone will eat depending on its deliciousness.*

CHOUÉE

Buttered Cabbage with Potato

CHOUÉE IS ALMOST IMPOSSIBLE TO MAKE BADLY and it's always very popular. It's just boiled cabbage mashed with butter and, optionally, boiled potatoes. The amount of potato is a matter of taste, and the amount of butter, in the rare recipe that specifies, is one part to eight of cabbage. Even more than most foods, cabbage has an affinity for butter. The dish comes from the dairy country of the French province of Poitou, where it is made in fall and winter and, with the year's first small green cabbages, in spring. The color can be near white from a tight, mature head or flecked with green from a Savoy or a young cabbage. The texture can be from fine to coarse. *Chouée* is rich yet it tastes light; it's good on its own and it goes especially well with pork and poultry, compensating for any dryness.

1 pound (450 gr) waxy or floury potatoes, peeled and cut in large pieces

3 pounds (1.3 kg) cabbage

salt

¾ cup (175 g) unsalted butter, in pieces

pepper, *optional*

Bring the potatoes to a boil in a large pot of cold water and cook until soft all the way through, about 12 minutes. While the potatoes are cooking, discard the coarse outer leaves of the cabbage, remove and discard the core, and cut the rest into chunks. When the potatoes are done, remove them from the pot with a slotted spoon.

Salt the same water in the same pot generously and return it to a boil. Add the cabbage and cook, uncovered, until it is completely soft but not falling apart, roughly 10 minutes. Drain it well. Either pass the vegetables through the coarse openings of a food mill or use a food processor: add and reduce the cabbage to a coarse texture, then add and reduce the potato. Add the butter and combine. Season with salt and, optionally, pepper, and serve very hot. *Serves 6.*

FAR AU CHOUX

Cabbage Pudding

THE BATTER FOR THIS RUSTIC PUDDING, FROM THE QUERCY in southwest France, is essentially the same as that for crepes, clafoutis, popovers, and Yorkshire pudding. Similar dishes are made in other French regions from other vegetables as well as fruits. When made without goose or duck fat, *far au choux* loses its regional reference and tastes much less interesting. Best of all is fat from a garlicky goose or duck confit. The *far* should be crisp-edged and tender—not at all stodgy. A lighter consistency comes from Savoy cabbage, whose heads are, as the cook and gardener Barbara Damrosch describes them, "ruffled and crinkly," with an "elegant" texture and a flavor "so much more delicate than that of the firm-headed types." The leaves are thinner and the heads looser than with regular cabbage, and the Savoy varieties don't keep as well, but their taste is sweeter and milder, less sulfurous when overcooked, faster cooking, and more tender. It's Damrosch's favorite kind, and the favorite of many cooks.

1 pound (500 gr) cabbage

¾ cup (100 gr) unbleached all-purpose flour

2 large eggs

1 cup (250 ml) milk

salt and black pepper

1 tablespoon rendered goose or duck fat (or chicken fat in a pinch)

Discard the coarse outer leaves of the cabbage, core it, and chop it in large pieces. Cook it for 5 minutes in boiling well-salted water, and drain it well. Heat the oven to 425° F (220° C).

Whisk the flour, eggs, and milk into a batter, mix in the cabbage, and season well with salt and pepper. With the fat, grease a gratin dish, such as an 8-by-12-inch (20-by-30-cm) oval, or a 10-inch (25-cm) cast-iron frying pan, and heat it in the oven until the fat is almost smoking, about 10 minutes. Stir the pudding mixture and fill the hot dish or pan. Bake until swollen and partly browned, 20 to 25 minutes. Serve hot. *Serves 4 as a first course.*

ERBAZZONE

Savory Pie of Greens

ERBA MEANS "GREENS"; -ONE MEANS "BIG." The pie, from Reggio in the Italian region of Emilia, is made with spring or fall greens, especially from beets. Similar pies, often from wild greens, are made elsewhere, in Liguria, for instance, and on the Greek island of Crete. For a lighter effect, in place of the pork fat, cook the onion and garlic in ¼ cup (60 ml) of olive oil and then add 1 ounce (25 gr) of finely chopped dry-cured ham, such as prosciutto di Parma, at the same time as the cheese. The crust is traditionally made with lard. Sometimes the pies are deep-fried.

about 2½ pounds (1 kg) greens such as beet, spinach, Swiss chard, or a mixture, well washed

2 tablespoons (25 gr) unsalted butter

¼ pound (100 gr) *lardo* (cured pork belly) or pancetta, chopped

1 or 2 cloves garlic, finely chopped

1 onion or half a dozen or more green onions, including most of the green, chopped

2 large eggs

¼ pound (100 gr) grated Parmigiano-Reggiano

salt and black pepper

dough to make a 10- to 12-inch (25- to 30-cm) 2-crust pie, chilled

Depending on your selection of greens, pull the tougher stems from the beet and spinach leaves and cut away the ribs from the chard. Put the greens, with drops of the washing water still clinging, into a large pot. Cook, covered, over medium heat, stirring once or twice, until wilted, 8 to 10 minutes. Drain and press on the greens to expel more moisture. Chop well.

In a small pan, gently cook together the butter, *lardo*, garlic, and onion, continuing until the garlic and onion are translucent but not at all colored. In a bowl, combine this *soffritto* with the greens, eggs, and Parmigiano. Season with salt and pepper.

Heat the oven to 425° F (220° C). Roll out the chilled pie dough to make two layers, one slightly larger than the other. Line a pie pan or baking sheet with the larger, and trim the edges so as to leave a ½-inch (1-cm) border. Fill the dough with the greens mixture, folding the border over the filling all around. Lightly wet the exposed dough. Top with the second layer of dough so it covers the damp border, and trim the extra. Press gently around the edges to seal the two layers and prick the top with a knife or fork. Bake until well browned, about 30 minutes. Serve hot or at room temperature; in the latter case, cool the pie on a rack so the bottom remains crisp. *Serves 4.*

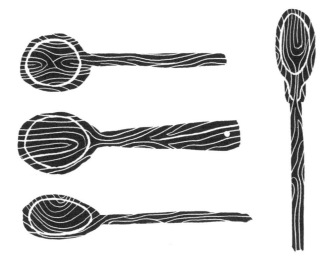

EGGPLANT AND TOMATO

THE SIMPLE COMBINATION OF EGGPLANT AND TOMATO excludes the squash and red bell pepper of ratatouille, which by comparison is a confused dish. Marius Morard, in his *Manuel complet de la cuisinière provençale,* an excellent Provençal cookbook published in 1886, called this *"aubergines à la marseillaise."* Tomatoes are used so often in southern European cooking that even when they are central, they don't necessarily appear in the name of a dish. To Morard's recipe I've added only such details as the size of the eggplant dice and the amount of salt. He was a grand-hotel cook and offered the option of passing the vegetables through a sieve, but then you lose the separate tastes from having cooked the vegetables apart. The purée, as he said, goes well with any sort of meat.

1 pound (500 g) eggplant, peeled and cut in ¾-inch (2-cm) dice

1 tablespoon salt

excellent, fresh-tasting olive oil

1 pound (500 gr) tomatoes, peeled, seeded, and coarsely chopped

black pepper

about a dozen branches flat-leafed parsley

1 clove garlic

Mix the eggplant with the salt and allow it to release its liquid for at least ½ hour. Rinse and drain it. In a wide nonreactive frying pan over medium heat, cook the eggplant until tender in ¼ cup (60 ml) olive oil, stirring from time to time, about 15 minutes.

While the eggplant is cooking, peel, seed, and chop the tomatoes (see page 74). In a separate nonreactive pan over medium heat, cook the tomatoes in a little olive oil until tender, about 10 minutes. Combine the two vegetables, seasoning well with salt and pepper. Finely chop the parsley leaves and garlic shortly before serving and sprinkle them on top of the vegetables (for appearance) or stir them in (for taste). *Serves 4 to 6.*

STEAMED NEW POTATOES

NEW POTATOES ARE READY, AND BEST, WHEN THE PLANTS BLOSSOM in early summer. Even floury varieties have an appealing waxy tenderness then, and I especially like the creamy texture and strong potato taste of certain less-common old varieties, such as La Ratte and Irish Cobbler. Some soils and climates produce a much more potatoey flavor than others, noticeable in new potatoes. You may say that the instructions below are hardly a recipe at all, just steaming. But when potatoes are truly new and freshly dug, they benefit from a degree of care that may rise to the level of a recipe.

3 pounds (1.5 kg) new potatoes

salt

2 tablespoons (25 gr) unsalted butter

chives

Very small new potatoes, in the range of an inch (2.5 cm) across, should be carefully washed and left whole and unpeeled. Larger new potatoes are better peeled and cut into roughly ¾-inch (2-cm) pieces. Steam the potatoes on a rack over boiling water, covered, until they are just tender, about 20 minutes. When they are just done — no softer than that, as they quickly become waterlogged and fall apart — remove the rack from the pot, pour off the water, and return the potatoes to the pot.

Then, over very low heat, season them promptly and carefully with salt; add butter and swirl to make an emulsion with any remaining water. Bunch the chives and slice them with a sharp knife to make fine, tiny rings — cut them at the last minute, so the taste is perfectly fresh. Mix in some of the chives, and once the potatoes are in their serving dish, sprinkle more chives over. *Serves 6 to 8.*

POMMES DE TERRE MACAIRE

Potato Cakes

THESE FRIED CAKES, ODDLY NAMED FOR A MALICIOUS 19th-century stage character, are especially good with grilled lean meat. As homey as they are, they appear in Escoffier's *Guide culinaire*, published at the opening of the 20th century. "Work this pulp with a fork," Escoffier wrote, meaning that he wasn't aiming at a refined, smooth purée. Modern recipes for *pommes de terre Macaire*, especially online, call for all sorts of additions—crème fraîche, Gruyère, nutmeg, egg yolk—and the ones in French call for lardons. Any of these distract from the potato, and putting in cheese and lardons would turn the cakes into a centerpiece rather than a complement. Escoffier's approach was simple, precisely like the one below, except that he used 200 grams of butter per kilo of cooked potato and called for a fast, hot frying in clarified butter. I've halved the butter that's mashed in with the potatoes, and I fry in regular butter over moderate heat. The original was a galette, a single large cake, but it's easier to handle smaller individual ones. Working with the hot baked potatoes, as below, may not be essential, but it avoids any possibility of a reheated taste, and the drier baked pulp absorbs butter up to Escoffier's amount without becoming too soft. For this purpose, I prefer potatoes with a more floury texture.

2 pounds (1 kg) floury potatoes, such as Russets

10 tablespoons (150 gr) unsalted butter

salt and white or black pepper

Bake the potatoes in their skins—about 50 minutes in a 450° F (230° C) oven, depending on their size—and slice them in half. One at a time, hold the hot potatoes in a hand protected with a pad or folded towel and spoon out the insides. Mash the potato pulp with a fork, incorporating 7 tablespoons (100 gr) of the butter and seasoning with salt and pepper. Melt the remaining butter in a large, heavy frying pan. Divide the mashed potato in four and form each portion into a cake roughly ¾ inch (2 cm) thick. Over medium heat, brown the cakes well on one side, 5 to 8 minutes, before turning to brown the other side. *Serves 4.*

GRATIN DAUPHINOIS

Potato Gratin

THESE POTATOES ARE SO GOOD, SUCH A SUPERIOR PARTNER to roast lamb or beef, that they may be the only vegetable gratin that has never gone out of fashion. *Gratin dauphinois* originated in the former province of the Dauphiné in southeastern France. I prefer using American light cream (20 percent fat) to heavy cream, which can be twice as fatty, and of course you can mix milk and cream to your taste, though milk alone is thin and uninteresting. Instead of rubbing the empty dish with garlic beforehand, as below, I often slice two garlic cloves paper thin to mix with the sliced potatoes, but that much garlic is distracting with roast beef.

1 or 2 cloves garlic

1 tablespoon (15 gr) unsalted butter

2 to 3 pounds (900 gr to 1.3 kg) baking potatoes, peeled and sliced ⅛ inch (3 mm) thick

black pepper

nutmeg

salt

1½ to 2 cups (350 to 475 ml) light cream

Heat the oven to 350° F (175° C). Peel the garlic and rub it all over the surface of an oval gratin dish about 8 by 12 inches (20 by 30 cm). Let the garlic juice dry and brush away the clinging bits of garlic flesh that might burn. Heavily butter the dish and fill it two-thirds full with potatoes (no more, or the dish will boil over). Over them, grind pepper and grate a trace of nutmeg; season well with salt. Pour cream over so as to wash the seasonings below the surface: just enough cream that the tops of the potatoes are barely covered. Bake to that key point at which the potatoes are done, the top is brown, and the cream is thick but still flows like a sauce—about 1 hour. *Serves 4 or 5.*

CIPOLLINE IN AGRODOLCE

Sweet-and-Sour Onions

THE COMBINATION OF SWEET AND SOUR ISN'T COMMON in Italian cooking, but it's essential to certain preparations, and I'm fascinated by it, probably because my own cooking tends to be strictly savory, apart from dessert. In fact, these *cipolline in agrodolce,* which go well with meats and poultry, are mild enough that you can eat them as a vegetable. They're best when first cooked. Sweet-and-sour preparations generally make wine taste sour and flavorless, although this mild dish is more adaptable than some.

2 pounds (1 kg) small onions, roughly 1 inch (2 to 3 cm) in diameter

2 tablespoons excellent, fresh-tasting olive oil

3 tablespoons red-wine vinegar plus more to taste

2 teaspoons sugar plus more to taste

2 whole cloves

1 bay leaf

salt and black pepper

Cook the onions in rapidly boiling water for no more than half a minute, peel them, and trim the ends, leaving enough root to hold them together. In a wide non-reactive pan over medium-low heat, cook the onions in one layer in the olive oil, turning to brown them lightly, about 15 minutes. Add an inch (2 or 3 cm) of water and the vinegar, sugar, cloves, bay leaf, and a little salt. Cook uncovered over low heat until the onions are tender, about 1 hour, turning them from time to time and adding a little water if the liquid becomes thick—don't let it burn. Remove the cloves and bay leaf. Taste the liquid, now reduced to a sauce, and, if needed, add more salt and a little more vinegar or sugar; grind in pepper. *Serves 4 to 6.*

Variation: **SWEET-AND-SOUR ONION CONDIMENT**

You can make the onions as a condiment, which will keep, refrigerated, for two weeks or more. Choose onions of any convenient size, and peel and slice them, rather than leaving them whole. Cook them over medium heat in a combination of ½ cup (125 ml) of white wine, ½ cup (125 ml) of white-wine vinegar, and ¼ cup (50 gr) of sugar plus the bay, cloves, and salt. Cover at first until the onions are soft, then uncover and cook until the liquid is reduced to a light syrup, about 10 minutes; stir the onions now and then and don't allow them to color as they cook. Find and remove the 2 cloves and the bay leaf. Cool to tepid and taste and season with salt and, if needed, additional sugar. Use white wine and white-wine vinegar here because, without the browning, the red would give an ugly color.

CALÇOTS AMB ROMESCO

Grilled Onions with Romesco Sauce

CALÇOTS, WHICH ORIGINATED IN THE TOWN OF VALLS in Catalonia, Spain, are a particular kind of onion, hilled up as they grow to have a longer section of thick, tender white stalk. *Calçots* resemble leeks, but don't taste like them. At their best for only three weeks each spring, they're grilled on a rack over hot coals until they're completely tender inside, by which time the outer layers are black. *Romesco* is an uncooked, creamy, orangey-pink sauce from around the nearby city of Tarragona; it's named for the mild red *romesco* pepper, which gives the sauce a slight piquancy. The pepper's taste isn't so specific that you can't substitute another mild sort. There are, not surprisingly, many recipes for the sauce. The bread with which it begins can be plain, toasted, or fried; the garlic may be cooked or raw, or there may be some of each; some cooks omit the tomato, though it adds color, flavor, and lightness; some add parsley and mint. The garlic and tomato for the sauce are often roasted over the same fire that will cook the *calçots*. In Catalonia, the oil that goes into the sauce comes from the sweet native Arbequina olive. Starting with the almonds and ending with the oil, all the ingredients are pounded in a mortar or pot.

    Calçots are eaten at a feast, a *calçotada*. As you eat the *calçots,* a dozen or more per person, depending on their size and the person, you peel and discard the black layers. You dip the tender, pale end generously into the sauce and then lower it into your mouth, a messy process that requires a bib. You eat only the tender part, discarding the green. Irving Davis—drawing, I believe, from experiences in the 1920s—wrote in *A Catalan Cookery Book* that *calçots* are "eaten only in the neighbourhood of Valls, in the open air under the almond trees in bloom." Like everyone else, he noted that eaters drink plentifully from the *porró,* the glass bottle passed from one eater to the next, tipped so a jet of wine comes out, the bottle never coming near anyone's lips. Of course, you may not have *calçots* at all, but the delicious sauce also goes well with grilled meats and fish and dresses salad—though some Catalans might consider those other uses to be heresy. The quantities given below are for one person—increase accordingly.

a slice of white bread

a small handful of peeled, toasted almonds

salt

1 *romesco*, *nyora*, or other mild dried pepper, crushed

1 or 2 cloves garlic

1 ripe red tomato — preferably grilled whole on a fire to blister and loosen the skin — peeled, seeded, and chopped

about ⅞ cup (200 ml) excellent, fresh-tasting olive oil

a dozen or more *calçots*, cleaned and the roots trimmed

In a mortar, pound the bread with the almonds and ¼ teaspoon of salt, or reduce them in a food processor. To the mortar or processor bowl, add the dried pepper and pulverize it along with the garlic, and then add and pulverize the tomato. When all these form a smooth paste, dilute it gradually with olive oil while stirring with the pestle or processing, until it's a thick, creamy, thoroughly emulsified sauce. Taste and season with salt as needed.

Cook the *calçots* whole over the hot coals, turning, until the outer layers are black and the insides are completely soft. Wrap the *calçots* in layers of newspaper and leave them to steam for about 15 minutes, which ensures complete cooking and softens the charred layers so they can be easily peeled away. Serve hot. *Serves 1.*

TURNIP GRATIN

ONE OF THE MOST UNDERAPPRECIATED OLD PREPARATIONS is a vegetable gratin made with white sauce—*béchamel* in French, *balsamella* in Italian. A turnip gratin wonderfully complements poultry, pork, ham, game birds, and lamb. (Cauliflower is not quite as good a complement to meats, but it's even better served as its own course, the vegetable being fully cooked just before the gratin is assembled, not added raw like the turnips.) The half-hour cooking of the béchamel eliminates the raw-flour taste, which is useful when a gratin will be cooked only briefly, though irrelevant when it will spend at least that long in the oven. However, the initial slow cooking of the béchamel also extracts flavor from the ham and onion. Those and the bay leaf and cloves go especially well with brassicas, the broad cabbage family, which includes turnips. The breadcrumbs, which can include crust, are easily made in a food processor from a very thinly sliced stale white loaf, but beware that sourdough is often too tough for breadcrumbs. You can also make crumbs from completely dry white commercial-yeast bread by breaking and crushing it with a rolling pin (a messier proposition). Cheese, particularly Gruyère, is a standard topping for a gratin, though it often detracts. Until 30 or 40 years ago in France, the surface of a gratin was typically colored very dark, in places nearly burned, which is much better than pale and insipid, and it's what I recommend.

BÉCHAMEL

6 tablespoons (85 gr) unsalted butter

½ cup (65 gr) unbleached all-purpose flour

1 quart (1 lt) cold milk plus more as needed

1 bay leaf

1 ounce (30 gr) dry-cured ham, in 1 or 2 slices, *optional*

continued

To make the béchamel: Melt the butter in a large, thick-bottomed saucepan, stir in the flour, and cook and stir the mixture for 1 minute. Add the cold milk all at once and immediately whisk the combination smooth, covering the entire bottom of the pan. Stir continuously, switching to a wooden spatula or spoon and still covering the whole bottom, until the mixture thickens and starts to bubble. Lower the heat, and add the bay leaf, ham, and the onion stuck with the cloves. Cook at a steady low bubble for at least 30 minutes, stirring occasionally across the whole bottom of the pan. Place a

1 or 2 small onions, peeled

2 cloves

salt and black pepper

nutmeg

2½ pounds (1 kg) white turnips, peeled and sliced about ⅛ inch (3 mm) thick

1 cup (roughly 100 gr) or more white breadcrumbs

unsalted butter

heat diffuser beneath the pan if necessary to keep the sauce at a bare bubble and prevent sticking and browning. Remove the bay leaf, ham, onion, and cloves. Taste and season well with salt, enough to season the vegetable, too; grind in pepper and add a few gratings of nutmeg, just enough to detect. If necessary, thin the béchamel with milk to an easily pourable consistency, whisking it together—a slightly lumpy consistency will make no difference in the end.

To assemble the gratin: Heat the oven to 350° F (175° C). Butter well a baking dish, an 8-by-12-inch (20-by-30-cm) oval or equivalent. Arrange half the turnips in one layer and pour half the béchamel over them. Arrange the rest of the turnips in an even layer and add the rest of the béchamel, so as to cover all the turnips. Bake until a knife or fork shows the turnips in the center are soft, about 1 hour. Take the dish from the oven, sprinkle breadcrumbs over the surface, and distribute over them a generous number of thin shavings of butter (more easily shaved from a cold stick). Brown the surface under the broiler, watching and taking care that the dish is far enough from the source that the crumbs don't blacken. *Serves 4 to 6 as a side dish.*

GRATIN D'ÉPINARDS

Creamed Spinach Gratin

A *GRATIN D'ÉPINARDS*, MADE WITH GOOD OLD CREAMED SPINACH, goes well with grilled steak and other meats. The following proportions yield extra white sauce, which could be used at another meal to make a gratin of another vegetable. Certain varieties of spinach, especially when the plants are young in early spring, are mild and not very astringent; other varieties, especially when the plants are older and the weather is hotter and drier, are stronger flavored. You don't know for sure until you taste. Mild spinach shouldn't be boiled but cooked in only the water that clings to it from washing. Adding some heavy cream to the gratin makes it richer and smoother (crème fraîche boosts flavor and acidity but takes away from the spinach). To make a dish that stands more on its own, add several hard-cooked eggs, halved and submerged in the spinach (before you cover it with breadcrumbs); they complement its taste.

6 tablespoons (85 gr) unsalted butter plus more for the gratin

½ cup (65 gr) unbleached all-purpose flour

1 quart (1 lt) cold milk

3 pounds (1.5 kg) very fresh spinach

about ½ cup (125 ml) heavy cream, *optional*

nutmeg

salt and black pepper

¾ cup (75 gr) fine breadcrumbs, dried or from stale bread

Melt the 6 tablespoons (85 gr) of butter in a large, thick-bottomed saucepan, stir in the flour, and cook and stir the mixture for 1 minute. Add the milk all at once and immediately whisk the combination smooth, covering the entire bottom of the pan. Stir continuously, switching to a wooden spatula or spoon and still covering the whole bottom, until the mixture thickens and starts to bubble. Lower the heat and cook at a steady low bubble for at least 30 minutes, stirring occasionally across the whole bottom of the pan. Place a heat diffuser beneath the pan if necessary to keep the sauce at a bare bubble and prevent sticking and browning. Set aside.

Clean the spinach carefully in a sinkful of water and remove it to a colander. Drain the sink, rinse away the grit, and repeat the washing until there is no sign of grit. Remove all the stems from the spinach, pulling them backward from the older leaves to take the tough veins. If the spinach is mild, cook it over medium heat, covered, in a 2-gallon (8-lt) pot, with only the washing water that clings to it, checking frequently and mixing and turning the mass. It will be done in about 5 minutes. If the leaves are stronger flavored, bring a 2-gallon (8-lt) pot of well-salted water to a rolling boil and cook the spinach for 2 to 3 minutes. Drain, and run cold water over it, so it is cool enough to touch. Form small balls of spinach in your hands, pressing to expel water and leave the spinach dry.

Chop the spinach coarsely. In a bowl, combine it with roughly an equal amount of white sauce by volume, adding the white sauce little by little along with, optionally, some heavy cream until you achieve the taste and texture you want. (The warm mixture will have the same consistency now that the browned gratin will have when it comes hot from the oven.) Grate in just enough nutmeg to reinforce the dairy taste—better too little than too much—and season with salt and pepper.

Heat the oven to 350° F (175° C). Put the mixture in a shallow oven dish in which the spinach will make a ½- to ¾-inch (1- to 2-cm) layer. Cover with breadcrumbs and then generously with shavings of cold butter. Bake until the contents are very hot throughout—30 minutes or more. Broil, watching carefully, until the surface is well browned. *Serves 6.*

PETITS POIS À LA LAITUE

Green Peas with Lettuce

THE PEAS FOR THIS DISH SHOULD BE VERY FRESHLY PICKED and at the height of their season — not at all starchy. The simple combination of green peas with new lettuce and spring onions is basic French home cooking. This version closely follows that of Édouard de Pomiane in his *Recettes nouvelles pour le printemps,* published in 1943 and designed for the austerity of wartime — which didn't keep him from recommending a wine to go with the peas. In an old-fashioned way, de Pomiane places the peas at the end of a meal just before dessert and, unexpectedly, suggests "a slightly sweet Barsac." I've made the quantities small because shelling peas is time-consuming; if you like — if you have children to help — don't hesitate to increase the amounts.

3 pounds (1.5 kg) peas in their pods to yield at least 1½ cups (175 gr) shelled peas — more mature pods may yield twice that amount

1 medium or 2 small new heads of butterhead, oakleaf, or other delicate lettuce

a dozen new onions with tiny bulbs

salt

1 tablespoon (15 gr) or more unsalted butter

Shell the peas. Discard the coarse outer leaves of the lettuce, carefully wash each head free of all trace of grit, and quarter the heads. Place the peas, the lettuce with the water still clinging, and the new onions in a pan. Salt lightly (no pepper). Cover the pan and, over medium heat, bring the small amount of liquid in the pan's bottom to a boil. When the peas are nearly done — about 10 minutes — uncover the pan, so that the water almost entirely evaporates by the time the peas are tender. Add salt to taste and flavor with a generous quantity of butter, boiling momentarily to emulsify it with the remaining liquid. *Serves 4.*

CELERY ROOT AND POTATO PURÉE

CELERY ROOT, OR CELERIAC, WITH ITS STRONG FLAVOR, is often mixed with potato in a white purée, which goes well with meats, especially flavorful ones such as roast beef, goose, and above all wild boar and other game. Try to find celery root that's young and white all through rather than old and threaded with tan fibers. And choose a drier, more floury potato to give more substantial texture to the purée. If you're wary of fat, you can reduce the amount of butter without much loss of flavor or texture. The proportions for the purée are partly a matter of taste — really, it's hard to go astray — and you can boil turnips or whole cloves of garlic with the potatoes and add them too.

2 pounds (900 gr) celery root, peeled and quartered

1 large onion, finely sliced

4 tablespoons (50 gr) or more unsalted butter

1½ pounds (700 gr) floury potatoes

salt and pepper

Boil the celery root until tender, roughly 15 minutes. Drain, reserving a cup of the liquid. Purée the celery root in a food processor, unless the roots have woody fibers. If they do, put them through the fine holes of a food mill and then through a fine strainer.

In a covered, heavy pot, stew the onion in ½ tablespoon (7 gr) of the butter over low heat, stirring occasionally, until the slices are entirely limp and translucent — don't let them color. Meanwhile, peel the potatoes, cut them into large pieces, and bring to a boil, starting in cold water; or, preferably, bake them whole in their skins in a 425° F (220° C) oven, then halve them and spoon them out of their skins. Reduce the hot potatoes to a purée together with the onion by passing them through the fine holes of a food mill (a food processor risks making glutinous potatoes).

Combine all three vegetables in a large saucepan, add the remaining butter, thin if necessary with some of the reserved cooking liquid, and season with salt and pepper. *Serves 4 or 5.*

ZUCCA ALL'AGRODOLCE

Sweet-and-Sour Winter Squash

SICILIAN *ZUCCA ALL'AGRODOLCE* IS ALSO CALLED *fegato di Settecannoli* (or *ficatu ri sette cannoli* in Sicilian) — liver from Settecannoli. That's the fountain with seven spouts in the piazza at the center of the Vucciria market in Palermo. Long ago, in the days when rich and poor lived close together, it's said that the poor smelled the liver cooking in the kitchens of the nobility and made their own humble version using winter squash. It's also said that there were only vegetable sellers in the piazza, and so the name was simply ironical. The yellow flesh coupled with the brown from frying looks slightly livery. The squash can be any dense winter variety that lends itself to slicing, though preferably not an American pumpkin — its distinct flavor isn't bad; it's just not Italian. I've used Rouge Vif d'Étampes, Blue Hubbard, and Long Island Cheese; butternut, though bland, would be all right. In Sicily, the mint for this and other uses is either garden spearmint or wild *mentuccia*.

Zucchini, in the Italian sense of any summer squash, are cooked in a related and delicious fashion without sugar: fry 1 pound (500 gr) of sliced *zucchini* in olive oil along with 1 peeled, partly crushed garlic clove; add salt and pepper, ¼ cup (60 ml) of white-wine vinegar, and 2 finely chopped mint leaves, and continue to cook until the liquid has evaporated.

1 pound (500 gr) winter squash, seeded, peeled, and sliced ½ inch (1 cm) thick

about ½ cup (125 ml) excellent, fresh-tasting olive oil

salt and black pepper

2 cloves garlic, finely chopped

¼ cup (60 ml) wine vinegar, preferably red

2 tablespoons sugar

4 or 5 spearmint leaves, finely chopped

In a large, nonreactive pan, fry the slices of squash in enough olive oil to come partway up the sides of the slices, working in batches as needed to keep a single layer. Stir and turn with a wooden spoon or spatula so as not to cut into the squash with a metal edge, and season with salt and pepper. Adjust the heat so the squash is only moderately brown by the time it's thoroughly cooked. Remove it to a serving dish as it's done.

Pour off all but a film of oil, add the garlic to the pan, and cook it over medium-low heat for a minute or two; don't let it color. Add the vinegar and sugar, cooking and stirring until the sugar is dissolved. Pour this sauce over the squash. Add the mint, and mix gently. Cool to room temperature and serve. *Serves 4.*

ZUCCHINI PUDDING

THIS ZUCCHINI PUDDING, A COMPLEMENT TO GRILLED MEATS, combines two elements from Richard Olney's essential *Simple French Food,* first published in 1974. Basically, it's his zucchini pudding soufflé treated like his onion pudding—that is, without having the egg whites separated and beaten. Many cooks dismiss zucchini as tiresome and uninteresting, but few vegetables are as richly flavored and as capable of withstanding frequent appearances on the table. The key is using the right variety: the only zucchini worth growing are not one of the neat bush kinds but an old-fashioned, less "improved" and more flavorful Italian variety, such as Costata Romanesco. As the plants grow, they slowly sprawl, forming vines several feet long and yielding heavily ribbed, irregular fruits. For the pudding, exact proportions don't matter, but it's better to use too much zucchini than too little.

2 pounds (1 kg) zucchini, no more than 10 inches (25 cm) long

2 teaspoons salt

5 tablespoons (75 gr) unsalted butter

5 tablespoons (40 gr) unbleached all-purpose flour

1 cup (250 ml) cold milk

1 onion, finely chopped

4 large eggs, beaten

about ⅜ teaspoon dried oregano or mixed dried herbs, especially thyme and Greek oregano, but optionally also marjoram and savory

salt and black pepper

Grate the zucchini coarsely and mix it with the salt in a large bowl. Set it aside for at least ½ hour. While the zucchini sits, make a quick béchamel sauce. Melt 4 tablespoons (60 gr) of the butter in a saucepan over medium heat, stir in the flour, and cook, stirring, for 1 minute. Add the cold milk all at once and immediately whisk the combination smooth, covering the entire bottom of the pan, then stir continuously with a wooden spatula or spoon until the mixture thickens and bubbles. Take the pan from the heat and cover it so the surface of the sauce doesn't dry out.

Drain the zucchini in a colander. Taking a quarter of it at a time, squeeze it hard between your hands to expel much of the moisture. Set the zucchini aside. Cook the onion in the remaining tablespoon of butter in a wide frying pan over low heat, stirring, until it is translucent but not colored. Add the zucchini and cook, stirring and turning until it is cooked through, about 15 minutes. Combine the vegetables with the béchamel in a large bowl and mix in the eggs. Add the oregano, taste and season with salt if needed, and grind in pepper.

Heat the oven to 400° F (200° C). Oil or butter a 7- to 9-inch (18- to 23-cm) diameter soufflé dish, or another oven dish such as an oval up to 8 by 12 inches (20 by 30 cm). Fill it with the pudding mixture and bake until swollen and brown — 30 to 40 minutes. *Serves 4 to 6.*

FISH, SEAFOOD, AND SNAILS

COD WITH TOMATO, HYSSOP, AND TARRAGON

FOR THIS, YOU NEED FRESH HYSSOP, A PERENNIAL with spikes of fine, small, edible blue-purple flowers, which are good in a salad. Hyssop was once an everyday garden plant, a potherb; it's not common now, but it's easily grown from seed. The flavor strikes me as medieval, like a resinous combination of thyme and savory with a little menthol. That's not surprising, since hyssop is a member of the broad mint family. I combined it with cod long ago when I was thinking about ways to use it. (If you don't have hyssop, do something entirely different with herbs. For instance, omit the tarragon, hyssop, and wine, and instead add ¼ cup or 30 grams of chopped green olives and 1½ teaspoons of chopped marjoram or oregano.) I serve the cod with rice and drink a basic light white wine (with the olives, drink the same or a fino sherry).

1 small onion, finely chopped

excellent, fresh-tasting olive oil

½ cup (125 ml) white wine

2 large tomatoes (together about 750 gr), peeled, seeded, and chopped

1 teaspoon coarsely chopped fresh tarragon leaves

4 teaspoons coarsely chopped fresh hyssop leaves

salt and black pepper

2 pounds (1 kg) filets of cod or haddock or another white-fleshed fish

1 cup (enough to fill a 250-ml measure) slightly stale bread in ½- to ¾-inch (1- to 2-cm) cubes

Heat the oven to 400° F (200° C). In a nonreactive metal baking dish (or a separate pan), cook the onion in olive oil over medium heat until it's translucent. Add the white wine and boil to reduce the quantity by half. Add the tomatoes, let them boil 1 minute, then add the tarragon and hyssop. Season with salt and pepper, and put the tomato sauce into a baking dish if it isn't already in one. Arrange the cod filets in the dish, tucking the thin tails under. Lubricate the fish with a thin stream of olive oil and season it lightly with salt. Bake until the point of a knife shows that the fish at its thickest point is no longer translucent, roughly 10 minutes if it's an inch (2.5 cm) thick. Meanwhile, fry the bread cubes in olive oil to make croûtons. As soon as the fish is done, serve it strewn with the croûtons. *Serves 4.*

MARYLAND CRAB CAKES

I GREW UP IN MARYLAND, AND THIS TO ME is a purist's recipe for crab cakes, meaning it calls for only enough bread to bind the crab and allows no flavorings that could possibly distract. Worcestershire sauce and too much green bell pepper take away from the crab taste. But even purist crab cakes allow some room for variation and individual taste. Parsley and cayenne are always good, though neither is required. There's nothing wrong with a little chopped, cooked onion, though it's not "Eastern Shore." Vinegar is an old flavoring for crab, and sherry is a 20th century one; I've borrowed the combined notion of sherry vinegar from John Taylor's *Hoppin' John's Lowcountry Cooking,* a collection of recipes from coastal South Carolina, where blue crabs are highly appreciated.

a large handful of soft but fairly substantial white bread, without crust

1 egg

a little heavy cream, if the crabmeat appears dry

1 pound (500 gr) lump or jumbo lump blue crabmeat

1 tablespoon sherry vinegar

2 tablespoons chopped parsley

salt and black pepper

red pepper (cayenne)

about ¾ cup (roughly 75 gr) dry bread crumbs, grated or crushed fine with a rolling pin

clarified unsalted butter

Soak the bread in water for 15 minutes, then squeeze out what water will come, leaving about ½ cup of pasty bread. Mash this smooth. Mix it with the egg and, if needed, the cream. Gently combine the bread paste, crabmeat, vinegar, and parsley; season with salt and black and red peppers. Form into 3 cakes and coat with dry breadcrumbs. Set a frying pan with ⅛ to ¼ inch (3 to 6 mm) of clarified butter over medium heat and brown the cakes on both sides, perhaps 10 minutes altogether. *Serves 3 as a main course.*

SALT COD CAKES

THESE FRIED SALT COD CAKES WOULD FIT INTO THE COOKING of various parts of the world, though the recipe happens to come from New England. Salt cod, not to be confused with stockfish (hard, unsalted dried cod), used to be commonplace throughout New England, but no longer. It's sold in Italian, Portuguese, Spanish, and certain specialty markets. Thick filets are best. The highest quality is found in Catalonia, where salt cod is appreciated more than it is anywhere else. With rare exceptions, before cooking, salt cod is soaked in cold water to remove much of the salt and restore some of the former texture. The degree of saltiness varies, and thicker pieces require longer soaking, but it's possible to remove too much salt and, along with it, flavor: salt cod dishes should be slightly salty. A good counterpoint to these cakes is a mound of cooked spinach or chard.

1 pound (500 gr) salt cod

1 large onion, finely chopped

2 cloves garlic, finely chopped

oil, lard, or unsalted butter

1 cup (250 gr) mashed potato

3 tablespoons finely chopped parsley

a good pinch of dried thyme

pepper

salt, *if needed*

about 1 cup (100 gr) dry breadcrumbs

1 lemon, sliced in wedges

Rinse the fish and leave it to soak in a large amount of cold water, changing the water twice a day, until the flesh has lost enough of its salt to make it easily palatable but is still notably salty, usually 24 to 36 hours.

Put the soaked cod in an open pot of fresh cold water and bring the water slowly to poaching temperature, when only a few bubbles disturb the surface. Don't overcook the fish: it should flake only under the influence of a probing knife or finger. Thin pieces of cod will be done almost immediately — remove them as that happens; thick pieces may take 10 minutes or longer. Drain the fish well and cool it briefly, then remove any skin. Feel the flesh carefully for bones, and remove them.

Cook onion and garlic in 2 teaspoons of oil over medium-low heat until soft, without allowing them to color. In a bowl, with light fingers, knead together the cod, onion, garlic, mashed potato, parsley, thyme, and pepper. Taste and add salt only if needed because the fish was oversoaked. Form 6 to 8 cakes, coat them with breadcrumbs, and sauté them briefly in fat until they are crisp and brown on both sides, pressing lightly with a spatula to flatten the cakes to less than an inch (2 cm) high. Serve with sliced lemon. *Serves 3 or 4 as a main course.*

ESCARGOTS À LA BOURGUIGNONNE

Snails in Garlic Butter

OTHER GOOD THINGS CAN BE DONE WITH SNAILS, but none is more pleasing in its simplicity and jolt of flavor than classic snails in garlic butter, as in this recipe from James. The strong butter balances the earth taste of the snails, which is not pleasing to all. More restaurants today might offer snails if the finer kinds hadn't been eclipsed 25 years ago by achatine snails from Indonesia and China, which are cheap but so mushy and muddy tasting that they only underscore how good a Burgundian or *petit gris* can be, even from a can.

The Burgundian snail, or *escargot des vignes* (*Helix pomatia*), is a large variety of northeastern France. The *petit gris* (*Cornu aspersum*) is smaller and found in the south and west of the country, from Provence through Brittany. In France, either kind can be bought live, canned, or frozen. Enthusiasts prefer live ones gathered in nature to cultivated ones. Consumption is so great in France that other varieties are imported from Turkey, Algeria, and central Europe. One reason for the success of canned snails is that preparing live ones from scratch is a long process. It used to be thought best to gather them in the fall after they had sealed themselves in their shells to hibernate. (These days, a better understanding of their anatomy allows for consumption year-round.) Old recipes called for first feeding them a plain diet of lettuce for a week and then putting them into a crock with salt and water to purge bitterness. After many washings in fresh water, they would be cooked for 3½ to 4 hours with water, lots of white wine, garlic, and a bouquet garni; the intestine was removed, and they were returned to their shells. North Americans have no choice but to buy canned. In the United States, you can order canned wild Burgundy snails put up by the French firm Henri Maire, which specializes in snails (a source is www.igourmet.com). The Grandjean brand, if you find it, belongs to Henri Maire and is said to be identical.

For basic *à la bourguignonne,* the snails are cooked in a simple garlic butter containing plenty of parsley. Some versions add chopped shallots, and others go so far as to put a shallot-and-white-wine reduction into the bottom of the shells before adding the snails, but these are unnecessary *grande cuisine* conceits. (An old chef from Nîmes used to tell James, "Those Parisians put shallots everywhere!") The generous amount of parsley helps the butter form a beautiful green foam as the snails cook. The assertive garlic will swallow up the flavors of a finer white wine, but the sharp acidity of a young generic Chablis or a lesser Sauvignon Blanc is just right, the parsley supporting the combination. Any leftover butter is excellent melted on a hot grilled steak.

1 medium clove (6 gr) garlic, coarsely chopped

⅜ teaspoon (2.5 gr) salt

black pepper

14 tablespoons (200 gr) unsalted butter, in 1-inch (2- to 3-cm) pieces, at cool room temperature

about 1 cup (50 gr) washed and dried parsley leaves, lightly compressed

a lemon, for juice

3 dozen large to extra-large snails, or at least 6 dozen small ones

Heat the oven to 450° F (230° C). Place the garlic, salt, and pepper in the bowl of the processor, and with the machine running, add the butter bit by bit. Scrape down the sides, and process again to be sure all is smooth and the garlic is reduced to a purée. Add the parsley to the processor along with a squeeze of lemon juice, and pulse until the leaves are chopped no more than fine.

Rinse the snails and dry them in a paper towel. Put them into ramekins holding about 6 snails in a single layer, and spread the butter mixture on top. Bake until the butter is very foamy and the snails are very hot, about 10 minutes. (Cooked too long, the foam subsides and the butter tastes simply greasy — some books warn against a sizzle, but it's a plus as long as there's foam with it.) *Serves 6.*

MOULES À LA MARINIÈRE

Steamed Mussels

THERE'S NO BETTER WAY TO COOK EXTREMELY FRESH MUSSELS than *à la marinière*, which is simply mussels steamed open in white wine and a few aromatics. That or some similar preparation forms the first step of most other mussel recipes, which, you might argue, exist only for the sake of variety.

A truly fresh mussel, especially a young one, tastes sweet. Use only the very freshest, cooking and eating the mussels as soon as possible after harvest, ideally within 24 hours, although up to three days seems fairly safe. Check for liveliness by pushing the top shell across the bottom, so the two rub slightly: you should feel the strong resistance of the adductor muscle at work. In a favorable environment, some of the mussels will relax and gape, and then close again on being tapped or put into fresh water, which they don't like. When they gape, they dry out, which is another reason to seek maximum freshness. During the short time before you cook them, keep the mussels in a colander in the refrigerator, with ice on top and a pan below to catch water.

In North America, the best season for blue mussels (*Mytilus edulis*) is October through May; for Mediterranean (*M. galloprovincialis*), it's July to October in the Pacific Northwest, earlier farther south; and for the Pacific blue mussel (*M. trossulus*), it's August through May. These days, most mussels for sale are farmed, though some are wild. It's best that any mussels be heavy for the size of their shells, indicating that the meats fill them, but keep in mind that rapidly grown farmed mussels have lighter shells. Like wild mussels that you might harvest yourself, even some commercial mussels retain the beard, or byssus, sticking out of the shell. That's the group of dark, greenish fibers that anchored the mussel to the spot where it grew.Among farmed mussels, there's some difference between those that have been suspended in the water, using ropes, rafts, and so on, and those seeded to the bottom. Sam Hayward, a chef in Portland, Maine, who has a profound knowledge of his coast, says, "The suspended tend to have thinner shells, less tough byssi, delicate flavor, no pearls or grit, fewer shell barnacles (hitchhikers), and smaller meats. Bottom-cultured mussels tend to have thicker shells, tough byssi, bigger flavor, some grit, and more barnacles. The public and restaurants seem to be gravitating toward cultured mussels and away from wild-debyssed, although the latter are less expensive." Good wild mussels may be rare but they exist. The best live below the low-tide line, where they are continuously submerged and grow faster. Hayward prefers those to cultivated, saying they have "more vigorous flavor, less fragile shells, fatter meats, better value per pound."

To clean mussels, stir them energetically in several changes of water and scrape off any barnacles with a dull knife. Wild ones may need an actual scrub. Discard any mussels with broken shells. Those for sale have normally had the byssus removed. Pulling it out before sending the mussels to market harms them, so commercial operations sometimes cut the beards off instead. If the mussels still have the beards, then it's up to you to pull or cut them off. After cooking, for a careful dish in which the meats are taken from the shells, you can remove any remaining bits of beard. In refined French cooking, the dark band around the cooked mussel is also removed, which seems wasteful and not worth the trouble.

The ingredients for *moules à la marinière* aren't at all fixed. Olive oil can take the place of butter, and one or more of the aromatic ingredients can be dispensed with; even the wine is sometimes left out. The simplest *marinière* variations are made by adding extra garlic, a little saffron, or a large tomato that has been peeled, seeded, and chopped. Enough salt is usually provided by the mussels themselves.

After a short cooking, the shells open, which inevitably some do before others; as soon as they open, the mussels are done. The meats inside have pulled back from the shells to form an oval. Further cooking only causes them to shrink more, lose more juice, and start to toughen. If the mussel meats will next be baked or otherwise recooked, the initial cooking should be just long enough to open them.

Mussels grown off the bottom don't contain sand, but others do, and if after cooking you find grit in the bottom of the pot, you can strain the liquid through a cloth. Serve this broth as is, to be eaten with a spoon or soaked up with bread or toast, or reduce it to a sauce; in the latter case, remove the top shells before pouring the sauce back over the mussels. (If you don't serve the broth, save it for another fish preparation.)

Having opened the mussels *à la marinière*, James sometimes serves them as an *amuse-bouche:* putting each mussel on a half shell, adding snail butter (page 138) and then fresh white breadcrumbs, ideally sourdough, and finishing them under the broiler. The crumbs turn crunchy before the meats overcook. Use olive oil instead of butter and you have a common Italian way to prepare mussels.

Classic accompaniments to *moules à la marinière* are french fries, of course, and good bread, fresh or toasted. Lighter beers go well with them, and so do flavorful Belgian *gueuze* and traditional Belgian ales with their spicy, hoppy taste. If a mussel dish contains cream, you can choose a more concentrated, aged Muscadet or one of the ripest Sancerres from the best plots—wines that also suit the saffron and tomato in some mussel dishes.

As a main course, allow roughly one pound (500 grams) of mussels per person, more for mussel lovers. You can multiply the amounts below.

1 onion (about 100 gr) or 1 shallot (about 35 gr), finely chopped

1 clove garlic, finely chopped or crushed

¾ cup (175 ml) white wine

1 tablespoon (15 gr) unsalted butter

2 pounds (1 kg) mussels, cleaned

finely chopped parsley for garnish

black pepper

Choose a heavy pot wide enough that the mussels form a single layer, or cook them in 2 pots or in batches. Cook the onion and garlic gently in the wine and butter for a few minutes, until they are soft. Raise the heat to high, add the mussels, and cover tightly. The mussels will open in 2 to 8 minutes, depending on their size, the intensity of heat, and the quantity in relation to the width of the pot. After about 2 minutes, stir to redistribute the mussels. When half have opened, to avoid overcooking, start removing the open ones with tongs or a slotted spoon to hot soup plates. Discard any that remain shut after 8 minutes. Sprinkle parsley over the cooked mussels.

Run a metal spoon over the bottom of the pot to see whether the liquid contains grit. If there's none, pour the liquid over the mussels, onion or shallot and all. If there is grit, either let it settle to the bottom for a moment and then add the liquid to the mussels, holding back the onion or shallot, or pour the liquid through a cloth-lined strainer before adding it. Serve the mussels immediately and have a peppermill on the table. *Serves 4 as a first course, 2 as a main course.*

MOUCLADE

Mussels in Cream Sauce

MOUCLADE IS A TYPICAL DISH OF THE CHARENTES, the pair of Atlantic departments of France also known for oysters, salt, melons, and Cognac. To make it, cooked mussels on half shells are covered generously with a sauce of mussel broth thickened with flour and egg yolk and sometimes a little cream, and usually flavored with saffron or curry. The spices are supposed to have been available because they were among the goods passing through the Charentais port of La Rochelle. Mussel recipes blur together, and *mouclade* recipes, all claiming to be true, are highly variable. Austin de Croze, in 1928 in *Les Plats régionaux de France,* left out the flour and egg, not to mention the spice, reducing the broth by half and adding "a little double cream." *Moules à la poulette,* made in the Charentes and other parts of France, contains the same ingredients as *mouclade,* except for the spice. Haute cuisine cooks, rather than thickening their *poulettes* with a flour-and-butter roux, used to add *velouté* (white stock lightly thickened with a blond roux and cooked carefully for a long time), one of the mother sauces of classical French cuisine.

The recipe for *mouclade* can be adapted to make an elegant sauced fish: after you cook the mussels to open them, use the broth to poach a tasty, meaty fish (grouper or halibut, for instance), whole or in filets or thick slices, in a snug pan so you can cover the fish halfway without adding water. Then turn the poaching liquid into the sauce for *mouclade,* as below, surrounding the fish with the mussels in their half shells and pouring the sauce over them.

Flour thickening has a certain unrefined homey appeal, and adding flour to a sauce containing egg allows the sauce to be overcooked, even partly boiled, without curdling. But the flour requires long, slow cooking to change its raw taste and perceptibly starchy texture to a smoother, more delicate one, and even then the result can be gloppy. Meanwhile, with mussels the flavor of egg yolk can distract. Yet a sauce containing neither flour nor yolk—just the reduced cooking liquor plus cream and further reduction—can be impossibly rich and salty. The way to do it is to reduce the broth by two-thirds, add 1½ cups (350 ml) of cream, and then further reduce the combination only a little, leaving the sauce thin. James and I have opted instead for as light a version of *mouclade* as we could, while still making something recognizable to a Charentais. To distract from the starchy texture, we reduced the amounts of flour and egg and included cream. The mussels are opened in wine only, so that any grit can be eliminated by straining through cloth without losing the vegetable garnish. The variation, a mussel-spinach gratin, is James's.

about 40 saffron threads or
½ teaspoon curry powder, *optional*

1½ cups (350 ml) white wine

4 to 5 pounds (2 kg) cleaned mussels

1 tablespoon (15 gr) unsalted butter

1 tablespoon all-purpose flour

1 clove garlic, finely chopped

1 onion (about 100 gr) or 1 shallot
(about 35 gr), finely chopped

¾ cup (175 ml) heavy cream

½ cup (125 ml) finely chopped parsley

black pepper

1 egg yolk, *optional*

a lemon, for juice

Pour ¼ cup (60 ml) of boiling water over the saffron threads, and leave them to steep.

Choose a heavy pot wide enough that the mussels form a single layer, or cook them in 2 pots or in batches. Pour in the wine, turn the heat to high, add the mussels, and cover tightly. The mussels will open in 2 to 8 minutes, depending on their size, the intensity of heat, and the quantity in relation to the width of the pot. After about 2 minutes, stir to redistribute the mussels. When half have opened, to avoid overcooking, start removing the open ones with tongs or a slotted spoon to hot soup plates. Discard any that remain shut after 8 minutes. Remove the top shell from each open mussel and place the mussels in a warm oven dish just large enough to hold them. Cover the dish and put it in a warm spot, such as a very low oven. Run a metal spoon over the bottom of the pot to see whether the liquid contains grit. If not, pouring it through a fine-meshed metal strainer will do; otherwise, line the strainer with a cloth.

Melt the butter in a large saucepan over medium heat, incorporate the flour, and cook 1 minute, stirring. Whisk in the warm mussel liquor, little by little, to make a smooth sauce. Add the garlic and onion; cook 10 minutes over low heat. Off the heat, add the cream, parsley, and curry powder or saffron threads in their water; grind in pepper. Then mix in the egg yolk and cook, stirring continuously with a wooden spoon or spatula so as to cover the whole bottom of the pan, just until the first tiny bubbles appear at the sides. Off the heat, squeeze in lemon juice to taste, and, if necessary, thin the sauce with water to the consistency of heavy cream. Pour it evenly over the mussels. Heat them through, 10 to 15 minutes in a 350 ° F (175 ° C) oven or, better, a few minutes under a broiler, carefully watched. *Serves 4.*

Variation: **MUSSEL-SPINACH GRATIN**

Open 2 pounds (1 kg) of mussels in wine, as above. Remove the mussel meats from their shells, and pour the broth, if it has no grit, through a fine-meshed metal strainer; otherwise, line the strainer with a cloth. Add about 40 saffron threads to this liquid, and reduce it nearly to a syrup. Add 1 cup (250 ml) of the heavy cream, and reduce further to a thin sauce. Whip another ½ cup (125 ml) of cream almost stiff, and fold half an egg yolk into it (you might use the other half in scrambled eggs). Add that to the sauce in the pan and whisk over high heat until the first tiny bubbles appear at the sides. Heighten the flavor with 1½ teaspoons of lemon juice. Line 4 individual gratin dishes with lightly buttered cooked spinach (you will need about 3 cups or 700 ml in all). Put the mussel meats in the center, and pour the lightly foamy sauce evenly over them. Broil until the sauce is golden brown. *Serves 4.*

DEEP-FRIED OYSTERS

BEER BATTER IS CLASSICAL FRENCH. IN SOME OLDER VERSIONS the beer is intended as leavening and the batter is set in a warm place to ferment. According to *La Bonne Cuisine de Madame E. Saint-Ange,* published in 1927, "You must allow the batter all the time necessary for the fermentation to start." But even without living yeast, an effervescent beer lightens the batter, and perhaps offers a trace of flavor and helps to inhibit the formation of gluten. The quantity of batter below is sufficient to fry, along with the seafood if you like: zucchini, zucchini blossoms, asparagus, artichoke hearts, mushrooms, or onions. I call for merely good oil, because the best is costly to use for deep-frying.

For eating raw, oysters are shucked just before they're eaten, and that's best for cooking, too, although it's reasonable to buy already shucked oysters from a prime supplier. I once wrote eight thorough paragraphs about oyster knives and how to use them. This isn't the place to dig in, nor to talk about the diverse kinds of oysters, but I will say I use a Dexter-Russell s122 oyster knife, which is the favorite of the champion shucker John Bil, of Prince Edward Island. Oysters in the shell will keep for a period of time, but my own preference, for any purpose, is to use oysters that are as freshly harvested as possible; I try to buy directly from the producer. Keep oysters as cold as you can, just above freezing if possible. Those in the shell should be kept out of the water, with damp towels above and below and ice on top.

1¾ cups (250 gr) unbleached all-purpose flour

¼ teaspoon salt

enough good olive oil or other light cooking oil for deep-frying

1 tablespoon brandy

¾ cup (175 ml) beer

¾ cup (175 ml) cold water

4 dozen oysters, assuming medium-sized meats, more oysters if they're small

a fat pinch of cream of tartar, if you use a noncopper bowl

2 egg whites

Place the flour and salt in a bowl and stir in 1 tablespoon of oil and the brandy, beer, and water, working the batter minimally, just enough to eliminate lumps. Set the batter aside to rest. Shuck the oysters, if they aren't already shucked, and place the meats in a colander to drain, with a bowl beneath. (With freshly harvested oysters, the liquor from shucking and from the colander is a luxury to save for fish soup and sauces.)

In a copper bowl, freshly cleaned with lemon juice or vinegar and salt, rinsed, and dried (or in a noncopper bowl, adding the cream of tartar), whisk the egg whites until they just form stiff peaks. Add them to the batter, mixing so there is no streak of white. In a high-sided pot suitable for deep frying, or in a special deep-fryer, heat approximately 1½ inches (4 cm) of oil to about 390° F (200° C) — when the temperature is right, a small spoonful of batter will brown in about a minute. Dry the oyster meats in a paper towel and, working in batches, coat them in batter and brown them in the oil without crowding the pot, turning once, about 5 minutes. Drain on paper towels and serve each batch as it's done. *Serves 4 as a main course.*

SARDELE IN SAOR

Sweet-and-Sour Sardines

VENETIAN *SARDELE IN SAOR* IS A TYPICAL SUMMER DISH, eaten either as a *cicheto,* a snack, or as a main course. As in the *escabetx* of the next recipe, cooking the fish and putting them in saor preserves them for a short time. Fresh sardines are one of the "blue" fish of the Mediterranean that have more fat and stronger flavor than other species. They were always poor people's food, never expensive. Before the sardines are floured and fried, they're sometimes dipped in egg, but they're never battered. Venetians prefer the light taste of vegetable oil, but light-tasting olive oil would be as good or better. Nowadays the oil from frying the fish is discarded, and fresh oil is added for the onions. Older recipes call for pine nuts and raisins and sometimes also cinnamon or mixed spices. At least one Venetian restaurant has served *scampi in saor:* a "corruption," a Venetian once told me. He didn't think it was wrong but "strange," because the taste of shrimp is too delicate for a *saor.* The fish, whatever the kind, are marinated in the sauce for at least 24 hours, and I was assured at one Venetian *bàcaro,* a neighborhood bar serving *cicheti,* that its *sardele* always marinate for at least a week. If you use another kind of blue fish (outside the Mediterranean, probably mackerel or the species called bluefish), choose small ones or cut them into pieces, so the sauce penetrates. Red-wine vinegar gives a deeper color (but red wine in place of white can stain the fish purple). Whether you add sugar, and how much, depends on the sweetness of the onions and the acidity of the vinegar. Raisins and pine nuts are in theory only used in winter, but they taste good at any time.

2 pounds (1 kg) whole fresh sardines, scaled and gutted

all-purpose flour

excellent, fresh- and light-tasting olive oil or another good, light cooking oil

salt

2 pounds (1 kg) sweet onions, sliced extremely thin

about ½ cup (125 ml) white- or red-wine vinegar

¼ cup (60 ml) white wine

several bay leaves

black pepper

a spoonful of sugar, if needed

a small handful (50 gr) of raisins, soaked for a few hours in water or white wine and then drained

a small handful (50 gr) of pine nuts

Rinse and dry the sardines well and flour them lightly. Pour enough oil into a nonreactive frying pan to cover the bottom. Fry the fish over medium-high heat, turning and salting, until they are just done — 4 or 5 minutes. Remove them to a platter to cool.

Wipe the oil from the frying pan and add fresh. Cook the onions in it gently, stirring now and then, until they are soft but not at all colored — 10 to 15 minutes. (If the onions seem dry, as they often do before a new crop is ready, cover the pan or add a little water.) Add the vinegar, wine, and bay leaves, and bring to a boil. Season this sauce with salt, pepper, and, if needed, sugar. Add the raisins and the pine nuts.

Choose a glass, glazed ceramic, or stainless-steel pan that will hold the fish in 2 or 3 layers. Spread onion sauce thinly in the bottom and then add a layer of sardines; spread with onions again, and continue, packing the fish closely together and surrounding them with onion. Cover and refrigerate for at least 1 day before eating; keeps for 3 days. Eat cool or tepid, not cold. *Serves 4 as a main course.*

ESCABETX DE VERATS

Marinated Mackerel

THIS RECIPE IS CATALAN, BUT AROUND THE MEDITERRANEAN, the method is an old one for preserving fish briefly when they are cheap, abundant, and at their best. *Escabetx,* like *escabeche,* comes from Persia and, along with the name, was brought by Arabs to Spain; Catalans claim that it was their form of the word, *escabetx,* that passed into other European languages. The fish—not only mackerel but other kinds (see the *sardele in saor,* preceding recipe)—used to be kept for a number of days, completely covered with the oil from frying, but even with refrigeration it seems better to keep them for only a few days. In preparing this or any food, use only European bay leaves, never the California species, which has a bolder, almost paintlike aroma.

2 pounds (1 kg) very fresh whole mackerel, cleaned

salt

excellent, fresh-tasting olive oil

branches of mixed fresh herbs, such as savory, thyme, oregano, and rosemary

several bay leaves

black pepper

1 clove garlic, chopped

ground sweet red pepper (*pebre vermell* or paprika), *optional*

1 cup (250 ml) good wine vinegar, less if the vinegar is very acidic

Dry the fish inside and out with paper towels, season well with salt, and fry just until the flesh at the thickest point is no longer translucent, keeping the oil well below the smoking point, in at least ¼ inch (6 mm) of oil—perhaps 4 or 5 minutes per side. Place the cooked fish in a deep platter, and over them distribute the fresh herbs and bay leaves, grindings of pepper, the garlic, and the ground sweet pepper. Pour on the vinegar and then the cooking oil, adding fresh oil if needed to cover the fish. Refrigerate. After 1 to 3 days, remove the herbs and serve, tepid. *Serves 4 as a main course.*

PIKE, PIKE-PERCH, OR SALMON WITH BEURRE BLANC

BEURRE BLANC, THE FAMOUS LOIRE VALLEY SAUCE TYPICALLY SERVED with poached fish, especially *sandre* (pike-perch), *brochet* (pike), and salmon, is made all along the middle and lower part of the river. But it probably comes from Anjou, and it's one of the region's many dishes suited to a glass of dry Chenin Blanc. Curnonsky, the great French gastronomic critic of the 20th century, was born in Angers, capital of Anjou, and credited this sauce to housewives. Despite all the butter, the taste should be delicate, not heavy. The tactic of first cooking the shallots to a purée, for a richer base, was that of the chef Charles Barrier of Tours.

1 pike or European pike-perch, cleaned, or a salmon filet, weighing about 2 pounds (1 kg)

2 shallots (about 50 gr)

½ cup (100 ml) white-wine or cider vinegar

1 cup (200 ml) white wine

¾ cup (175 gr) unsalted butter, in 1-inch (2- to 3-cm) pieces

salt and white pepper

Chop the shallots extremely fine, almost to a paste, and cook them slowly in the vinegar and white wine to the consistency of thin applesauce, 15 or more minutes. Take them from the heat. Poach or grill the fish, just until the thickest part, investigated with the point of a knife, is no longer translucent, about 10 minutes if the fish is an inch (2.5 cm) thick. Take care not to overcook it, or it will taste dry.

Meanwhile, over very low heat, or on and off the heat—don't let the butter melt into oil—little by little whisk the pieces of butter into the shallots to form a light cream. Season with salt and white pepper. Temperature is key: serve the sauce, without too much waiting, from a slightly warm vessel together with the fish. *Serves 4.*

Variation: **FENNEL SAUCE**

English fennel sauce, for salmon and other fish, is based on English butter sauce, and since this version omits the usual flour, it's really a *beurre blanc* made with plain water. Use freshly cut fennel.

Blanch 1 cup (a 250-ml measure) of lightly compacted chopped fennel foliage (no stems) for 30 seconds in boiling water. Drain it well in a fine strainer and press it dry in a towel. Optionally, reduce it to a purée in a mortar or food processor. In a small pan, heat 2 tablespoons of water. Then, over very low heat, or on and off the heat—don't let the butter melt—add ½ pound (250 gr) of unsalted butter cut into 1-inch (2- or 3-cm) pieces, whisking it in little by little, so it forms a light cream. Whisk in the blanched fennel. Season with salt and white pepper and enliven the sauce with some freshly squeezed lemon juice. *Serves 4.*

FISH QUENELLES

ALONG FRANCE'S MANY RIVERS, JAMES WRITES, FORCEMEATS were a way to deal with impossibly bony fish, like pike. (This recipe is purely James, and certain gram weights reflect his professional precision.) You see this not only in the airy and decidedly *cuisine bourgeoise* pike quenelles with crayfish of Lyon, but also in humble preparations, such as *pain de brochet,* made with plenty of floury filler. More luxuriously, in classical French cuisine, fish *mousselines* were served on their own with sauce or inside *paupiettes* of sole, accompanied by rich sauces and opulent garnishes, such as lobster or crayfish and sliced truffle.

Making these forcemeats once required pounding the fish into a paste using a mortar and pestle, adding egg whites or whole eggs, then forcing the mixture through a sieve and cooling it in a bowl over ice before finally incorporating the rest of the ingredients by hand. Most often the forcemeats were bound with a *panade,* not the usual mixture of breadcrumbs and boiled milk but commonly a puddinglike mixture similar to pastry cream without the sugar. The amount of *panade* was half or even more of the weight of the fish. As a *stagiaire* in Lyon in the late 1970s, the only restaurants James could afford served impossibly cakey quenelles ("Where's the fish?" he asked himself) in gluey béchamel sauce made pink with not crayfish but tomato paste.

The disappearance of fish quenelles, pâtés, and the like probably had much to do with the arrival of Nouvelle Cuisine and, simultaneously, the food processor. Flour was taken out of sauces, and *panade* out of fish forcemeats. The latter left a *farce mousseline,* a purée of raw fish bound with egg whites and mounted with cream: simple, relatively inexpensive, and easy as pie to make with a Cuisinart. Suddenly, these preparations were on every menu, until critics and diners cried, "Enough!" The *farce mousseline* was nothing new, for in 1907 Escoffier had praised its "incomparably delicate results," adding that it could replace all other forcemeats but no other could replace it. He was right. Even apart from the considerable filler in the form of *panade,* other forcemeat recipes involved unnecessary richness from butter or, in older Lyon recipes, beef tallow, as though to do away with any vestigial flavor of fish.

In fact, the very delicacy of *mousseline* forcemeats can make them somewhat problematic; they must be used judiciously to avoid monotony. Poached in individual ramekins and served on their own as *mousselines,* forcemeats satisfy best as small first courses, and they can be used in a supporting role with fish and shellfish. The perfect smoothness and delicate flavor of a forcemeat scream for contrast: assertive sauces and a bit of tender crunch. Easy to make are a sweated julienne of vegetables, sweated finely sliced fennel, or wilted spinach, any of which work well with a brazenly acidic *beurre blanc* (page 151) or a white-wine sauce flavored with saffron or curry. Various pike and pickerel, including walleye pike (similar to European pike-perch), have a dense fleshiness perfect for forcemeats, but they must be fastidiously boned—or passed twice through the fine plate of a meat grinder. Very firm sole and flounder filets also work, as does salmon, but cod, haddock, and other fish that release lots of liquid during cooking don't. Impeccably fresh scallops, however, contribute an ethereal lightness, and combining one part of these with three of the base fish gives the *mousseline* a wonderful silkiness.

Farce mousseline works best in warm preparations (see the first variation, below). Served cold as a fish pâté (second variation), it has a slight graininess; counter that by adding to the ingredients some *panade*—25 percent of the weight of the fish. Remember that the fish must be kept as cold as possible throughout the process and that, before the cream is added, the fish-and-egg-white mixture must be completely smooth. Quenelles are ovals, shaped with two large spoons, of smooth, egg-bound meat or fish mixtures—in this case the fish forcemeat—that are poached. Classically, fish quenelles are often served with *sauce Nantua* (crayfish sauce) and garnished with crayfish tails or lobster meat.

The *mousselines,* quenelles, and pâté have enough flavor for a wine such as a *premier cru* Chablis, and if you turn the lobster coulis into a lobster stew (see next recipe), that can stand up to the greater concentration of a *grand cru* Chablis.

PANADE

½ cup (125 ml) milk

3 tablespoons (45 gr) unsalted butter

⅝ cup (85 gr) all-purpose flour

1 large egg

To make the *panade:* Bring the milk and butter to a boil over medium-high heat in a small pot. Remove from the flame, stir in the flour, and return to the flame, continuing to stir until the mixture forms a ball. Put this into the food processor; wait a minute while it cools slightly. Add the egg and process until smooth. Spread the mixture on a plate, cover with plastic wrap, and refrigerate until completely chilled.

To make the *panade* forcemeat: Cut the fish into roughly ½-inch (1-cm) cubes. Put them onto a plate and in the freezer until the edges begin to freeze, about

14 ounces (400 gr) extremely fresh fish, traditionally pike or pickerel (alternatively very firm sole or flounder, or salmon), without bones, skin, or dark fatty bits

egg whites from 5 large eggs (150 ml whites)

1¼ cups (300 ml) heavy cream

1½ teaspoons (10 gr) salt

¾ teaspoon (2 gr) white pepper, freshly ground

1 quart (1 lt) Crayfish or Lobster Coulis for Quenelles (see next recipe)

cooked crayfish tails (8 to 10 tails and a whole crayfish on each plate) or pieces of cooked lobster from two 1¼- to 1½-pound (500- to 750-gr) lobsters, to garnish the quenelles

20 minutes. Put about ½ cup (100 gr) of the *panade* in the food processor, and process until well incorporated. Add the chilled fish and reduce it to a fairly smooth purée, processing about 90 seconds. With the machine running, gradually add the egg whites, taking about 90 seconds to do so — don't add them too quickly or chunks of fish may remain in the purée. At the end, if the mixture is no longer ice cold, put it, still in the bowl of the food processor, into the freezer for a few minutes.

With the bowl of purée back in place and the machine on, add the cream in a thin stream; turn off the machine as soon as the cream is incorporated. Especially in warm weather, overprocessing may curdle it. Season with salt and white pepper, and process very briefly. (White peppercorns aren't as aromatic as black, but they can be pretty good, and in these pale sauces, they're conventional. Better, however, to use black or no pepper at all than preground white.)

To make quenelles: Classic quenelles are simply the *panade* forcemeat, nothing more, shaped in ovals using 2 tablespoons dipped in cold water. The ovals are dropped into barely simmering water and briefly poached. (It's faster and requires less skill to instead oven-poach the mixture in ramekins, as with mousselines in the variation below.) The quenelles can be formed in advance, cooked, cooled, put into a container of cold water, and well chilled in the refrigerator before later being reheated and served, which probably gives better results.

To serve the quenelles, reheat them in gently simmering water for about 5 minutes until warmed through, and then, using a slotted spoon, add them to a pot filled with the crayfish or lobster coulis. Cover, and heat in a 400° F (200° C) oven for a few minutes until the quenelles are slightly puffy (left too long, they puff so much that they turn overdelicate and vulnerable). Serve immediately with plenty of the coulis and the crayfish or lobster garnish. *Serves 6.*

Variation: **FISH MOUSSELINES**

Warm *mousselines* need a sauce or they're pretty boring—if not the coulis in the recipe that follows, then a *beurre blanc* (page 151) flavored with saffron or the recipe for Mouclade (page 143) made in a small amount so that there is enough liquid to make some sauce and a few mussels to garnish each serving.

To make *mousselines,* purée the chilled fish and mix in egg whites, cream, salt, and pepper as for the quenelles, but omit the *panade.* Instead, divide the mixture among 6 to 8 buttered ramekins (nonreactive muffin tins will work). Place them in a roasting pan, surround with boiling water, cover with foil, and poach in a 325° F (165° C) oven to an internal temperature of 165° F (72° to 75° C), about 10 minutes. Overcooking leads to unpleasant sulfur flavors, and *mousselines* forgotten in the oven will rise like soufflés but fall quickly and disastrously. They aren't good cold or reheated, but you can keep them warm for up to 2 hours. *Serves 6 to 8 as a first course with the crayfish or lobster coulis.*

Variation: **FISH PÂTÉ**

To make pâté, to the *panade* forcemeat add a garnish of 14 ounces (400 gr) of raw fish—for instance, a mix of about 4 ounces (100 gr) of salmon, 5 ounces (150 gr) of shrimp, and 5 ounces (150 gr) of scallops. These can be either cut by hand into ¼-inch (5-mm) cubes or pulsed in the food processor with a cup or so of the forcemeat to pea-sized pieces. Too much fish as a garnish or pieces that are too big will make the pâté taste dry. Having mixed the pieces with the forcemeat, put the combination in a large buttered mold or 10 individual ramekins and poach as for the *mousselines.* With the pâté, it is of even greater importance not to exceed an internal temperature of 165° F (72° to 75° C), the ramekins taking about 10 minutes and the loaf about 45 minutes. Once cooked, the pâté will hold in a warm place for a couple of hours. *Serves 10, with or without the crayfish or lobster coulis to accompany, and it can be served cold with a mayonnaise or, better yet, cucumbers in sour cream with dill.*

CRAYFISH OR LOBSTER COULIS FOR QUENELLES

THE CLASSIC CRAYFISH SAUCE, *SAUCE NANTUA*, WAS A BÉCHAMEL finished with crayfish butter and cream. It could be improved a little by substituting a white-wine sauce for the béchamel, but the flavors remained timid, and the crayfish butter — cooked crayfish shells puréed with butter and simmered for a long time, then strained through cheesecloth — gave a greasy, overcooked taste.

The recipe that follows is an attempt to combine the best of both methods and keep things simple. Cooking the shells in hot oil until they are bright orange is key, for it imparts a delicious flavor of grilled crayfish or lobster. The taste is rounded out by simmering the lobster body in white wine, shallots, and plenty of fresh tarragon; the thickening is accomplished by reduction. Lobster pieces can be reheated in the sauce to make a fine, if rich, lobster stew, and the sauce with smaller amounts of lobster can accompany meaty fish, such as halibut, or the *mousselines* or the warm fish pâté. The crayfish version is more suited to freshwater fish, or pike or pickerel quenelles.

2 lobsters, each weighing 1¼ to 1½ pounds (500 to 750 gr), cooked, or about 4 dozen cooked crayfish

¼ cup (60 ml) mild, fresh-tasting olive oil or another good, light cooking oil

1 quart (1 kg) heavy cream

¼ cup (50 gr) unsalted butter

2 large shallots, chopped, to make at least ½ cup (80 gr)

1¼ cups (300 ml) dry white wine

short branches of fresh tarragon

continued

The lobsters or crayfish must be freshly cooked and not overcooked. Extract the lobster meat or crayfish tails and reserve. To avoid possible damage to your blender (typically more rugged than a food processor), choose only the more tender sections of shell (of course, tenderness also reflects how recently the lobster molted), such as the part surrounding the lobster's body, breaking it into 1-inch (2- or 3-cm) pieces. Use only about 1¾ cups (100 gr) of well-broken-up shell — too much will overpower the sauce.

In two 9- to 10-inch (about 25-cm) pots (1-gallon or 3-lt capacity each), heat the oil to smoking. Carefully add the shells and stir for about 2 minutes, until they salt

white pepper

Cognac

Tabasco sauce

a lemon, for juice

turn from red to bright orange. Cool to room temperature, pour off any excess oil, add half the cream to each pot, and simmer over low heat for approximately 15 minutes. Cool to room temperature.

In another pot, melt the butter and sweat the shallots until tender. Add the nonmeat insides of the lobsters (but no tomalley or coral) plus the legs, or else the crayfish body sections left after the tail meat has been removed, with the empty claws — broken into small pieces — and sweat for 1 or 2 minutes. Add the wine, tarragon, and just enough water to cover. Simmer gently for about 15 minutes.

Pass the wine-and-shallot mixture through a fine strainer. Return it to the pot, and reduce over medium-high heat to about a quarter of its original volume.

Pour the cooled shell-and-cream mixture into a blender. Grind for about 2 minutes, until the color is pale pink and the texture is like coarse sand. Line a fine strainer with fine cheesecloth to catch the shell grit, and pass the mixture through it into the reduced wine mixture. Simmer over medium heat until the sauce just coats the back of a spoon. If it becomes too thick, thin with water. Season with salt, grindings of white pepper, some drops of Cognac, two or three shakes of Tabasco, and a good squeeze of lemon juice. *Makes about 1 quart (1 lt), enough to serve 6 people as sauce for quenelles, along with a lobster or crayfish garnish, or, with lobster added to make lobster stew (see note, above), enough for the same number.*

PESCE SPADA ALLA STEMPERATA

Swordfish with Olives, Celery, Garlic, Vinegar, and Mint

ALLA STEMPERATA IS A FULL-FLAVORED SICILIAN WAY to prepare swordfish or tuna (and sometimes rabbit or hare). For guidance on ecologically friendly fish choices, see Seafood Watch (www.montereybayaquarium.org). Giuseppe Coria, in his essential tome *Profumi di Sicilia*, published in 1981, attributes the dish to Ragusa and Siracusa and says the obligatory ingredients are green olives, celery, garlic, vinegar, and mint. Nonetheless, I've found recipes that use onion and not garlic, and omit the mint, and I like a somewhat larger group of ingredients, as below, including carrot, if only for color. If you want to include pine nuts, taste before you buy to be sure they're fresh. This dish is good hot, but it's traditionally served at room temperature.

6 swordfish or tuna (not bluefin) steaks (about 3 pounds or 1.3 kg total)

excellent, fresh-tasting olive oil

4 to 6 cloves garlic, finely chopped

1 onion, finely chopped

1 celery heart, thinly sliced, to make about 1 cup (100 gr)

1 carrot, finely chopped

¼ cup (25 gr) capers in salt, well rinsed

20 (about 90 gr) green olives, pitted

½ cup (125 ml) white-wine vinegar

⅓ cup (50 gr) raisins, softened in hot water and drained

4 or 5 spearmint leaves, chopped

⅓ cup (40 gr) pine nuts, *optional*

salt and black pepper

Fry the fish in olive oil over medium heat just until the translucent flesh turns opaque, about 10 minutes for an inch (2.5-cm) thick steak, and remove it from the pan to stop the cooking. In a separate large, nonreactive pan with a lid, cook the garlic, onion, celery, and carrot gently in olive oil until soft but not colored, 5 minutes or more. Add the capers, olives, vinegar, raisins, mint leaves, and pine nuts. Cook another 2 to 3 minutes. Taste and season with salt, if needed, and grind in pepper. If the pan seems in danger of drying, add up to ½ cup (125 ml) of water. Return the fish to the pan, cover, and cook gently to partly meld the flavors, not much more than 5 minutes. *Serves 6.*

SALMON WITH LEEK AND SAFFRON SAUCE

THE TRIO OF LEEKS, SAFFRON, AND CREAM COMPLEMENTS many kinds of fish and shellfish. The quality and price of saffron vary greatly. Generally, the more consistently red the threads, the better, although there are effects of age and provenance, fine saffron coming from Spain but also other countries, including Iran. Too much saffron gives a medicinal flavor; enough is oceanic. There's no perfect way to measure small amounts of saffron threads, whose potency in any case varies; although the threads come in different sizes, the most accurate thing to do is to count them. The use of cornstarch in this recipe is somewhat arbitrary: the thickening for any sauce shouldn't call attention to itself, and here the cream distracts from whatever starch is used.

several leeks weighing roughly 2 pounds (1 kg) altogether

1 teaspoon (5 gr) butter

¾ cup (175 ml) white wine

1½ cups (350 ml) heavy cream

a pinch (about 25) saffron threads

5 tablespoons (75 ml) mussel broth (see page 140)

½ teaspoon cornstarch

salt

3-pound (1.4-kg) salmon filet in one piece

Cut off the green tops and the roots of the leeks. Open the upper end of each with 2 lengthwise cuts at 90-degree angles to one another, and wash each leek thoroughly upside down under running water to remove the grit hidden between the layers. Cut the leeks into lengthwise strips roughly ⅛ inch by 2 to 3 inches (3 mm by 5 to 7 cm), and sweat them in butter in a covered pan over low heat, stirring now and then. In about 25 minutes they will have completely softened. Take the pan from the flame. Heat the oven to 500° F (260° C).

In a small pan over high heat, reduce the wine by half. Add the cream, and reduce the combination again by half. Off the heat, add the saffron threads and the broth. Mix the starch with a little cold water and stir it in. Heat the sauce again, stirring continuously, until it thickens slightly and bubbles. Shellfish broth is salty; taste the sauce and add more salt only if needed. Keep the sauce covered and warm.

Butter a roasting pan or a gratin dish that will hold the salmon and is suitable for the table. Place the salmon in it, salt the fish lightly, and bake it in the upper part of the oven until the flesh at the center only just loses its translucence, perhaps 10 to 12 minutes. Arrange the leeks around the salmon and coat it with some of the sauce; pass the rest of the sauce at the table. *Serves 4 to 6.*

SALMON "SOUFFLÉ"

THE HOMEY TEXTURE OF THIS SALMON "SOUFFLÉ," which my grandmother used to make, is more like that of a pudding. While she used canned salmon, it makes good use of a leftover piece. Key to the flavor is a generous quantity of parsley. Unfortunately, there's no precise way to measure parsley, if only because the intensity of the flavor varies, but in the cooked dish green and pink should be almost equally present. When I've had a lush crop of chervil—at the risk of undoing the simplicity of the dish—I've made the recipe by replacing plain parsley with fines herbes (mostly fresh chervil plus parsley, chives, and a little tarragon). And at the risk of further complication, a little paprika complements the flavor and deepens the pink color.

1 small to medium onion, finely chopped

a small inner stalk of celery with a few of its leaves, finely chopped

3 tablespoons (45 gr) butter

¼ cup (60 gr) all-purpose flour

1¼ to 1½ cups (300 to 350 ml) cold milk

6 large eggs, separated

2 cups (400 gr) cooked salmon, skin discarded, broken up fine

roughly ¾ cup (40 gr) finely chopped flat-leaf parsley, measured without compacting

nutmeg

¼ to ½ teaspoon Worcestershire sauce

salt and black pepper

¾ teaspoon cream of tartar, if you use a noncopper bowl

Cook the onion and celery gently in the butter until they are translucent and somewhat soft. Stir in the flour and cook 1 minute. Add the milk all at once and immediately whisk the combination. Stir continuously, preferably with a square-edged wooden spatula that will easily cover the whole bottom of the pan, until this béchamel sauce thickens and comes to a steady bubble. Off the heat, stir in the egg yolks.

In a large bowl, combine the béchamel, salmon, and parsley. Grate in a little nutmeg, barely enough to detect, and add Worcestershire sauce to taste. Season well with salt and pepper, bearing in mind that the egg white foam, yet to be added, will dilute the taste. Heat the oven to 375° F (190° C).

Butter and flour an 8-inch (20-cm) soufflé mold. In a large copper bowl, freshly cleaned with salt and vinegar or lemon juice, rinsed, and dried (or in a noncopper bowl, adding the cream of tartar), whisk the egg whites until they just form stiff peaks. Whisk a quarter of the beaten whites into the salmon mixture. Fold in the rest by thirds. Fill the mold, and bake until fully set, when a small blade inserted in the center comes out clean — about 30 minutes. *Serves 4 to 6 for lunch or a light supper.*

MARINATED TUNA IN OLIVE OIL

THE PREDECESSOR OF CANNED TUNA IN OIL, A 19TH-CENTURY innovation that at its best is extremely good, was tuna cooked with a large amount of salt and preserved for a time under oil, stored in clay jars in a cool cellar. Probably this was done in many Mediterranean places, and certainly near the large tuna fisheries on the coasts of Provence and Italy. If you do it yourself, you can control the quality of the fish and the oil, introduce other seasonings, and avoid over-cooking—and there's no fishy taste or taste of can. Don't choose the fatty belly, and don't use threatened species such as bluefin, which is slow to mature and is currently being caught faster than it can reproduce. This Provençal-influenced version is based on recipes in Marius Morard's *Manuel complet de la cuisinière provençale* (1886), J.-B. Reboul's *La Cuisinière provençale* (1899), and Jacques Médecin's *La Cuisine du comté de Nice* (1972). I call for less salt than is necessary for preservation, so the cooked fish should be refrigerated and kept no more than a week. Bay leaves appear in all three recipes, which variously propose a quartered lemon in place of wine, coriander seed, a fennel branch, an onion, thyme, saffron—not to be used all at once. The fish is excellent dressed with lemon juice or a little good vinegar and some of the oil that covered it.

1 pound (500 gr) tuna (Atlantic or Mediterranean), sliced 1 to 2 inches (3 to 5 cm) thick

2 tablespoons (40 gr) salt

4 bay leaves

12 black peppercorns

4 cloves garlic, halved lengthwise, any green sprout removed

1 cup (250 ml) white wine

7 cups (1.75 lt) water

excellent, fresh-tasting olive oil

Remove the skin, dark meat, and any bones from the tuna. To a nonreactive pot, add the salt, bay leaves, peppercorns, garlic, white wine, water, and tuna, and bring them to a very slow simmer. Poach the fish until it is barely cooked through, perhaps 20 minutes. Take the pot from the heat, and cool the fish in the poaching liquid. Drain it, and arrange it, cutting as necessary, to fit tightly in a jar or other deep, relatively narrow container. Pour in olive oil until the tuna is completely immersed, tapping the jar to eliminate air pockets. Optionally, add another bay leaf, peppercorns, or other seasonings (see above), and the garlic from the cooking pot. Store in the refrigerator for up to a week. Serve at room temperature. *Makes a little less than 1 pound (450 gr).*

PEPERONI RIPIENI CON TONNO

Bell Peppers Stuffed with Tuna

THE FORERUNNER OF THIS ANTIPASTO FROM PIEDMONT IN ITALY was probably peppers with anchovy sauce; both are excellent. The tuna in question is canned (see preceding recipe), and it's important to avoid bluefin and any other threatened species (see Seafood Watch at www .montereybayaquarium.org) and to use a better-quality brand than the usual North American ones, which taste slightly fishy at best. Two good European brands, though not inexpensive, are Flot and Ortiz, both of which put up tuna in jars as well as cans. To fill the peppers, most *piemontese* restaurants quickly reduce the tuna to a paste in a food processor, which makes the texture dry, even sandy. It's much better to work with your hands.

4 yellow or red bell peppers, preferably at the peak of their season

2 salted anchovies

12 ounces (350 gr) excellent imported canned tuna in oil

about ¼ cup (50 ml) excellent, fresh-tasting, mild olive oil, such as Ligurian

a lemon, for juice

salt and black pepper

Bake—don't roast and scorch—the whole peppers in a 350° F (175° C) oven until tender, putting a little water in the pan, or cook them, halved and seeded, in boiling water: they can be soft but not flaccid and shapeless. Cool the peppers in a covered bowl. Peel them, and remove stems, seeds, and inner membranes. Clean the anchovy filets of salt, strip them from the bones, and rinse them. Mash the anchovy to a paste with the back of a fork. Drain the tuna, and with your fingers break it up into a fine, even consistency. Mix in the anchovies and then enough olive oil so the mixture appears very moist. Squeeze in just a little lemon juice, grind in pepper, and season with more salt (the tuna is already salted) as needed to contrast with the sweet, unseasoned peppers. Fill either whole or half peppers with the mixture. *Serves 4 as a first course.*

POULTRY AND RABBIT

COQ AU VIN

Chicken in Red Wine

COQ AU VIN, A VARIABLE DISH, APPEARS IN MUCH OF FRANCE and under various names. In Alsace, it's *coq au riesling* with cream and mushrooms; in Britanny it's *poulet au cidre* with hard cider, cream, and sautéed apples; a Basque might add tomato. In the Berry, *poulet en barbouille* is on the fringe of the form; made with red wine and the chicken's blood, it's really a *civet*. Wherever coq au vin appears, the essence is this: the chicken is cut into pieces and browned in fat, wine is added, and a little flour is used for thickening. The difference between coq au vin and bœuf bourguignon is mainly that a young chicken cooks faster than beef. But a year-old cock, as in the name of the dish, requires a long cooking time to allow it to give more flavor as well as gelatin to the sauce. For most of us, though, that's hard to come by. Today a tender young bird is normal, and if more gelatin seems needed you can always add some gelatinous stock. Once a housewife would commonly have had her own dooryard chicken. Today purchased chicken should be well raised outdoors and, preferably, come from an old-fashioned breed with fine flavor. Very freshly killed is best. Cutting it into eight pieces allows each of four people to have both light and dark meat.

Many coq au vin recipes call for brandy, but that easily distracts, all the more so because we are no longer used to its taste in sauces. Many recipes also call for adding stock, which softens the taste of the red wine, but below the taste is softened instead by well-cooked onions, which are passed through a strainer to provide thickening, a 1970s tactic that reduces — can even eliminate — the need for flour. (Even without stock or onions, the wine used should be pleasant to drink and not too tannic.) The Burgundian trinity of garnishes — lardons, tiny onions, and mushrooms — as good as they are, can be omitted. Croûtons by themselves are very good. Coq au vin is usually served with steamed potatoes, but in Alsace there might be fresh egg noodles, in Provence rice, and in the southwest potatoes sautéed in goose fat, which would also be used to brown the chicken. It makes sense to drink the same sort of wine you've put in the pot, but maybe a better example from a better producer.

unsalted butter, lard, or excellent, fresh-tasting olive oil or another good, mild cooking oil

continued

Melt 2 tablespoons of fat in a large, heavy nonreactive pot with a cover. Lightly salt and pepper the pieces of chicken and brown them in the fat, turning to color all sides — about 30 minutes. Remove the chicken and

salt and black pepper

a chicken, weighing 4 to 5 pounds (about 2 kg), cut into 8 pieces: 4 sections of breast roughly equal in size (including the wings attached to 2 of them) plus 2 thighs and 2 drumsticks

2 carrots, peeled and cut in short pieces

2 large or 3 medium onions, quartered lengthwise

¼ cup (30 gr) all-purpose flour

2 cloves garlic

a bundle of herbs (1 bay leaf, a few fresh celery leaves, 2 or 3 branches of fresh thyme—or add dried thyme directly to the pot—and half a dozen branches of fresh parsley, tied together)

1 to 2 cups (250 to 500 ml) chicken stock

1 to 2 cups (250 to 500 ml) red wine

15 to 20 baby onions, *optional*

1 or 2 slices (100 gr) lean salt pork or pancetta without rind, about ¼ inch (6 mm) thick, cut crosswise into lardons, *optional*

½ pound (250 gr) white button mushrooms, left whole if they're small, otherwise quartered, *optional*

set it aside. Add the carrots and quartered onions and cook them slowly, stirring and turning until the onion is nearly cooked. Add the flour, and turn and stir the vegetables for a couple of minutes so the flour begins to cook.

Return the chicken to the pot, add the garlic and herbs and enough stock and wine to nearly cover the meat. Cook very slowly, covered, using a heat diffuser if necessary so that the contents barely bubble, until the chicken is tender—about 15 minutes for the breast of a young bird (a little more for the piece with the wing), and about 10 minutes more for the legs. (The ideal temperatures are about 150° F, or 65° C, for the white meat and 160° F, or 70° C, for the dark.) Remove the pieces as they are done to a warm, covered dish. Discard the carrots.

Put the cooking liquid along with the onions, garlic, and herbs through a sieve, pressing so the soft onion and garlic pass through and discarding whatever remains. Boil the onion-filled liquid slowly in the pot to reduce it slightly, placing the pot off center and two or three times removing the fat and skin that form on the surface, for as long as half an hour. The sauce should be almost free of fat, and just thick enough to coat the meat. Taste and season as needed.

While the sauce is slowly bubbling, cook the baby onions slowly to golden in a covered pan with 1 tablespoon (15 gr) of butter and a few spoonfuls of water. Put the lardons into a pan of cold water, bring them to a boil, strain, and rinse in cold water. Sauté them, uncovered, in 1 tablespoon (15 gr) of fat until the edges just begin to crisp; drain them on a paper towel and keep them warm. Sauté the mushrooms in butter. Reheat the chicken briefly in the sauce, and add the garnishes of mushrooms, tiny onions, and lardons. *Serves 4.*

FRICASSÉE DE POULET ANGEVINE

Chicken with Cream and Mushrooms

A *FRICASSÉE*, PROBABLY FROM THE FRENCH WORDS FOR "FRY" AND "BREAK," in modern times is often a dish of chicken cut up, or "broken," into pieces that are cooked briefly in fat without browning, to heighten but not alter the flavor; the pan is deglazed with an acidic liquid, and the chicken is cooked in that liquid (not necessarily enough for a proper braise), which is then reduced to a sauce. That makes it nearly a coq au vin, except that the *fricassée* is usually light colored, and at the end, to set off the acidity, the sauce is often finished with rich cream or egg yolk or both. The main ingredients of this Anjou version — the chicken, mushrooms, white wine from Chenin Blanc, and cream — are all common in the province and in its cooking. A more refined *fricassée* would contain well-made stock and egg-yolk thickening. This one instead is thickened partly with a little flour and partly by reduction. The Cognac, with its potential rough edge, should be partly consumed by the initial flames and then softened by cooking and the addition of cream. North American heavy cream is more watery than French, and if you add it and then reduce the sauce, it will break, the fat rising as oil to the surface. The simple solution is to reduce the sauce before adding the cream. Many sauces benefit from being brightened with a squeeze of lemon juice just before serving. To know for certain, add a few drops to a spoonful of the sauce, and taste and compare. Other acids, in tiny amounts, such as vinegar, can also point up a sauce, but none has quite the energy of lemon. You shouldn't be quite aware of it; if you can taste lemon, you've put in too much. The same dish is very good, though non-traditional, made with a sweet Anjou wine rather than a dry one. Serve with steamed potatoes or simply with bread, and drink a good Anjou Chenin Blanc.

salt and black pepper

a chicken, weighing 4 to 5 pounds (about 2 kg), cut into 8 pieces: 4 sections of breast roughly equal in size (including the wings attached to 2 of them) plus 2 thighs and 2 drumsticks

all-purpose flour

¼ cup (60 gr) unsalted butter — less if the chicken is fatty

1 onion, chopped

¾ pound (350 gr) cultivated white mushrooms (or wild ones, such as chanterelles), chopped

¼ cup (60 ml) Cognac or other eau-de-vie

½ bottle (375 ml) white wine, preferably from Anjou

1 clove garlic, crushed

a small bundle of fresh herbs (parsley, thyme, savory) or about ¼ teaspoon mixed, crumbled dried herbs (thyme, savory, a hint of oregano)

1 small or ½ large bay leaf

1 cup (250 ml) crème fraîche or heavy cream

a lemon, for juice

Salt and pepper the pieces of chicken, and coat them lightly with flour, shaking off extra. In a large, heavy, nonreactive pot, such as enameled cast iron, cook the chicken for a few minutes over medium heat in butter, turning, without coloring (work in batches, if necessary). Remove the chicken, and cook the onions and mushrooms, again without coloring, for a few minutes, until the onions are translucent and the mushrooms are cooked through. Take them from the pot.

Move the pot to an area where there is nothing flammable overhead — *be aware that the flames may rise 2 feet!* Pour in the Cognac and light it with a match. When the flames die out, add the wine, garlic, herb bundle and bay leaf, along with the chicken, onions, and mushrooms.

Cook slowly over low heat, below a simmer, using a heat diffuser if necessary. Turn the meat once or twice, and as the pieces become tender, remove them to a warm, covered platter. The breast of a young bird may take 15 minutes (more for the piece with the wing), and the legs about 10 minutes longer. Using a slotted spoon, remove the onions and mushrooms to the platter, and discard the bay leaf, herb bundle, and garlic. Place the pot off center, and adjust the heat so it bubbles slowly on one side. As fat rises and a skin forms on the surface, two or three times gather and remove them, which will take as long as half an hour. Take care to skim all the fat, then raise the heat and boil the liquid to reduce it to a thick sauce.

Add the crème fraîche or heavy cream. Taste the sauce and brighten it as needed with a good squeeze of lemon juice, and season it with salt and pepper. Return the chicken, onions, and mushrooms to the pot. Bring just to a boil and serve promptly. *Serves 4 to 6.*

POULET AU VIN JAUNE ET AUX MORILLES

Chicken with Cream, Morels, and Vin Jaune

CHICKEN, CREAM, MORELS, AND *VIN JAUNE* form one of the great flavor combinations. The dish comes from the Jura Mountains in the Franche-Comté region of eastern France, and yet it doesn't appear in Pierre Dupin's classic *franc-comtois* cookbook of 1927, which offers only a recipe for morels in cream sauce, containing "the most perfumed white wine you have," served on croûtons. Being a native of the region, possibly he meant *vin jaune,* the great, curious wine of the Jura that is matured *sous-voile,* "under a veil" of yeast, like sherry, and, loosely speaking, recalls sherry's flavor. Chefs in the region don't use the best *vin jaune,* because it's costly and its finest flavors are lost in cooking. However old the combination may or may not be, by 1961 *poulet* (or *chapon* or *coq*) *au vin jaune* was well-enough established that the Michelin red guide named it as a specialty of all three of the starred restaurants in Arbois, the most important town in the wine region. The dish was perhaps not invented by, but was given a push by, the great Arbois chef of the period, André Jeunet. Dried morels, outside the season, have always been used in place of fresh, but not all morels are equal—not from the same species of *Morchella,* not from the same soil or kind of tree. (Very good, if expensive, dried French morels from the French dealer Plantin are sold by Joie de Vivre in Modesto, California.) Because the intensity of mushroom flavor varies, and even ardent gatherers don't agree on dried-to-fresh equivalents—proposing anywhere from 1:4 to 1:10, by weight—no simple formula is possible, and the amount I call for is little more than a guess. Any quantity of good morels, fresh or dried, however few, is a luxury. Even without them, the trio of cream, chicken, and *vin jaune* is excellent. "Why do you flour meat?" a chef asked me, thinking it might be an improvement to eliminate the flour here. He may be right. In my view, the flour protects the surface of meat during the initial cooking in fat (in this recipe, the cooking is so gentle that that hardly matters); at the same time the flour itself cooks, losing some of its raw taste; and afterward it helps to thicken the sauce. (Too much browning in fat takes enough thickening power from the flour that it won't do the trick.) If you like, you can omit the flour below, reducing the sauce further but accepting a thinner result. The acidity from the final squeeze of lemon juice counters the richness of the sauce. Serve the dish with rice.

¼ pound (100 gr) dried morels or
1¼ pounds (500 gr) fresh ones

salt and black pepper

all-purpose flour

a chicken, weighing 4 to 5 pounds
(about 2 kg), cut into 8 pieces: 4
sections of breast roughly equal in size
(including the wings attached to 2 of
them) plus 2 thighs and 2 drumsticks

¼ cup (50 gr) unsalted butter

1 cup (250 ml) white wine, preferably
from the Jura

2 cups (500 ml) chicken stock

¼ to ⅜ cup (65 to 100 ml) *vin jaune,* or
a less expensive Jura *sous-voile* white
wine

2 cups (500 ml) heavy cream or crème
fraîche, or a combination

a lemon, for juice

Dried morels may be clean or slightly gritty; brush them with a dry brush and feel whether any of the dark particles that come off include grit. If so, decide whether you can brush all the grit away or you need to rinse it away under running water, knowing that some flavor will be lost along with the dirt. Afterward, soak the dried morels in warm water for at least 20 minutes, then drain, reserving that liquid to add later to the pot. Clean fresh morels by first brushing away dirt with a dry brush and then immersing them in water, stirring vigorously and changing the water repeatedly, until there is no sign of grit.

Lightly salt and pepper and lightly flour the pieces of chicken. In a wide, heavy-bottomed pot with a lid, cook the pieces gently in the butter without coloring. Add the cup of wine, the stock, and the liquid from soaking the dried morels, if you are using them. Cook, covered, over low heat, turning from time to time, and as the pieces become tender remove them to a warm, covered platter. The breast of a young bird may take 15 minutes (more for the piece with the wing), and the legs about 10 minutes longer.

Skim the fat carefully from the surface of the liquid in the pot, and reduce the liquid almost to a glaze, add ¼ cup (65 ml) of *vin jaune,* the cream, and the morels. Cook several minutes to get rid of the raw-wine taste, and, if necessary, reduce the combination slightly, so the sauce is just thick enough to coat the wooden spoon you may be stirring with. (If the sauce must wait, it may lose enough moisture that it will need a little water.) Add the chicken and heat. Just before serving, stir in a little more *vin jaune,* bringing the sauce momentarily to a boil. Taste the sauce, and, as needed, season it with salt and pepper and add a squeeze of lemon juice. *Serves 4.*

SAUTÉED CHICKEN WITH TOMATOES AND OLIVES

VARIATIONS ON THIS PROVENÇAL TREATMENT ARE ALSO APPLIED to rabbit and pork as well as salt cod and fresh fish such as *rougets* (mullets). As for the fat, salt pork is only sometimes called for; instead, some recipes use more olive oil and then, about 10 minutes before the end of cooking, add two salted anchovies (just the filets, stripped from the bones and rinsed) pounded in a mortar with the cloves of garlic. You can skip the flour and boil further to concentrate the sauce a little, but don't make it intense. The old recipes call for fresh tomatoes, but you could use store-bought canned tomatoes, whose taste of can is largely hidden here, and the ones you put up in jars of course don't have that problem.

¼ pound (100 gr) lean salt pork, *lardo*, or pancetta without rind, cut crosswise in ¼-by-¼-inch (6-by-6-mm) lardons

excellent, fresh-tasting olive oil

salt and black pepper

a chicken, weighing 4 to 5 pounds (about 2 kg), cut into 8 pieces: 4 sections of breast roughly equal in size (including the wings attached to 2 of them) plus 2 thighs and 2 drumsticks

all-purpose flour

2 onions, finely chopped

½ cup (125 ml) white wine

2 cloves garlic, very finely chopped

1 teaspoon fresh thyme leaves or ½ teaspoon dried thyme

continued

Put the lardons into a pan of cold water, bring them to a boil, drain, and rinse in cold water. In a large, heavy pot, sauté the lardons in 2 tablespoons of olive oil until their edges just begin to crisp and they render some of their fat; remove them to a paper towel to drain.

Salt and pepper the chicken, and coat the pieces lightly with flour. Sauté the chicken in the fat from the lardons, turning, until the pieces are golden on all sides. Remove the chicken to a warm plate.

Over low heat, cook the onions in the same fat, adding more oil if needed, stirring until they are translucent but not colored. Add the wine, raise the heat, and stir to deglaze the pan. Add the garlic and thyme and cook briefly to reduce the amount of liquid by about half. Add the tomatoes and bay leaves, and simmer until the liquid is reduced again by about one-third, depending on how juicy the tomatoes are, to a strong but not intense flavor.

Return the chicken to the pot, and cook over

5 tomatoes, peeled, seeded, and chopped

2 bay leaves

¾ cup (150 gr) green or black Niçoise or other olives cured in brine

a large handful of parsley, chopped not long before serving

medium-low heat, covered, until the chicken is done—perhaps 20 minutes, according to how thoroughly you sautéed it beforehand. During the last few minutes of cooking, add the sautéed lardons and the olives. Remove the bay leaves. Taste and season as needed with salt and pepper. Sprinkle with chopped parsley. Warn everyone that the olives have pits. *Serves 4.*

CHICKEN LEGS BRAISED IN RED WINE

FOR TENDER, JUICY MEAT, A BRAISE REQUIRES GENTLE COOKING. If you're cooking on top of the stove rather than in the oven, very gentle cooking takes place in earthenware, perhaps the oldest material for a cooking vessel, because the heat from below is transmitted poorly—that is, slowly. (In the oven, there's no advantage to earthenware, because with the all-around heat, after a short time the pot reaches and stays at the same temperature as any other container.) To protect earthenware from cracking, heat it gradually, protect it from the direct heat of a stove burner with a metal heat diffuser, and avoid pouring cold liquids into the hot pot. For a braise, another sort of heavy, nonreactive pot, such as enameled cast iron, will also do very well, and if your container lacks a lid you can always use a plate. With just chicken legs, overcooking is less likely (dark meat doesn't dry out as quickly as white), and all the meat is done at the same time.

For the most flavor, just as for sauce, stock, or soup, it's important that the braising liquid be unmuddied by extraneous particles (mainly protein) from the meat: remove the scum that forms early on. But it's easy to forget to watch, and then the pot comes to a boil and the particles are dispersed through the liquid. You can partly recoup later by cleansing the liquid, which also removes fat. Even the clearest liquid benefits from being cleansed, especially if there's flour in it (the protein is taken away while most of the starch remains to thicken); this is done by removing the skin that forms at the same time the fat rises out of suspension. A heavy skin will form on a large quantity of flour-thickened liquid; you can pull the skin off and a new one will form several times. (The egg-white clarification of stock in classical cooking is at best imperfect: at the same time that it removes particles it also takes away flavor, which is why the beaten egg whites are mixed with ground meat.)

Great taste comes from an accumulation of large and small things, and in soups and braises I always use gray sea salt in the belief that its greater flavor makes a small contribution. As with a pot-au-feu, serve the broth first in shallow bowls. Follow it with the meat and vegetables with a little of the remaining liquid poured over them. Good bread is essential.

2 cups (500 ml) red wine

1 quart (1 lt) chicken stock

excellent, fresh-tasting olive oil or another good, light cooking oil

4 whole chicken legs

4 leeks

3 carrots, peeled and cut in ¼-inch (6-mm) dice

an inner stalk of celery, cut in ¼-inch (6-mm) dice

an herb bundle: a few celery leaves, half a dozen branches of fresh parsley, 1 or 2 branches of fresh thyme, and a bay leaf, tied together

2 garlic cloves, peeled and crushed

salt and black pepper

Pour the wine and stock into a pan and set them to simmer at the back of the stove. Remove any scum that rises to the surface (a long-handled skimmer with a fine screen is useful). Pour some oil into a large, non-reactive pot and, two at a time, brown the chicken legs well on both sides.

Trim the leeks, leaving only an inch (2 or 3 cm) of green top and just enough root to hold each one together. Cut the upper part of each leek in half lengthwise, turn it 90 degrees, and cut it again lengthwise, so that the upper half is quartered. One at a time, hold the leeks upside down in running water to rinse away every trace of grit hidden among the layers. So the leeks stay intact in the pot, tie them in a bundle, wrapping it 4 or 5 times with string. Heat the oven to 250° F (120° C).

Temporarily remove the chicken legs from the pot. Put the leeks, carrots, and celery in the bottom, and then arrange the chicken legs compactly on top of them, tucking the herbs and garlic in the middle. Add the simmering liquid, which should fully, or almost fully, immerse the chicken; if it doesn't, add water.

Season the liquid with salt and pepper. Bring the whole again to a boil, remove any further scum, cover the pot tightly, and place it in the heated oven. When the chicken is tender — in roughly 45 minutes — remove the pot from the oven. Discard the herb bundle and garlic cloves, and remove the chicken and the leeks to a warm plate, cutting the string around the leeks. Set the pot so it heats mostly from one side and simmer lightly. Over 15 minutes (half an hour or more if you have time), remove the skin that forms, once or twice, and skim off almost all the fat. Taste for salt. Return the chicken and leeks to the pot, simmer long enough to heat the meat through, and carry the pot to the table. *Serves 4.*

CHICKEN "ROASTED" IN BUTTER WITH SAUTERNES SAUCE

THIS VARIATION ON THE CLASSIC FRENCH *POÊLÉE* TECHNIQUE for cooking meat in butter in a covered pot — itself derived from an elaborate roasting method — yields a surprisingly flavorful sauce. Because the Sauternes in the sauce is sweet, the wine you drink should also be sweet — logically also Sauternes. But the combination makes a very rich taste without refreshment, a recurring dilemma with sweetness in main courses. In this instance, my solution is to start the meal with a large vegetable course (an unadorned plate of buttered green beans, spinach, or whatever is in season), then serve small portions of the main course with boiled or steamed potatoes and a glass of sweet wine, and follow that with salad, cheese (Roquefort and other moist blue cheeses will go with the sweet wine), and dessert. A neatly trussed chicken looks attractive, but trussing only makes it more difficult to cook the dark meat fully without overcooking the light; there are tricks, but some unevenness is inevitable with a whole bird. If the bird isn't trussed, however, the legs poke out oddly as it cooks, and it doesn't fit compactly into a pot, nor does it allow turning during *poêlée* cooking. James's solution is to pull the legs out forcefully, before cooking, so they fully straighten out and will stay that way, and then tuck them back where they would be if trussed — they'll mostly remain there. Of course, the wine added to the pot doesn't have to be Sauternes; it can be another sweet wine made from grapes concentrated by noble rot.

a chicken, weighing about 4 to
5 pounds (roughly 2 kg)

salt and black pepper

dried thyme

¼ cup (50 gr) unsalted butter

2 bay leaves

1 carrot, finely diced

1 stalk celery, finely diced

1 onion, finely diced

1 slice (about 1 ounce or 25 gr) dry-
cured (prosciutto-style) ham or twice
as much mild ham

¾ cup (175 ml) or more Sauternes

a lemon, for juice

Dry the chicken with a paper towel, and season it all over with salt, pepper, and thyme. In place of trussing, jerk each leg so it remains straight, and then fold it back into place. Choose a heavy nonreactive pot just large enough to hold the chicken; place a metal heat diffuser beneath it, and in it gently melt the butter. Add the bay leaves and the chicken, cover, and cook over low heat, turning the chicken once or twice so it browns top and bottom; but keep the breast mostly up so as not to overcook it by much. After about 30 minutes, add the carrot, celery, onion, and ham so they brown in the bottom of the pot. Keep the pot covered except to stir the vegetables once or twice. When the chicken is done—perhaps 50 minutes altogether—remove it to a warm platter. If the vegetables aren't yet fully brown, uncover and cook them further, stirring. Discard the bay leaves and ham. Deglaze the pot with the ¾ cup (175 ml) of Sauternes, add ½ cup (125 ml) of water, and then carefully skim off all the fat. Reduce the liquid to the consistency of a sauce. Taste and, as needed, add salt, a little lemon juice, and perhaps more wine. Transfer the chicken to a platter, and carve it at the table, passing the sauce. *Serves 6.*

GÂTEAUX DE FOIES DE VOLAILLE

Chicken Liver "Cakes"

THESE LYONNAIS "CAKES" ARE ACTUALLY FLANS WHOSE CUSTARD is typically thickened with béchamel or bread soaked in milk and then lightened with beaten egg whites. The following recipe is more delicate than that, containing less liver and garlic and no starch, and the egg whites aren't beaten. Usually specified are pale, fat-filled blond chicken livers, which are sold separately in France; but when, as here, the proportion of liver is relatively small, red livers will do. Common garnishes in Lyon restaurants are slices of quenelle and green olives, but they don't enhance the taste and I leave them out. I've eaten a large serving as a main course, but a little goes a long way.

SAUCE

1 pound (500 gr) ripe red tomatoes

1 or 2 shallots (together about 50 gr), chopped

½ tablespoon unsalted butter

salt and black pepper

GÂTEAUX DE FOIES

2 cups (500 ml) milk

2 cups (500 ml) heavy cream or crème fraîche

3 cloves garlic, finely chopped

½ pound (250 gr) chicken livers, trimmed of the nervy connections

continued

To make the sauce: Peel, stem, and quarter the tomatoes, keeping the seeds and their gel (which provides needed acidity). Cook the shallots over medium-low heat in the butter until they are translucent. Add the tomatoes and cook until they are fully soft, about 10 minutes. Strain this sauce, working it with a plastic spatula (this is easier if you first pass it through the fine holes of a food mill), and discard the seeds. Boil, as needed, to reduce the sauce to the consistency of heavy cream. Season with salt and grind in pepper.

To make the *gâteaux:* Bring the milk, cream, and garlic to a boil, and take the pan from the heat. To the bowl of a food processor, add the chicken livers one by one, pulsing each time to make a purée, and then add the marrow or butter, pulsing until smooth. Add the eggs and yolks, again one by one, pulsing each time until smooth. With the machine running continuously, slowly pour in the hot mixture of milk, cream, and garlic, allowing the machine to run for a few moments

¼ pound (100 gr) beef marrow, or
2 ounces (50 gr) unsalted butter

4 large whole eggs

3 large egg yolks

salt and black pepper

until the garlic is reduced and the purée is again smooth. Pass the whole through a fine strainer. Season with salt and grind in pepper.

Heat the oven to 350° F (175° C). Heavily butter 10 small molds, such as ceramic custard cups, each holding about ¾ to 1 cup (roughly 200 ml), and divide the mixture among them, filling each about halfway. Place a roasting pan in the oven and pour in enough simmering water to come about two-thirds of the way up the sides of the molds. Set the molds in the pan and poach until the custard is set, about 20 minutes—the interior color should be rose. Serve the *gâteaux* promptly on warm plates together with the heated sauce. *Serves 10 as a small first course.*

GUINEA FOWL WITH GREEN PEPPERCORNS

GUINEA FOWL, NATIVE TO AFRICA, ARE ALWAYS FARMED in Europe and North America. As with most other domesticated poultry, the meat isn't aged. The taste of guinea fowl is fresh and mild, even elegant—delicate enough that a sauce made with chicken stock can overwhelm it. The main concern with guinea fowl is that overcooking turns it dry and insipid. In this dish, the complication is brandy, whose old-fashioned flavor in cooking suggests a gaminess that's alien to guinea fowl. But the extended boiling here takes away the alcoholic edge, and with the clean spice of green peppercorns, there's no question of a gamey taste. If you have a choice, buy female guinea fowl, which are more tender and have larger breasts. (The males weigh more but yield less meat because of their bigger bones.) Guinea fowl goes well with buttery mashed potatoes and with carrots and salsify slowly cooked in butter.

2 guinea fowl, each weighing 2½ to 3 pounds (1.2 to 1.4 kg)

mixed dried herbs, mostly thyme, without stems and finely crumbled

salt and black pepper

3 ounces (85 gr) salt pork, pancetta, or *lardo* without rind

¼ cup (60 ml) brandy

½ cup (125 ml) white wine

2 cups (500 ml) veal or guinea fowl stock (or chicken or turkey stock)

¼ cup (60 ml) heavy cream

4 teaspoons green peppercorns, preserved in brine and not vinegar, rinsed and drained

Using a heavy chef's knife or poultry shears, cut out and discard the backbone of each guinea fowl. Separate the legs from the rest of the carcass, keeping them whole. Then, with a sharp knife, slit the skin over the breastbone in a straight line. Inside that opening, make a shallow cut on either side of the breastbone between the bone and the meat. Slide your thumb through these openings, pushing down to expose the filets, which are the long, narrow pieces of white meat that are somewhat separate from the rest of the breast meat. Make a shallow cut on either side between the filets and the breastbone, and slide your thumb under the filets to expose both sides of the breastbone completely. Cut through the narrow base of the bone on either side so as to separate the breast of each guinea fowl into halves with the rib bones and wings still attached. (Less neatly but more quickly, you can use a heavy chef's knife to make a cut straight down on either side of the breastbone and remove it.) Dry all the pieces with a paper towel, rub them with the herbs and salt and pepper, and set them aside.

Cut the salt pork or bacon across the grain into ¼-inch (5-mm) cubes. Brown these, without letting the fat smoke, in a heavy-bottomed pot just large enough to hold the birds (or use 2 pots). When the fat is mostly rendered, discard the crisp pieces (or eat them—the lean is a little tough but they're delicious). Cook the birds slowly in this fat in the covered pot, turning so they brown evenly, until the meat is done, about 20 minutes for the breasts with wings and another 15 minutes for the legs (check the inside of a thigh with a knife). As the pieces are done, remove them to a hot serving dish, and set it in a warm spot. Discard the fat in the pot. Add the brandy and the wine, stirring and scraping with a wooden spoon or spatula to dissolve the brown material on the bottom, and boil to reduce the amount of liquid by half. Add the stock and again reduce the liquid, this time by two-thirds. Pour it through a strainer into a small pot, add the cream and green peppercorns, and reheat the sauce to a boil. Taste for salt. Pour the sauce over the birds. *Makes 4 large portions consisting of a half breast and a whole leg per person.*

PERDRIX AUX CHOUX

Partridges with Cabbage

THE CABBAGE-PARTRIDGE COMBINATION IS ESPECIALLY GOOD. Traditional French *perdrix aux choux* calls for tough older birds and long cooking, about 2 hours in a closed pot, so the birds surrender almost all their goodness to the cabbage and broth and their meat has little to offer. Restaurants often used to take out those old birds before serving and replace them with tender young ones. Few of us have access to stewing partridges, however, and the following assumes tender farm-raised ones.

2 medium-small cabbages, roughly 4 pounds (1.8 kg) altogether

4 partridges, about 1 pound (450 gr) each

3 ounces (75 gr) lean cured pork belly or pancetta, without rind

4 small fresh sausages (roughly 4 ounces or 100 gr each), without fennel seed or other marked flavoring

2 carrots, peeled and cut in thick slices

1 stalk celery, finely chopped

1 onion, finely chopped

¾ cup (175 ml) white wine

about 3 cups (750 ml) rich stock from, in order of preference, partridges, other game birds, or veal

salt and black pepper

Remove the coarse outer leaves from the cabbages, slice away the thick outer part of the exposed ribs, and quarter the heads, leaving the core intact so the pieces hold together. Blanch for 10 minutes in boiling water and drain well, pressing to expel water. Cut out the cores and finely chop the cabbage. Dry the birds with paper towels and truss them.

Cut the pork belly into ¼-inch (6-mm) cubes; lightly brown them over medium heat in a heavy pot large enough to contain the entire preparation of cabbage and birds. Remove the crisp cubes to a warm platter. Then, in the rendered fat, brown the birds together with the sausages, and remove them all to the platter. Cook the cabbage, carrots, celery, and onion in the fat for 7 to 8 minutes, stirring now and then. Add the wine, 2 cups (500 ml) of the stock, and the brown cubes of pork belly, and cook very slowly, covered, for about 20 minutes. Season lightly with salt and pepper.

Nestle the partridges, breasts up, in the cabbage without allowing them to touch the bottom of the pot. Add more stock as needed so the partridges are almost fully immersed. Bring the liquid to a simmer, cover, and braise at a bare but steady bubble over very low heat (you may need a metal heat diffuser), until the partridges are cooked to medium (check the inside of a thigh with a knife), about 20 minutes. Transfer the partridges to the center of a deep, very hot serving platter and remove the trussing strings. Carefully skim all but a trace of the fat from the cabbage-filled liquid in the pot. Taste for salt. Slice the sausages on a board and mix them with the cabbage. Arrange the cabbage around the birds and over them pour the rest of the liquid in the pot. Serve in heated deep plates or wide bowls. *Serves 4.*

LAPIN À LA CRÈME

Rabbit in White Wine with Cream

LAPIN IS THE FRENCH WORD FOR RABBIT, but the rabbits commonly cooked are farmed and young and are properly called *lapereaux*, a word that sometimes appears on menus. The tiny kidneys are usually still attached to the body cavity and can be left in place during cooking (or sautéed along with the liver and devoured by the cook as the dish simmers). Although the sauce is often thickened with a little flour, James here exploits the ease and lightness of thickening solely by reduction. A garnish isn't required, but if you don't use the chanterelles below, you can add ½ pound (250 gr) of button mushrooms and 2 dozen baby onions, prepared as in the next recipe (don't use the lardons there as a garnish here—they would be too fatty with the cream).

unsalted butter

a rabbit, weighing 3 to 4 pounds (about 1.5 kg), cut into 2 front legs, 4 sections of loin, and 2 back legs each cut into 2 pieces, plus the bony parts without much meat on them (the neck and rib cage, the lower backbone, and so on)

1 onion (about 100 gr), chopped

1 carrot (about 75 gr), chopped

a 2-inch section (about 30 gr) of celery, chopped

1 or 2 (about 60 gr together) shallots, finely chopped

1¼ cups (300 ml) white wine

1¼ cups (300 ml) good chicken stock

salt

continued

In a pot with a cover, wide enough to hold all the rabbit pieces without crowding (or in two batches), and using enough butter to melt and cover the bottom of the pan by ⅛ inch (3 mm), sauté the bones and pieces of meat without browning until the latter have stiffened. Remove the meat and bones, and discard the butter. Add a small amount of fresh butter and cook the onion, carrot, celery, and shallots over low heat without browning until they are soft, about 10 minutes.

Return the rabbit meat and bones to the pot, and add the white wine and stock and just a little salt (the liquid will later be concentrated). Cover and simmer over low heat, so the liquid lightly bubbles, until the rabbit is tender—when probed with a fork or the point of a knife, the meat will separate from the bone—45 to 60 minutes. Remove just the pieces of meat.

Boil the bones and vegetables in the cooking liquid until it is reduced to ½ to ⅔ cup (100 to 150 ml). Add the heavy cream and simmer for a few more minutes,

1 cup (225 ml) heavy cream

a handful of chanterelles per person, halved or quartered depending on size, *optional*

white pepper

a lemon, for juice

or longer if the sauce is too thin to coat the meat—add water if it becomes too thick. Strain it and return it to the pot.

In a separate frying pan, sauté the chanterelles in 2 tablespoons (25 gr) or more of butter, as needed. Add this garnish along with the rabbit pieces to the sauce, and simmer 5 to 10 minutes. Taste and season as needed with salt, adding a grinding of white pepper and a squeeze of lemon juice. *Makes 4 modest portions.*

Variation: **LAPIN À LA MOUTARDE** (*Rabbit with Mustard, Breaded and Grilled*)

The most common version of rabbit with mustard is made simply by preparing rabbit in white wine with cream, and, off the heat and immediately prior to serving, stirring in mustard. The following alternative, from James and probably dating from the late 1960s, is based on an attractive premise—tender rabbit is coated with bracing Dijon mustard to hold in place fresh breadcrumbs and then grilled to brown and crisp the crumbs. The reality, however, often disappoints. Grilling raw rabbit can be precarious, what with the meat sticking to the rack and small pieces falling through, and getting the heat right so the meat is neither undercooked nor burned—and even if you escape these pitfalls, the meat can turn dry and tough. Yet the alternative of partially grilling or sautéing the pieces and then finishing them in a roasting pan in the oven can yield soggy breadcrumbs and the acrid flavor of overcooked mustard. James's tactic for ensuring a moist, tender result is to first braise the rabbit. Afterward, if you want, you can reduce the strained cooking liquid to thicken and concentrate it and add mustard for still more punch. With or without that sauce, a salad of watercress or other strong greens goes well.

Prepare the rabbit as above, but instead of removing it from the cooking liquid when it is done, cool the meat in the liquid to warmish room temperature—no cooler or the pieces won't heat through as they broil or grill. Meanwhile, trim the crusts from several thick slices of 1- to 2-day-old white bread, tear it apart, and reduce it to breadcrumbs in a food processor. Remove the rabbit pieces and dry them with paper towels, brush them thinly but evenly with Dijon mustard (from a fresh jar with some zippy heat), and coat them with the soft breadcrumbs. Under a broiler or on a grill, brown the pieces on all sides, turning. (The broiler is safer, if you watch continuously and turn as needed. With a grill, keep the fire mostly to one side and sloping, so you can move the meat back and forth from hotter to cooler spots as needed.) *Makes 4 modest portions.*

LAPIN À LA BOURGUIGNONNE

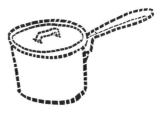

Rabbit in Red Wine

IN FRENCH COOKING, WHEN YOU THINK OF RABBIT IN RED WINE, what springs to mind is the *civet* with its last-minute enrichment with blood and, often, the puréed liver. Before the wine goes in, *civet* recipes often call for flaming the pieces of meat with brandy, which in James's view is overkill because the rabbit is too delicate. And in North America, unless you raise your own rabbits or know someone who does, you don't have access to the blood, although you may be able to find pork blood. In any case, blood makes the dish impossible to reheat without curdling, and especially when the puréed liver is added, the taste often is muddy and overpowers the domesticated rabbit. Without the blood and liver, French chefs give the dish a name such as *lapin à la bourguignonne.*

The usual garnish for either *civet* or *à la bourguignonne* is the combination of brown-glazed baby onions, sautéed quartered mushrooms, and sautéed lardons. The last are cut from fresh or mildly cured pork belly or, rarely, smoked belly (whose smoke can overwhelm). Any of this pork is sliced for lardons and then, before frying, it's blanched—placed in cold water and brought to the boil, then drained—to make the pork more tender, rehydrate it, take out excess salt, and keep it from rendering as much fat into the sauce. The lardons are sautéed until golden. Although they are floating in the sauce rather than inserted into the lean meat, they give the rabbit a rich flavor and sense of juiciness. White-wine versions of the same dish, called *lapin au vin blanc* or *lapin en gibelotte,* are usually served with the same garnishes. These rabbit dishes belong to the family of preparations that includes coq au vin and bœuf bourguignon, and any of them are almost always accompanied by steamed potatoes and sometimes a further garnish of croûtons sautéed in butter and then (sometimes) rubbed with garlic. You can also put a little very finely chopped garlic into the pot during the last two or three minutes of cooking, which, besides adding flavor, gives a heady aroma if you bring the pot to the table.

2½ cups (600 ml) dark but not overly tannic fruity red wine

a rabbit, weighing 3 to 4 pounds (about 1.5 kg), cut into 2 front legs, 4 sections of loin, and 2 back legs each cut into 2 pieces, plus the bony parts without much meat on them (the neck and rib cage, the lower backbone, and so on)

unsalted butter

1 onion (about 100 gr), chopped

1 carrot (about 75 gr), peeled and chopped

a 2-inch section (about 30 gr) of celery, chopped

1 or 2 shallots (about 50 gr together), finely chopped

1 clove garlic, minced

¼ cup (30 gr) all-purpose flour

1¼ cups (300 ml) good chicken stock

a ½-by-½-inch (1-by-1-cm) piece of orange zest without white pith

salt

5 ounces (150 gr) lean salt pork or pancetta without rind, or 7 ounces (210 gr) lean, skinless fresh pork belly

2 dozen baby onions

½ pound (250 gr) white cultivated mushrooms, left whole if they're small, otherwise quartered

continued

Boil the wine until it is reduced by half, and set it aside. Sauté the rabbit pieces along with the bones in 2 tablespoons (25 gr) of butter. Remove the meaty pieces when they are golden (too much cooking makes the outside meat stringy), and continue cooking the bony bits until they are fully brown but not at all burned. (If the oven happens to be on for another purpose, cook the meaty pieces on top of the stove and roast the bony bits for more even, deep browning.)

In a pot just large enough to hold the entire preparation, cook the onion and carrot over medium-low heat in 1 tablespoon (15 gr) of butter until the onion is translucent and light golden brown. Add the celery, shallots, and garlic, and cook, stirring, for 90 seconds more. Add the flour, and stir for 45 seconds. Add the reduced wine, the stock, the orange zest, and just a little salt. Return the pieces of meat to the pot and simmer over low heat, covered, so the liquid lightly bubbles — this will almost certainly require a metal heat diffuser under the pot. Cook until the rabbit is tender — when probed with a fork or the point of a knife, the meat will separate from the bone — 45 to 60 minutes. Remove the pieces of meat and strain the sauce to remove the vegetables and bones; discard these. Return the sauce and meat to the pot, keeping it off the heat.

Slice the salt pork, pancetta, or fresh pork belly across the grain, about ¼-inch (6-mm) thick for salt pork or pancetta and ⅜-inch (1-cm) thick for fresh belly, which shrinks more. Then, maintaining the same thickness, cut each slice again to obtain long rectangles, so that each lardon is composed of alternate sections of fat and lean. Place the lardons in a pot of cold water and bring to a boil; drain, and cool under cold

black pepper

a little Madeira, tawny port, lemon juice, as needed, *optional*

running water, then drain well. Sauté them in 1 tablespoon (15 gr) of butter (lard will do at least equally well) over medium-high heat until light golden (cooked too much, they become tough). Drain on a paper towel and reserve.

Put the baby onions in a pan that will just hold them in one layer, and add 1 tablespoon (15 gr) of butter and enough water to come halfway up the onions. Cover and cook over medium-high heat until the onions are tender and the liquid is gone, about 10 minutes (the exact amount of liquid required is difficult to guess, and when the onions are nearly done, sometimes it's necessary to uncover the pot early to encourage evaporation). Then take the lid off and keep cooking, stirring, until the onions are golden brown all over, perhaps another minute or two, if that. Meanwhile, sauté the mushrooms in butter or in the fat left from sautéing the lardons.

Add the lardons, onions, and mushrooms to the rabbit in the sauce, and simmer gently for 5 to 10 minutes. Just before serving, thin the sauce if necessary with a bit of water (not with wine), and taste and season as necessary with salt and a grinding of pepper. If the wine flavor seems too aggressive, soften it with 1 or 2 teaspoons of slightly sweet Madeira or tawny port; if the taste is flat, squeeze in a little lemon juice. *Makes 4 modest portions.*

Variation: **LAPIN AUX PRUNEAUX** *(Rabbit with Prunes)*

Rabbit is cooked with prunes in southwest France as well as in the north, where the dish is sometimes called *à la flamande*. It retains the lardons and sometimes adds or substitutes raisins (or, on occasion, fresh Muscat grapes), and, like British jugged hare, it is often made slightly sweet and sour by vinegar and red-currant jelly. To convert rabbit in red wine to rabbit with prunes, increase the red wine to a total of 3 cups (700 ml). Put 20 prunes, ideally from Agen (the famous source, where the plums are perhaps harvested slightly riper and sweeter than they are in California), into a pot with the wine, bring to a boil, and set aside to cool. Remove the prunes with a slotted spoon, then reduce the wine and continue with the recipe. Garnish the rabbit with the prunes as well as the lardons prepared as above (skip the onions and mushrooms). The sweetness of prunes makes this one of the dishes for which it's difficult, if not impossible, to find a wine that has enough sweetness to match and yet still refreshes — choose an everyday dry or barely sweet wine that refreshes, and don't worry.

LAPIN À LA KRIEK

Rabbit in Beer

THIS MODERN BELGIAN SUMMER DISH COMBINES ELEMENTS OF THE *CARBONADE* (page 222) and of rabbit with prunes (preceding recipe). Here the fruit is cherries and the liquid, instead of stock or broth, is the beer named *kriek,* which in Flemish means "sour cherry." Traditionally, the beer is made by putting fresh cherries into lambic, the curiously tart Belgian beer fermented by wild yeast. After three months, the lambic has taken on the cherries' flavor, color, and sugar, the last provoking a fresh fermentation and bubbles. Like other Belgian fruit beers, *kriek* was originally always dry, although most today is sweet, and some tastes repulsively like cough syrup. The breweries Cantillon and De Ranke are two that make excellent *kriek,* one of the rare drinks that smell sweet but surprise in the mouth with a dry taste. In cooking, the *kriek* loses all but a memory of its cherry flavor; its lightness, however, complements the cherries that you add. In season, use fresh, though I admit I've used only dried. (In North America, most dried fruit is sold already pitted, which surely harms the flavor at least a little. When there's a choice, I opt for pits.) With the rabbit, don't drink *kriek,* whose cherry flavor wouldn't provide a contrast; choose a regular lambic or a *gueuze.*

about 2½ pounds (2 kg) fresh sour cherries, or 1¼ cups (225 gr) dried

a 1-liter bottle (or 2 500-ml bottles) dry *kriek*

2 rabbits, together weighing 6 to 8 pounds (roughly 3 kg), cut in serving pieces

lard or excellent, fresh-tasting olive oil or another good, light cooking oil

3 large (about 900 gr together) onions or a dozen large (about 600 gr together) shallots, chopped fine

continued

Soak the dried cherries, if you use those, overnight in enough *kriek* to cover.

The next day, dry the pieces of rabbit with paper towels. In a large, heavy pot with a lid, brown them well in fat — about 30 minutes over medium heat — working in batches so as not to cool the pan by crowding. Remove the meat to a warm dish.

Cook the onions or shallots slowly in the pot, adding more fat if needed, until they show some color, roughly 10 minutes. Add the flour, mixing it with the fat and cooking it for 1 minute. Add the rest of the *kriek* to the pot (or all of it, if you did not use some of it to soak dried cherries) while stirring, and, still stirring, heat

¼ cup (35 gr) all-purpose flour

an herb bundle: 1 bay leaf, several branches of parsley, and half a dozen or more branches of fresh thyme, tied together (or use ½ teaspoon dried thyme)

salt and black pepper

about ¼ cup (50 gr) brown or white sugar

the liquid until it bubbles. Return the rabbit to the pot, and add the herb bundle (sprinkle in the dried thyme if you use that), salt, and pepper, mixing everything together. The meat should be almost fully immersed; if not, add more beer or water (or broth or stock from rabbit or veal). Cook at a *very* low bubble, placing a heat diffuser under the pot, if necessary, and setting the lid either more or less ajar to further control the temperature. Beware of drying out the rabbit: cook it only until a skewer slides easily into, and especially *out* of, the meat — about 1 hour. Add the soaked cherries and their liquid, or the fresh cherries, about 15 minutes before the meat is done.

With a slotted spoon, remove the meat, the fruit, and most of the onions to a warm dish; discard the herb bundle. Carefully skim the fat from the liquid, and boil the liquid, if need be, to reduce it to the consistency of rich but runny cream. Add salt and sugar to taste. Return the rabbit, fruit, and onions to the pot, and heat them through. If the cherries contain pits, be certain to warn your eaters. *Serves 6 to 8.*

PIGEONNEAUX AUX OLIVES

Squabs with Olives

THE FLAVOR OF THIS DISH, ASSOCIATED WITH THE SOUTH OF FRANCE, depends heavily on the olives, so be sure to taste before you buy. For green olives, you can substitute black, though not a dry and withered kind. Rather than aiming at well-done meat, as you would with most braises, cook squabs to only about medium so they aren't dry. The same method is often applied to duck, which can stand being more fully cooked.

about ¾ cup (150 gr) pitted green olives

4 squabs, weighing about 1 pound (450 gr) each

3 ounces (85 gr) fresh pork belly or fatback, without rind

2 cups (450 ml) rich veal or game-bird stock or, in a pinch, poultry stock

about ⅜ teaspoon mixed dried herbs, mostly thyme, without stems and finely crumbled

salt and black pepper

Pit the olives, unless they are very small, and, unless they are both very small and delicate, blanch them for several minutes in boiling water. Drain and set aside. Remove the birds' wingtips and, if present, the feet. Cut the pork belly into ¼-inch (5-mm) cubes, and brown them over medium heat, without letting the fat smoke, in a heavy pot just large enough to hold all the squabs comfortably in a single layer. When the fat is rendered, discard the crisp pieces (or eat them with a little salt). Add the squabs, and brown them, turning so as to color all sides, about 15 minutes in all; set them aside. Add the stock and stir up the brown material from the bottom of the pot. Add the herbs and return the squabs to the pot. Cover and cook over very low heat, so the liquid barely yet steadily bubbles, turning the squabs once, until they are done to medium (check the inside of a thigh with a knife), about 15 minutes. Remove them to a hot platter.

Carefully skim the fat from the braising liquid with the sharp edge of a large spoon. Pass the liquid through a fine strainer, and return it to the pot. Over low to medium heat, set the pot to one side of the burner and, over at least 15 minutes, let a skin form and remove it; skim the fat again. Boil to reduce the liquid by one-third. Reduce the heat, add the olives, and simmer for a few more minutes. Taste and season, if needed, with salt, and grind in pepper. Remove the olives with a slotted spoon and place them around the squabs; moisten them with several spoonfuls of the sauce and pass the rest in a heated sauceboat. *Serves 4.*

CANARD AUX CERISES

Duck with Sour Cherries

THIS OLD FRENCH DISH IS A COUNTERPART TO DUCK *À L'ORANGE* and, like it, is often made cloyingly sweet. Both are descended from duck *à la bigarrade,* meaning "with sour oranges," such as Seville, and old recipes for that add no sugar at all. With duck, I prefer cherries to citrus. And small fruits with the pits left in hold more flavor during cooking. Dried sour cherries can be excellent; they have often been slightly sweetened in drying, so you may need no further sugar. Any main course with sweetness is difficult with dry wine and raises the question of what to drink. Duck with sour cherries would go in a rich, show-offy way with a glass of Banyuls or Maury (*vins doux naturels* from southwest France), but the wine must be slightly sweeter than the sauce, and the only way to ensure that is to open the bottle and taste the two together. A greater problem is that a sweet wine doesn't give refreshment. The imperfect solution is to barely sweeten the sauce and serve an especially flavorful dry red wine, not too special, that will more or less stand up to the dish.

about 2 pounds (900 gr) fresh sour cherries or 1 cup (175 gr) dried cherries

a duck, weighing 5 to 6 pounds (about 2.5 kg)

1 carrot, peeled and cut in large pieces

1 onion, halved

duck fat, lard, or excellent, fresh-tasting olive oil

½ bottle (375 ml) white wine

continued

Put the cherries, if dried, to soak in just enough hot water to cover them and set them aside. In a heavy pot just large enough to hold the duck, and having a tight-fitting lid, brown the duck, carrot, and onion slowly and well in fat over medium heat, uncovered, turning to color all sides—as long as 1 hour, with very low heat. Add the wine, scraping to dissolve the brown material on the botom of the pot, and then enough water to almost immerse the bird. Add the herb bundle, and season lightly with salt (the sauce will later be concentrated). Cover and cook at a very low bubble, turning the duck from time to time, until the meat is thoroughly tender—at least 1 hour.

a bundle of herbs: 1 bay leaf, several fresh parsley branches, a section of celery stalk with leaves, and several branches of thyme, tied together (if you have no fresh thyme, add a large pinch of dried to the pot)

salt and black pepper

1 to 2 tablespoons sugar

When the duck is done, remove it to a warm platter, and discard the carrot, onion, and herb bundle. Carefully skim the fat from the remaining juices and then strain them and return them to the pot. Drain the soaked dried cherries, if you use those, setting the fruit aside and adding the soaking water to the pot. Over high heat, reduce the combined liquids to about ¾ cup (175 ml). Add the cherries and cook about 3 minutes for soaked dried cherries or 15 minutes or more for fresh. If they yield juice, boil for a few more minutes to thicken the sauce. Taste it, and add salt, pepper, and sugar as needed. Carve the duck at the table, ladling some cherries and sauce over each serving. If the cherries have pits, warn your eaters. *Serves 4.*

MEAT

POLPETTE DI CARNE

Meatballs

MEATBALLS, *POLPETTE*, ARE MADE ALL OVER ITALY, commonly with additions such as garlic, parsley, grating cheese, and forms of cured pork. (One recipe from the Veneto for *polpette* includes some sweetness, from lemon zest, sugar, almonds, and cinnamon; I made it and for me the taste didn't work.) Most recipes can be applied to chicken, veal, or beef, and the choice of herbs follows the choice of meat. For any, a mix of dried, crumbled thyme, oregano, and savory is safe; with chicken, I opt for fresh sage or rosemary. If I'm adding pecorino, I tend to fry in olive oil, since butter is more typical of northern Italy, while pecorino is more typical of the south. You can fry up a sample meatball to check the taste, but the ingredients below provide so much flavor that more isn't likely to be needed.

1 or 2 cloves garlic, finely chopped

excellent, fresh-tasting olive oil or unsalted butter

1 pound (500 gr) ground chicken, veal, or beef

a slice of white bread, torn in pieces, enough to fill about 1 cup (a 125-ml measure)

a little milk or water

¾ cup (about 60 gr) grated Parmigiano-Reggiano or pecorino cheese

a handful of chopped parsley

½ teaspoon dried or roughly 3 times as much very finely chopped fresh herbs (see note above)

3 large eggs

salt and black pepper

soft or dry breadcrumbs for frying

1½ cups (350 ml) broth, stock, or tomato sauce

Cook the garlic in a little olive oil or butter over medium-low heat until it is translucent but not colored. Reduce the meat to a rough paste in a mortar or food processor, and place it in a large bowl. Soften the bread in a little milk or water for a few minutes, then squeeze out most of the liquid and add the bread to the meat, along with the garlic, cheese, parsley, other herbs, eggs, and salt and pepper. Mix thoroughly.

Form the seasoned meat into *polpette,* which is to say balls about the size of a small mandarin orange and similarly flattened; roll them in breadcrumbs. (The bread-coated, uncooked *polpette* can be held in the refrigerator for a few hours until mealtime.) Brown them in butter or oil over medium heat, turning, until cooked through, about 15 minutes. Add the broth, stock, or tomato sauce, and simmer to lightly reduce the liquid to a sauce, turning the *polpette* again. Add salt and pepper to taste. *Serves 4 to 6, after a bowl of pasta with a meatless sauce.*

BAECKEOFFE

Oven-Braised Pork, Lamb, and Beef

THE NAME OF THIS ALSATIAN STEW MEANS "BAKE OVEN"; the dish used to be assembled at home and carried to a nearby baker to be put into the oven after the bread came out. The marinade traditionally includes onions and leeks, but they convey a rank raw-onion flavor, perceptible in the finished dish. Instead of putting them in the marinade, I delay, and then just before cooking I slice them and add directly to the pot. Choose a somewhat waxy potato that won't fall apart too much in cooking. The pig's foot contributes important gelatin, but if you can't find it or a pig's tail, don't let that keep you from making the dish. The meats of a *baeckeoffe*, as those of any braised dish, must cook very gently if they are to remain moist. Sealing the lid with a piece of dough compensates for any loose fit and gives the pleasure of breaking the seal at the table, which releases a burst of steam and aroma. The same tactic can be used with other braised dishes whose liquid doesn't have to be reduced and cleansed before it is served. The only accompaniment needed is bread.

1 pound (500 gr) pork shoulder or loin from the more marbled shoulder end (*échine* in France, sometimes sold in the US as "blade loin roast" or the "rib end of the pork loin")

1 pound (500 gr) lamb or mutton shoulder

1 pound (500 gr) lean beef chuck or top blade (better is the related French cut *paleron*)

1 pig's foot

1 pig's tail, *optional*

continued

The evening before, trim most of the fat from the three meats, and cut them into 2- to 3-inch (5- to 8-cm) pieces without bone, following where possible the divisions between muscles. In a large bowl, mix the meats and the pig's foot and tail with the carrots, herb bundle, garlic, and a generous amount of ground pepper (no salt); add white wine to cover. Set in a cool place to marinate overnight.

The next day, heat the oven to 350° F (175° C). Fill the bottom of an appropriately large oven pot, with a cover, with half the potatoes. Drain and set aside the meats, carrots, herb bundle, and garlic, reserving the marinade. Add the meats, carrots, onions, and leeks to the pot, and insert the bundle of herbs and the garlic in

2 carrots, peeled and sliced in rounds

a bundle of herbs: 2 branches of fresh thyme, 1 bay leaf, half a dozen branches of parsley, and a short section of celery with a few leaves, tied together

2 cloves garlic, peeled and crushed

black pepper

2 cups (500 ml) or more white Alsace wine such as Edelzwicker, Sylvaner, Pinot Gris, or Riesling; no Gewurztraminer or Muscat or anything sweet

3 pounds (1.5 kg) somewhat waxy potatoes, peeled and sliced ⅛ inch (3 mm) thick

2 onions, chopped

2 leeks, white only, sliced crosswise

salt

roughly 2 cups (500 ml) homemade stock or water

a piece of bread dough or a soft dough made of just ⅞ cup (100 gr) of flour kneaded with ⅓ cup (70 ml) of cool water

the middle. Season generously with salt and top with the rest of the potatoes; salt again. In a separate pan, bring the marinade almost to a boil, skim it, and strain it into the oven pot. Add enough stock or water (or, optionally, more wine) to just cover the closely packed contents.

Roll the dough to make a long strip that will fit the rim of the pot. Dampen the rim and attach the dough, and then dampen the top of the dough and set the lid firmly in place. Put the pot in the oven for 20 minutes, then reduce the setting to 200° F (95° C) and bake for 3½ more hours. Break the seal of dough at the table, using a dull tool to pry gently at the edges. *Serves 6.*

SAUCE PIQUANTE

Herb-Vinegar Sauce for "Boiled" or Roasted Meats

THERE'S MORE THAN ONE VERSION OF THIS FRENCH SAUCE, which goes especially well with roasted or grilled pork but also with boiled or roasted lamb or beef as well as leftover meats. Here are two home variations, one with dried herbs and one with fresh. (In either case, a professional would add demi-glace or *sauce espagnole* and finish the sauce, off the heat, with butter.) If the vinegar is very strong, cut it with water. The pan juices come from whatever meat you're cooking. If instead you use only stock, the *sauce piquante* can be prepared mostly in advance, with the capers, cornichons, and fresh herbs added just before serving. The fresh-herb variation closely follows that of the redoubtable Madame Saint-Ange from the 1920s.

Dried-Herb Variation

1 onion (about 100 gr), finely chopped

2 shallots (about 70 gr), finely chopped

1 tablespoon (15 gr) unsalted butter

½ cup (125 ml) red-wine vinegar or to taste

several branches of parsley

1 bay leaf

a large pinch of dried thyme

6 whole black peppercorns

1 clove

1 teaspoon sugar, if needed

1 cup (250 ml) pan juices or veal or chicken stock, or a combination

continued

In a small nonreactive saucepan, cook the onion and shallots in butter until they are soft but not brown. Add the vinegar, parsley, bay leaf, thyme, peppercorns, clove, and sugar, stir, and then boil to reduce by half. Add the pan juices or stock, and cook slowly for 15 minutes, while the fat and impurities rise to the surface. Carefully, with a wide metal spoon, remove the fat and the skin that has formed, and then strain the sauce. Just before serving, add the capers and cornichons to the hot sauce. Taste and, if needed, add salt and pepper, and vinegar or sugar. *Makes about 1 cup.*

2 tablespoons (35 gr) pickled capers, well drained

2 tablespoons (35 gr) well-drained, finely sliced cornichons

salt and black pepper

1 very small onion (25 gr), finely chopped

1 small shallot (about 25 gr), finely chopped

1 cup (250 ml) vinegar

2 cups (500 ml) pan juices or veal or chicken stock, or a combination

1 tablespoon (20 gr) unsalted butter

2 tablespoons all-purpose flour

1½ tablespoons (25 gr) capers, well drained

2 dozen cornichons, well drained and finely chopped

freshly chopped parsley, chervil, and tarragon, in equal amounts, to make about ½ cup (perhaps 20 to 25 gr altogether)

salt and black pepper

Fresh-Herb Variation

Boil the onion and shallot in the vinegar in a nonreactive pan until the amount of liquid is reduced to 3 tablespoons (about 45 ml). Add the pan juices or stock and boil 2 to 3 minutes. In a second nonreactive pan over medium heat, melt the butter, stir in the flour, and cook for 1 minute. Over low heat, add the hot liquid little by little, each time whisking the combination smooth. Bring the sauce to a boil over high heat, still whisking. Then reduce the heat so the liquid bubbles slowly, and cook it for 15 minutes. With a wide metal spoon, remove the fat and the skin that has formed on the surface. If needed, thin the sauce with a little water or stock. Just before serving, add the capers, cornichons, and fresh herbs. Taste and season with salt and pepper. *Makes about 2 cups.*

PORC AUX PRUNEAUX

Pork with Prunes

THIS RECIPE IS BASED ON THE DISH AS JAMES SAW IT MADE in 1980 at the former bistro La Marmite in Tours, run by the chef Charles Barrier next door to his three-Michelin-star restaurant. Prunes hadn't been produced in the area for a long time, but they were still used in local cooking—even in, strange as it may seem, eel stew. Pork with prunes wasn't at the forefront of regional specialties, although it was fairly common, usually made with white wine from nearby Vouvray and with cream, and finished with red-currant jelly. Barrier's red-wine version, made slightly sweet by the prunes and slightly sour by vinegar, makes more sense. For a balanced taste, the sauce needs a certain meatiness, provided in professional kitchens by *glace de veau*. James proposes that at home one use a pork rib roast instead, so the role of the *glace* is filled by deglazing the roasting pan and adding the bones to the simmering liquid for the sauce. Usually, the dish is made with *noisettes,* which are essentially boneless chops; the thick slices of the boned roast below are very much like them. Boiled potatoes are a good accompaniment, and the wine could be a Bourgueil or Chinon, made from Cabernet Franc just downriver from Tours.

a pork rib roast, weighing 2¼ to 2½ pounds (about 1 kg), bone in, preferably from the end nearest the shoulder

salt and black pepper

1 cup (about 250 ml) dark red wine, fruity but not overly tannic

16 prunes, preferably from Agen

1 small onion (about 70 gr), in ½-inch (1-cm) dice

½ carrot (about 50 gr), in ½-inch (1-cm) dice

continued

Heat the oven to 325° F (165° C). Put the meat into a roasting pan just large enough to hold it (too much empty pan will scorch). Season the meat with salt and pepper, and put it into the oven. In a small pot, bring the wine and prunes to a boil, then set aside.

After 45 minutes of roasting, place the onion, carrot, and celery around the meat and stir briefly to coat them with fat. After another 15 minutes, begin checking the roast for doneness (if the vegetables are browning too quickly, add a bit of water to the pan). In about 20 more minutes (making a total of roughly 80 minutes), the meat next to the bone will reach 145° F (63° C)—this is an old-fashioned dish, so it shouldn't be pink. Remove the meat to a plate to cool for 10 to 15 minutes.

a 2-inch (5-cm) piece of celery stalk (about 30 gr) in ½-inch (1-cm) dice

2 tablespoons finely chopped shallot

2 teaspoons good red-wine vinegar

1 teaspoon cornstarch

sugar

Separate the meat from the bones with a long, straight carving knife: place the blade flat along the extremity of the ribs and, keeping the blade flush with them, cut the ribs free, being careful to leave the meat intact. Depending on the butcher, the chine bones (the thin bones that formed half the spine) may be present; if so, repeat the process to separate them.

The removed ribs will look like spare ribs. Separate them one from another with a knife, or by tearing, and return all the bones to the roasting pan. Add any juices that have run from the roast as it cooled and was cut, and place the pan in the oven for another 10 to 15 minutes. This step is important. The goals are to brown the ribs slightly and, even more, to evaporate the bit of juice in the bottom of the pan so it forms a beautiful brown glaze. Beware of spattering fat as you remove the pan from the oven and carefully pour off the grease.

Place the roasting pan over a burner set at medium-low; add the shallots and stir for about 10 seconds. Then add the red-wine vinegar and about ⅔ cup (150 ml) of water and use a wooden spatula or spoon to dissolve the glaze. Place the entire contents, including the bones, in a pot. Add the wine from the prunes, but not the prunes themselves. Simmer for about 10 minutes, strain, and return the liquid to the same pot. There should be about 1 cup (225 ml); if not, add some cold water.

Bring the liquid back to a simmer and add any juices that have flowed from the meat on the platter. Make a slurry of the cornstarch and ¼ cup (50 ml) of cold water and add it to the pot in small doses, stirring until you have a saucelike consistency. It won't take much (the amount needed depends on the gelatinousness of the bone-wine reduction) — err on the thin side.

Taste the sauce for salt and pepper, and adjust as necessary. Now taste it again for sweet and sour. It should have an edge but shouldn't be puckery. You can add just a bit of sugar — be careful not to make it too sweet — or, better yet, chop one of the prunes very fine and add it to the sauce. Heat the prunes in the sauce.

Slice the roast ½ inch (1 cm) thick, arrange the slices on a warm platter, put the prunes around, and pour the sauce over the meat. *Serves 4.*

ROAST PORK WITH ROSEMARY AND GARLIC

ROASTING IS COOKING BY RADIANT HEAT. IN ITS PURE FORM that means in front of, not over, a fire, where a large cut requiring long cooking would become too smoky, distracting from the taste. Grilling over a fire is for thin, tender cuts that cook quickly. For roasting, since most of us don't have a hearth, we settle on a hot oven, which, though the results aren't quite the same, can be very good. A classic roast provides a contrast of deeply browned exterior—even crisp in places—with a succulent rare interior, an effect impossible to achieve with low-temperature methods. Roast pork, to me, has the most flavor cooked to medium, which is more than the current fashion, but pork is naturally less juicy than beef or lamb, so it's especially important not to take it beyond medium—not to let the temperature rise higher than 140° to 145° F (60° to 63° C). The easy sauce that follows is equally good with roast leg of lamb, especially pale young lamb. There are many varieties of shell beans, familiar and obscure, sometimes with colorful names (Red Kidney, Soldier, Marafax, Jacob's Cattle, Cranberry, Sulfur, Cannellini, the flageolet family), but I've never been drawn far into the distinctions of taste. More important is the way they're cooked—with a bouquet of herbs, a carrot, a celery stalk, and an onion pricked with two cloves, salt being added only at the end of cooking—and any sauce that may go with them. Many different wines can accompany roast pork, both whites and light reds, from Loire Valley Chenin Blanc to Pinot Noir grown in cool places to light Nebbiolo and a good dry Lambrusco.

1 head garlic

a pork loin, weighing roughly 7 pounds (3.2 kg) with the bones or 4 pounds (1.8 kg) without, cut from the center or shoulder end

good olive oil

salt and black pepper

¾ cup (175 ml) white wine

1 or 2 branches of fresh rosemary

For a milder taste, peel the garlic cloves (if green sprouts show, split the cloves and pry out the sprouts); bring them to a boil in cold water, and cook for about 30 minutes, until a clove, removed and pressed with a fork, dissolves into purée; drain and set aside. *For a stronger taste,* separate the cloves but leave them in their skins to prevent burning, and roast them in the pan together with the meat, placing a little wine or water in the roasting pan at the start, again to prevent burning.

Heat the oven to 450° F (230° C). Coat the exposed lean meat of the pork loin with oil and season the entire surface with salt and pepper. Place the meat in a roasting pan, surrounded by the unpeeled garlic cloves (if you prefer a stronger flavor), and roast for 15 minutes. Reduce the setting to 325° F (165° C), and cook until the center of the meat or the center next to the bone reaches 140° F (60° C). Remove the meat to a warm platter, where the internal temperature—especially if the bones are present—will continue to rise, at least another 5° F (3° C).

Skim or pour off most of the fat from the pan, set the pan over medium to high heat, and deglaze with the wine. Put the contents of the roasting pan, including the garlic if you roasted it, into a saucepan together with the rosemary, and boil until the liquid is reduced to a light syrup. If you prefer a milder taste, add the boiled garlic now, mashing the roasted or boiled cloves to a paste and mixing it with the liquid in the pan. Strain this sauce, pushing the soft garlic through the strainer, pressing and then scraping the purée from the other side and stirring it back into the sauce. Thin the sauce, if necessary, with water. Season well with salt, grind in pepper, and bring to a boil. Pour the sauce over the roast to mingle with the juices in the platter or, if you're serving shell beans, mix the sauce with the cooked beans. *Serves 6 to 8.*

JAMBON À LA CRÈME

Ham with Chablis and Cream

BURGUNDY'S *JAMBON À LA CRÈME* AND *JAMBON AU CHABLIS* are closely allied to its *saupiquet*. Each consists of slices of ham, fried (originally in lard) and then cooked gently in wine. There are no firm boundaries between these dishes: *à la crème* contains more cream, *au Chablis* relies more on wine, and *saupiquet* calls for vinegar. (This *saupiquet* has diverged almost entirely from the one of southern France for roasted rabbit, which typically contains garlic, anchovies, capers, parsley, the rabbit's liver, and only sometimes vinegar.) In the Burgundian countryside, the ham was cut from a fully cured whole leg smoked in the chimney, and it required soaking to get rid of some salt. James and I prefer lightly cured unsmoked ham, the kind called *demi-sel* in France (to make your own, see page 28), cooked beforehand (poached as a whole piece and then sliced); or you can use already cooked ham. *Jambon à la crème* and related dishes are a good way to use leftover ham that isn't too smoky. Frying the ham, though typical, makes it tough and doesn't add much because the slices aren't afterward simmered, so the brown flavors don't enter the sauce. We assume full-strength wine vinegar of about 7 percent acidity (most North American vinegar is diluted to about 4 percent); the bit of tomato, though not always used, has a buffering effect on it. We've suppressed the classic thickening with flour (a couple of spoonfuls cooked in the fat after frying) in favor of adding stock and thickening by reduction. And we've added tarragon. This makes it a more refined, less homey dish, yet also quicker, since the old dish required the sauce to be cooked slowly for a long time to get rid of the raw-flour taste, and the ham was sometimes included in that long cooking so it would add its flavor. Optionally, serve lightly sautéed mushrooms alongside the ham and sauce. A good *premier cru* Chablis has the right degree of richness.

2 pounds (1 kg) lightly cured ham,
either a whole raw piece or cooked
ham in ¼-inch (6-mm) slices

1 cup (250 ml) Chablis or other
dry white Burgundy

1¾ cup (400 ml) chicken stock

¼ cup (50 ml) red- or white-wine
vinegar

2 or 3 shallots, chopped, enough to
make about ½ cup (75 gr)

3 or 4 branches fresh tarragon

3 or 4 juniper berries, crushed

½ cup (125 ml) puréed tomatoes,
either good ripe fresh ones or
ripe-tasting canned

2 cups (500 ml) heavy cream

salt and black pepper

If the ham is raw, poach it in water in a single piece and keep it warm and ready in the poaching liquid while you prepare the sauce. If the ham is already cooked and sliced, moisten the slices with a bit of broth or stock and heat, covered, very gently at a low temperature in the oven or on top of the stove in a pan protected with a heat diffuser.

In a nonreactive pot, boil together the wine, stock, vinegar, shallots, tarragon, and juniper berries until the volume is reduced by three-fourths or more. Add the tomato purée and boil 1 minute. Add the cream and boil again to reduce the sauce until it just coats the back of a wooden spoon, like the familiar dessert sauce *crème anglaise* (pourable custard). Strain, taste, and season with salt and pepper. Return the sauce to the pot, and bring it momentarily to a boil; if it's too thick, thin it with a splash of water. Slice the ham, if it isn't already sliced, arrange it on a hot platter, and cover with the sauce. *Serves 4.*

CHOUCROUTE GARNIE À L'ALSACIENNE

Sauerkraut with Sausages and Other Cured Pork

CHOUCROUTE GARNIE, A COOL-WEATHER DISH FROM ALSACE, VARIES from place to place and cook to cook. Some of the elements are cooked partly or entirely together, and yet the flavors remain distinct and complement one another, with a balance between the cured meats and the sauerkraut. Success depends on the quality and variety of the meats and sausages. The selection of meats is sometimes reduced but there is always bacon. Three kinds of sausages are commonly called for: *saucisses de Francfort, saucisses de Strasbourg* (also called *knack*), and *saucisses de Montbéliard,* but other good lightly smoked sausages without strong added flavors will do well, and can include veal. The thing to look for is a variety of textures. And the quantity of pieces isn't important; just keep in mind the number of people you will serve. Some North American butchers have appropriate sausages, and you may even find rendered goose fat. Good sauerkraut doesn't require more than draining, then a quick rinse and draining again, and perhaps not a rinse at all. But some naturally made and preserved sauerkraut, especially as time passes, becomes strong and sharp. The cooking times sauerkraut needs may vary, but it should retain a slight crunch. There's no need for a first course before a *choucroute*.

2 pounds (1 kg) salted pork loin or *échine* (page 28)

1½ pounds (600 gr) smoked *jarret de porc* (the lower part of the ham or shoulder, extending into the leg) or a substitute

⅔ pound (300 gr) fresh, unsmoked bacon, rind removed

⅔ pound (300 gr) smoked bacon, rind removed

continued

Poach the pork loin, the *jarret de porc,* and both kinds of bacon until tender, about 2 hours. About three-fourths of the way through that time, drain the sauerkraut, taste it, and if it is very sharp, rinse it in one or more changes of water, and drain again. In a large pot, cook the onions in the goose fat or lard until soft, without browning; tip the pot and spoon off and reserve the fat. Add the sauerkraut, seasonings, wine, and water or stock to the pot.

Cook the sauerkraut for about 45 minutes alto-

5 pounds (2 kg) sauerkraut

2 onions, chopped

½ cup (150 gr) rendered goose fat or lard

a bundle of seasonings: 3 cloves, 6 juniper berries, 4 or 5 coriander seeds, a dozen black peppercorns, and 1 bay leaf, tied in a piece of cloth

½ bottle (375 ml) Riesling, Sylvaner, or good Edelzwicker

1 cup (250 ml) water or stock

5 pounds (2 kg) potatoes, preferably waxy, peeled and cut, as needed, into large pieces

4 *saucisses de Francfort* (smooth-ground pork sausages) or a substitute, about 1¼ pounds (600 gr)

4 *saucisses de Strasbourg* (smooth-ground smoked beef and pork sausage) or a substitute, about 1¼ pounds (600 gr)

4 *saucisses de Montbéliard* (coarsely ground smoked pork sausage), or a substitute, about 1¼ pounds (600 gr)

2 *boudins noirs* (blood sausages), if possible, about 1¼ pounds (600 gr)

salt

gether, adding the poached meats, after they are done, during about the last 20 minutes of cooking the sauerkraut—if the meats aren't quite ready, turn off the sauerkraut and wait—and saving the hot poaching liquid. Boil the potatoes, or steam them on top of the sauerkraut for 30 minutes. Poach the sausages in the water that held the meats, and sauté the *boudins noirs* in the reserved fat from the onions. Remove the bag of spices, and taste the sauerkraut for salt. Pile it in the center of a serving platter, leaving the liquid behind, and arrange the potatoes and meats impressively over it. *Serves 8 to 10.*

SCALLOPINI AL VINO BIANCO O AL LIMONE

Veal Scallops with White Wine or with Lemon

IF VEAL SCALLOPS ARE FLOURED BEFORE COOKING, THEY'RE MORE TENDER, although also more bland, since the flour prevents the meat and juices from browning in the pan. You can compromise by flouring just one side of the meat. Instead of white wine, you can use dry or slightly sweet Madeira or sweet Marsala; with the last, add enough lemon juice to balance the sweetness. Marsala has for a long time been generally a sweet, insipid wine used largely for cooking, like most Madeira, but a little good, dry Marsala can be found at a much higher price, and that would be better. If you use white wine and then add the juice of half a lemon, you have a lemon sauce.

1 pound (500 gr) veal scallopini, preferably from top round, cut across the grain ¼ inch (6 mm) thick

salt and black pepper

all-purpose flour

unsalted butter or excellent, fresh-tasting olive oil

¾ cup (175 ml) white wine

a lemon for juice

2-square-inch (5-square-cm) shaving of the yellow zest, *optional*

several fresh sage leaves, *optional*

Pound each slice of veal with a mallet to flatten it and spread it slightly. Season the slices with salt and pepper, and flour them lightly. Brown them briefly in very hot fat, a minute or less per side. As each slice is done, remove it from the pan to a warm platter.

Deglaze the empty pan with the wine and, if you choose, the juice of the lemon and the shaving of zest. Add the sage leaves, and return the meat to the pan. Over medium heat, simmer while shaking or stirring the pan to mix the flour adhering to the meat with the liquid and thicken the sauce, about 1 minute. Remove the fresh sage leaves, if you use them, and season as needed with salt. If you haven't added lemon juice up to now, squeeze in just enough to brighten the taste. Transfer the slices to a warm platter or warm plates, and pour the sauce over the meat. *Serves 4.*

SALTIMBOCCA

Veal Scallops with Ham

THE VARIOUS NORTHERN ITALIAN RECIPES FOR ROLLED-UP THIN SLICES of veal form a loose group, including *uccelletti scappati* (birds that have flown), *quagliette di vitello* (little veal quails), and *braciolette* (little skewers). The best known of the type, though, is usually cooked flat: the Roman dish saltimbocca (jump into your mouth). To make it, Pellegrino Artusi's classic cookbook, *La Scienza in cucina e l'arte di mangiar bene*, first published in 1891 and still widely used, calls for simply pinning together with a toothpick half a sage leaf, a slice of ham with its fat, and a slice of veal, and sautéing. That's it. Saltimbocca is still often made that way. However, it's not only easy to overcook the thin scallops — certainly if you want browning — but the ham side, as Artusi notes, must be cooked less or it turns hard. Instead, for saltimbocca I like to form the veal and ham into little rolls. Sometimes the simple dish contains an addition of Marsala or white wine to make a sauce. For me, the white wine ties together the ham and veal. With flavorful ham, you need only a thin slice, and the ham's salt is sufficient. Any of these veal dishes goes well with almost any vegetable and with buttered rice or polenta, the latter enriched in the usual way with butter and grated Parmigiano.

1 pound (500 gr) veal scallopini, preferably from top round, cut across the grain ¼ inch (6 mm) thick

black pepper

2 to 4 ounces (60 to 100 gr) paper-thin slices of raw, dry-cured ham (prosciutto, Southern country ham), depending on the ham's salty intensity

fresh sage leaves

clarified unsalted butter or excellent, fresh-tasting olive oil

¾ cup (175 ml) dry white wine, *optional*

Pound each slice of veal with a mallet to flatten and spread it slightly. Season it with a grinding of pepper, and place a paper-thin slice of ham on it — the ham should almost but not quite cover the veal — and then half a sage leaf. Roll them up together, and secure with a toothpick. Brown the rolls in hot fat over medium heat for several minutes, turning. Add the wine, reduce the heat to a low simmer, and cook about 10 minutes. Serve the rolls with the wine in the pan as a sauce. *Serves 4.*

Variation: **UCCELLETTI SCAPPATI** *(Grilled Veal Rolls)*

For any of these scallopini recipes, the methods are not at all fixed—some recipes for saltimbocca are identical to some for *uccelletti scappati*. The latter, always rolled, typically contain a thin slice of veal over a very thin slice of ham, and the rolls are cooked like small birds: they're threaded onto a skewer with, between rolls, a piece of pancetta, a leaf of fresh sage, and a cube of firm, stale bread. Sometimes, instead of the fat being placed between the rolls, a thin slice of it is wrapped around each one, which protects the meat. The "birds" are grilled slowly over a fire. Equally, they can be cooked in a pan with butter or other fat, with wine added to make a sauce. Sometimes the slices are rolled around a filling that contains cured pork or cheese, and then they are called *involtini* or *imbottiti*. A French name for the filled version is *alouettes sans têtes* (larks without heads); in America they're "veal birds" or "veal olives." Pork loin or turkey breast could substitute for veal.

To make *uccelletti scappati*, prepare the scallopini as for saltimbocca: pounding to flatten and spread them slightly, seasoning each with a grinding of pepper, and placing a paper-thin slice of ham on top, and rolling the two up together. Wrap each roll with a very thin slice of cured pork fat (lardo, pancetta, or salt pork). Thread the "birds" onto skewers, about four to a skewer, placing a sage leaf on either side of each and between them a 1-inch (2- to 3-cm) cube of somewhat dense white bread. Grill them slowly over hot coals just beginning to die down, until the meat is medium rare in the center, perhaps 10 minutes. Beware—dripping from the pork fat will make the fire flare; move the skewers as needed to avoid the flames. *Serves 4.*

VITELLO TONNATO

Veal in Tuna Sauce

USUALLY TODAY, *VITELLO TONNATO* TAKES THE FORM of dry slices of veal accompanied by a tuna mayonnaise. The original, as here, called for marinating the veal slices in the tuna sauce. Serve with salad and, of course, bread.

2 pounds (1 kg) boneless veal, eye of loin or another tender cut that yields neat slices

a short inner celery stalk with leaves

several branches of fresh parsley

1 bay leaf

1 onion, halved

1 carrot, peeled and cut in large pieces

2 salted anchovies, the filets cleaned of salt, stripped from the bones, and rinsed

¼ cup (25 gr) capers in salt, rinsed

juice of 1 lemon

1 cup (225 ml) excellent, fresh-tasting olive oil

4 ounces (100 gr) tuna in oil, drained

salt

another lemon, olives, and more capers, for garnish

Put the meat into a pot just large enough to hold it; add the celery, parsley, bay leaf, onion, and carrot and just enough water to cover. Cook at a low bubble, monitoring to be sure it doesn't boil. Poach to an internal temperature of about 130° F (54° C), which with the gentlest poaching—the surface of the water is barely troubled—may take up to 2 hours. Cool the meat in the liquid, where its temperature will rise a few degrees more.

Put the anchovies, capers, lemon juice, oil, and tuna into the bowl of a mortar or food processor, and reduce them to a slightly coarse-textured sauce. Taste and season, if needed, with salt. Remove the cooled meat from the liquid, and slice it across the grain about ⅛ inch (3 mm) thick. Thinly coat the bottom of a platter with sauce; on that arrange about a third of the slices of meat, without overlapping; cover with a little more sauce; and continue, making two more layers of meat with sauce and ending with a good coating of sauce. Cover with plastic and chill 24 hours. Garnish with slices of lemon, olives, and a scattering of rinsed capers. *Serves 4 to 6.*

ROGNONS DE VEAU À LA MOUTARDE

Sautéed Veal Kidneys with Mustard

SAUTÉED VEAL KIDNEYS IN MUSTARD SAUCE is one of the most typical old Paris bistro plates. The mustard should give some peppery bite, but the Dijon mustard sold in France is much hotter than the examples exported to the United States (Maille "Extra Hot" made for the United States, for instance, is milder than the standard Maille in France), and anyway most jars are old enough by the time they get to the United States that they are losing power and flavor. You can't compensate by adding more mustard, because the extra acidity and other flavors throw off the balance. It's better not to worry about the absence of heat, though you could add some mustard powder (mix first with water and wait 10 minutes before using). The best solution, if you happen to visit France (or Quebec), is to buy a jar of mustard and carry it back. Don't chop parsley more than about half an hour before you serve it; the closer to last-minute the better. The kidneys could be preceded by a vegetable course. Serve them with mashed potatoes, fresh egg noodles, or simply bread, followed by salad. The dish is excellent with a glass of Beaujolais, which is of course one of the traditional bistro wines of Paris.

½ pound (250 gr) cultivated white mushrooms

unsalted butter

2 veal kidneys, together weighing roughly 1 pound (500 gr), cleaned of outer fat and membrane and inner gristle

salt and black pepper

1 small shallot, finely chopped, making at least 1 tablespoon

½ cup (125 ml) white wine

continued

Quarter the mushrooms and sauté them in butter in a wide nonreactive pan just until cooked through; remove and set aside. Separate the kidneys into pieces following the wrinkles. Salt and pepper them. Heat 2 tablespoons (30 gr) of butter to sizzling in the same pan over medium-high to high heat, and sauté the kidneys for about 5 minutes, leaving them still partly rare and red inside—cooked further, they become rubbery. Transfer them to a warm plate. In the fat that remains in the pan, cook the shallot until translucent. Add the wine and boil to reduce the amount by half. Add the cream and boil again to reduce to sauce consistency. Stir in the mustard—and then don't boil the sauce

½ cup (125 ml) heavy cream or crème fraîche

2 tablespoons Dijon mustard, optionally half regular and half coarse-grain

a little white-wine vinegar or lemon juice

parsley

again. Taste and add just a little vinegar or lemon juice—up to ½ teaspoon—if needed, and season with salt and pepper. Return the kidneys and mushrooms to the pan. Chop the parsley. Heat the kidneys and mushrooms through, without boiling, stirring to coat them with the sauce, and serve immediately on heated plates with a sprinkling of parsley. *Makes 2 bistro-sized portions, or 4 moderate ones.*

FIGÀ A LA VENEXIANA

Venetian-Style Calf's Liver

FEGATO ALLA VENEZIANA (TO USE THE ITALIAN rather than the Venetian) — liver and onions sparked with lemon, wine, or vinegar — is a quickly made dish. The only danger is that the liver will be overcooked: dry and tough. To protect against that, the onions are cooked first and the liver goes on top. The onions also help to counteract any dryness as well as the mild bitterness of liver. If you add enough acidity, then the sweetness of the onions — often half the weight of the liver — makes the dish slightly sweet and sour. One Venetian I've met uses only grated lemon zest, nothing acidic at all. Giuseppe Maffioli, a deep student of the city's cooking, in *La Cucina veneziana,* published in 1982, gives the option of *figà a la sbrodega,* using fewer onions but adding garlic, rosemary, and fresh sage leaves; then he adds wine or vinegar or both, and seasons the dish at the end with a tiny pinch each of cinnamon and clove. Calf's liver is best. (At times the stronger, cruder pork liver is used and, occasionally, beef liver, stronger still.) But in Venice, the livers of chicken or other fowl are sometimes chosen; kidneys can be treated the same way, but with them be sure to add vinegar to go with the stronger taste.

You eat *fegato alla veneziana* with polenta, usually soft and hot, though it can be cooled on a platter, cut into pieces, and fried or grilled slowly, so the surface firms and the pieces don't fall apart. The Veneto traditionally eats a lot of corn; pasta and bread have become widespread everyday food only recently. As throughout northern Italy, much of the bread in Venice has a washed-out-looking tan crust over an ultrawhite cottony interior, and very little taste. Polenta from freshly ground cornmeal is hugely superior.

½ pound (250 gr) sweet onions, thinly sliced

¼ cup (60 ml) excellent, fresh-tasting olive oil or 2 tablespoons each oil and unsalted butter

¼ cup (60 ml) white wine

1 tablespoon white-wine vinegar, *optional*

1 pound (500 gr) calf's liver, outside membrane removed, sliced no more than ¼-inch (6-mm) thick and cut again to make strips roughly 1-inch (2- to 3-cm) wide

a small handful of parsley, finely chopped just before cooking

salt and black pepper

Cook the onions slowly in the fat in a very large frying pan (enough space to later fit the liver in a single layer), stirring now and then, until they are soft but not at all fried or brown—10 to 15 minutes. (If the onions seem dry, cover the pan or add a little water.) Raise the heat to high, stir in the wine, and taste; if you prefer a slightly sharper taste, add the vinegar. Put the liver in a layer on top of the onions. Cook 2 to 3 minutes, turn the liver, and, stirring several times, cook 2 more minutes, or until the liver just ceases to be bloody—*do not overcook*. Take the pan from the heat, and immediately stir in the parsley so it cooks in the residual heat. Season with salt and grind in pepper. *Serves 4.*

CARBONADE À LA GUEUZE

Beef Braised in Tart Belgian Beer

GUEUZE IS A YOUNGER, EFFERVESCENT FORM OF LAMBIC, the otherwise flat Belgian beer brewed with wild yeast, which gives distinctive flavors and tartness. This recipe for *carbonade à la flamande*—to use the more general name—reflects a conversation I once had with a Belgian chef named Yvon Schenkeveld, who might not agree with all my details. Traditionally, the liquid was either dry lambic, including *gueuze,* or the lambic mixed with sugar and called *faro.* *Carbonade* is also very good made with other amber and dark Belgian beers, and similar beer-braising is applied to other meats, including pork and rabbit (see Lapin à la Kriek, page 193). The beef for *carbonade* is often the French cut *paleron* (a muscle covering the shoulder blade, not an American cut) or *aiguillette* (bottom sirloin flap, from the hind leg), which provides marbling and gelatin. American butchers don't break down a carcass into as many different cuts for different purposes, and when they slice the chuck crosswise into slabs, the best you can do is select one with marbling and cartilage, the latter for gelatin. Usually in Belgium the meat for *carbonade* is sliced ⅔- to ¾-inch (about 1.5-cm) thick, but I use thicker pieces in the hope of a moister result. The old cooking fat was lard. Restaurants reflexively add brown stock, but in the days when soup was always on hand, a housewife might add *bouillon.* The *carbonade* is sometimes thickened by cooking in it a piece of bread spread with coarse Flemish mustard; it would be better to stir the mustard in at the end, off the heat, to preserve all its flavor and bite—except that it doesn't matter, since the mustard only distracts. A modern idea is to use a slice of gingerbread (*pain d'épices*), but the spices are at least as distracting—plain, simple flour is best. Traditional *carbonade* is sweet from plenty of onions, but if you use dry lambic, the onions don't supply enough sugar and you must add some sugar to balance the beer's tartness. Serve the *carbonade* with mashed, steamed, or boiled potatoes. Drink a beer whose bitterness or sweetness is similar to that of the dish.

3½ pounds (1.5 kg) beef chuck (shoulder)

lard or excellent, fresh-tasting olive oil or another good, light cooking oil

4 or more large onions, totaling as much as 2¼ pounds (1 kg)

¼ cup (35 gr) all-purpose flour

1 quart (1 lt) excellent *gueuze* or other lambic beer, such as from the Cantillon brewery

a bundle of herbs: 1 bay leaf, half a dozen parsley branches or roots, and a couple of branches of fresh thyme, tied together (or use dried thyme, loose)

salt and black pepper

brown or white sugar

Dry the beef with a paper towel, and cut it into roughly 2-by-2-inch (5-by-5-cm) pieces, following as much as possible the breaks between muscles. In a large, heavy pot with a lid, brown the meat well in fat, working in batches so as not to cool the pan by crowding — for 30 minutes or more. While the meat is browning, chop the onions coarsely. Remove the browned meat to a warm dish.

Over medium heat, brown the onions in the pot, adding more fat as needed, about 12 minutes. Add the flour, mixing it with the fat and cooking it for 1 minute. Add the beer while stirring. Return the meat to the pot, and add the herb bundle, 1 teaspoon of salt, and grindings of pepper, mixing all together. The meat should be almost fully immersed; if not, add more beer (or water, broth, or stock). Cook at a very low bubble, placing a heat diffuser under the pot if necessary and setting the lid either more or less ajar to help control the temperature. Cook the meat until a skewer slides easily in and, especially, out — about 3 hours. Remove the meat and about half the onions with a slotted spoon; discard the herb bundle. Carefully skim the fat from the liquid. Boil it, if necessary, to reduce it to the consistency of rich but runny cream. Return the meat and onions to the pot, and heat them thoroughly. Taste, and add salt and a little sugar, as needed. *Serves 6.*

GRILLADE DES MARINIERS DU RHÔNE

Sliced Beef Stewed in Red Wine

THE RHÔNE RIVER BOATMEN HAVE DISAPPEARED, but they leave behind a reputation for certain dishes, including *matelotes* (red-wine-and-onion fish stews) and *grillades,* such as this one. André Besson, a retired chef who lives in Montreal, worked for two years at La Pyramide in Vienne, just south of Lyon. That was the restaurant of Fernand Point, the greatest French chef of the 20th century. (Point had already died but he had been Besson's godfather and had poured Champagne into the baptismal font.) Point used to walk along the banks of the Rhône, talking with the *mariniers* and sometimes sharing their meals. The following rustic dish is from La Pyramide, and Besson believes it is the *grillade* just as the boatmen cooked it, though Point's classical training must have had an effect. The word *grillade* suggests something grilled, but Besson explains that around Lyon, it refers to the cut of beef called *pointe de culotte,* a small piece between the sirloin and the rump (it's also called *pièce de bœuf,* as when it is braised for *bœuf à la mode*). American butchers divide the carcass differently, and the cut is unobtainable here. Rump roast comes closest. Probably better, if less traditional, are cuts from the blade or shoulder (in slices an inch, or 2 cm, thick or a little thicker), including short ribs. Optionally, Besson says, marinate the meat for 2 hours in ⅜ cup (100 ml) of vinegar, ground black pepper, and ⅜ cup (100 ml) of walnut oil. You can find recipes for *grillade des mariniers* that marinate for one or two days. The simplest old methods call for moistening with vinegar and water. Wine, when used, was probably more often red than white. The *grillade* was served, says Besson, with steamed potatoes, tagliatelle, turnip gratin, salsify with *persillade* (very finely chopped parsley and raw garlic), or Jerusalem artichokes. Besson may have made some small alterations in Point's recipe, and in a few places where I thought more specificity was needed, I've done so as well.

²/₃ pound (300 gr) white onions, finely chopped

8 tablespoons (100 gr) unsalted butter

1 tablespoon sugar

1 large ripe tomato, peeled, seeded, and diced

¾ cup (200 ml) good red-wine vinegar

1¼ cups (300 ml) dry white wine

3 salted anchovies, the filets cleaned of salt, stripped from the bones, and rinsed

1 tablespoon chopped herbs (parsley, chives, chervil)

1¾ pounds (800 gr) *pointe de culotte* or rump roast (see note above for other possible cuts), sliced across the grain in 4 pieces

³/₈ cup (100 ml) excellent, fresh-tasting olive oil

salt

black pepper

In a nonreactive pan, cook the onions with half of the butter and the sugar over high heat for 5 minutes, and continue to cook over low heat for another 5 minutes, until the onions have a golden color. Add the tomato. Deglaze the pan with the vinegar, and reduce the mixture over high heat by two-thirds to tame its acidity. Add the wine and cook slowly for 10 minutes. Mash the anchovy filets with the remaining butter and the herbs; set aside.

In a separate nonreactive pan over medium-high heat, brown the slices of meat on both sides in olive oil. Pour off the fat, add the onion mixture to the meat, salt very lightly, and cook over very low heat, covered, for at least 2 hours. Divide the slices of meat among 4 heated plates. Return the sauce to the heat, skim most of the fat from the surface, boil to thicken just a little, as needed, and whisk in the anchovy-herb butter — then don't let it boil again. Taste for salt and pepper. Coat each slice of meat with a good spoonful of sauce. *Serves 4.*

OXTAIL STEW

THE RICH FLAVOR OF *POT-AU-FEU À LA QUEUE DE BŒUF* recalls that of *brasato al Barolo* (beef braised in Barolo wine) from Piedmont in northeast Italy. Most oxtails are sold already trimmed of much fat and cut into short pieces. To prepare a whole tail, slice away all but a thin layer of the fat, which thickens toward the base of the tail; flex the tail, feeling for the wide meetings of the vertebrae, and with a sharp knife slice through the cartilagelike material between them.

Serve the soup first in warm bowls, and pass fresh bread or, if you have older bread, place toasted slices in the bottom of the soup bowls. Then serve the oxtails with a little more of the liquid spooned over. Accompany the oxtails with waxy potatoes, egg noodles, or thick polenta. At the table, it's hard to remove the meat from the bones effectively with any degree of decorum. The best response may be, so what? But you can, in advance in the kitchen, cool the sections of tail enough to remove the meat from the bones and then reheat it in the liquid. In that case, push the vegetables through a sieve to reduce them to a purée and to remove the salt pork, and add the vegetables back to the soup to thicken it into a sauce, and serve the meat and sauce together. Or serve only the clear soup at a first meal, followed by an unrelated main course; the next day, coat the sections of tail with soft or melted butter, roll them in dry breadcrumbs, and brown them, turning once, in a very hot oven. Serve the oxtails with mustard or a sauce made by reducing the soup, if any is left, to a slightly thick sauce.

(If lack of stock is an impediment to cooking this red-wine oxtail stew, instead braise them in dark beer. Use the recipe for *carbonade* on page 222, replacing the chunks of beef with sections of two oxtails — there will be twice as much oxtail, but roughly half is bone — and replacing the *gueuze* with a dark but not intense beer. There will be sauce but no soup. Use only half the amount of salt pork, adding oil if needed to brown the meat, and assemble the braise compactly using all the vegetables and seasonings. Moisten the braise with 2 cups or 500 ml of dark beer and enough water to immerse the uppermost pieces of oxtail halfway.)

The oxtail stew below stands up to a rich red wine, or back off and drink a minor red just for refreshment.

1 quart (1 lt) chicken stock

¼ pound (125 gr) salt pork or unsmoked bacon (such as pancetta), diced

2 oxtails, roughly 6 pounds (3 kg) total, cut into sections at the vertebrae

1 celery stalk, halved and cut in sections

2 carrots, peeled, halved, and cut in sections

3 onions, quartered

1 parsnip, peeled, quartered lengthwise, and cut in sections

2 cups (500 ml) red wine

1 cup (250 ml) white wine

a dozen fresh parsley branches and the top of an inner stalk of celery with leaves, tied together with a string

4 garlic cloves, peeled and crushed

½ teaspoon dried thyme

¼ teaspoon mixed dried herbs, such as oregano, savory, and marjoram

a pinch each of ground allspice and ground clove

2 bay leaves

black pepper

salt

Set the oven to 200° F (95° C), put the stock in a 5- to 6-quart (5-lt) covered oven pot, and set it in the oven to heat slowly. In a large frying pan, render the fat from the salt pork or bacon and remove the crisp pieces to the oven pot. Sauté the oxtail sections in batches in the fat, turning so as to brown all the sides well and removing the finished pieces to the pot of stock—20 to 25 minutes altogether. Sauté the celery, carrots, onions, and parsnips in the same fat, long enough to caramelize their edges, and add them to the pot of stock. Use some of the wine to deglaze the frying pan, scraping the bottom and adding all the material to the pot.

Tuck the parsley bouquet in the center, and add the garlic, the other herbs and spices, and the remaining wine. Grind in pepper, but add no salt. Return the pot to the oven, still at 200° F (95° C). Check now and then during the first hour, adjusting the setting as needed (ovens are often inaccurate) to ensure that the liquid is bubbling below a simmer but more than intermittently. Cook until the meat is completely tender but still attached to the bones, 3½ to 4 hours.

Remove the oxtails to a large plate and put that in the oven. With a slotted spoon, transfer the vegetables, parsley bundle, and salt pork to a colander held over the pot; press to expel their liquid, and discard them. Carefully skim all but a few drops of fat from the soup in the pot. Set it off center on a medium-low burner, and wait 10 to 15 minutes for more fat and impurities to rise to the surface and form a skin. Draw it to the side and remove it. Allow the skin to re-form once or twice more, removing it each time, to make the flavors cleaner and clearer, a process that will take at least half an hour; if you have the time, a longer cleansing is even better. Taste the liquid for salt. Put the meat back into the pot, return the liquid to a boil, and bring the pot to the table. *Serves 4 to 6.*

NAVARIN PRINTANIER

Spring Lamb Stew

A *NAVARIN*, THOUGH THE ORIGINAL CALLS FOR MUTTON, is excellent with flavorful lamb. The name refers to *navets,* or turnips, and the spring version, a *navarin printanier,* combines mutton with new potatoes and other young vegetables ready in the garden or market; tomato is optional at any season. Reheated the next day, the stew has lost its freshness, partly because of the potatoes, and the dish is not nearly as good. The admirable and ever-meticulous Madame Saint-Ange, in *La Bonne Cuisine de Madame Saint-Ange* of 1927, asserts that a *navarin* is "one of those excellent simple dishes whose preparation demands the same time and close attention to details as a dish of the *grande cuisine.*" Citing its importance in home cooking, she devotes five dense pages to it; her chief fear is that the vegetables will be harmed by overcooking. She rounds the cut-up pieces of potato into the shape and size of "an elongated pigeon egg," because sharp edges would disintegrate and thicken the sauce. She belabors her concerns, but care does yield more distinct, delicious flavors. In the following recipe, if the sometimes-called-for peas and green beans were added, they would go into the pot in the last minutes of cooking.

a lamb shoulder, weighing roughly 4½ pounds (2 kg) with bones or half as much without

6 tablespoons lard (90 gr) or oil (90 ml)

¼ cup (35 gr) all-purpose flour

⅛ teaspoon sugar

½ cup (125 ml) peeled, seeded, and chopped fresh tomato, or canned tomato, broken up, *optional*

water

2 cloves garlic, peeled

continued

Trim surface fat from the shoulder, and cut it into roughly 2-inch (5-cm) pieces, discarding the bones or saving them for stock. Select a large, heavy oven pot, such as enameled cast iron, with a tight-fitting cover. Heat 4 tablespoons (60 gr) of the fat over medium-high heat, and in a single layer without crowding (or in two batches), brown the meat well on all sides, roughly 15 minutes. Sprinkle the flour and sugar over the meat; turn the pieces to cook the flour briefly and caramelize the sugar.

Heat the oven to 350° F (175° C). Add the tomato and enough water to immerse the meat almost completely. Crush the garlic cloves with the flat of a knife, and add them. Push the herb bouquet into the center

a fat bouquet of herbs, including fresh parsley, fresh thyme, and bay leaf, tied with a string

salt

3 pounds (1.4 kg) spring root vegetables — mostly potatoes but also new turnips, small onions, and, optionally, carrots

black pepper

of the pot. Bring the whole to a boil, stirring to prevent the flour from adhering to the bottom. Salt the liquid only lightly, to allow for reduction. Cover the pot and place it in the oven. After 30 minutes, lower the setting to 300° F (150° C). Bake until the meat is very tender, about another 1½ hours.

While the meat is cooking, peel the vegetables, except for small new potatoes, and as needed cut them into 1-inch (2- to 3-cm) pieces. Hold the potatoes and carrots in a bowl of cold water. Lightly brown the onions in the remaining 2 tablespoons of fat. If you use mature potatoes, add these and the carrots and onions to the *navarin* about 45 minutes before the meat is done, discarding the herb bouquet at the same time. Add young turnips and other spring vegetables, including small new potatoes, about 30 minutes before the meat is done. Pack the vegetables tightly in the pot, and add hot water only if necessary to cover them.

When the meat and vegetables are cooked, remove them to a warm dish. Tip the pot to reduce the surface area of liquid, and with a large, thin-edged metal spoon meticulously skim off all the fat. Strain the liquid into another container, and wipe or rinse away the debris clinging to the pot. Return the liquid to the pot. If this sauce is not just slightly thick, boil to reduce it. Season with salt and pepper as needed. Remove any outer gristle from the meat, and return the meat and vegetables to the pot. Bring the *navarin* momentarily to a boil, and serve promptly in deep, well-heated plates. *Serves 4 to 6.*

CINGHIALE COLLE CASTAGNE

Wild Boar with Chestnuts

MARIA PIERA QUERIO, CHEF OF THE LOCANDA DELL'ARCO in the Alta Langa village of Cissone, in Piedmont, gave me this recipe. In North America, you're much more likely to cook meat from farm-raised wild boar than from a truly wild one, and the farmed meat will become tender more quickly, about as fast as pork shoulder. In fact, most *wild* wild boar meat will never have perfect texture. The chestnuts sold in North America aren't as reliably good as the ones in Italy or as easy to peel. Querio warns against too much clove. And she says: "Use good wine. It can be Barolo or old Barbera, but Barbera has a violet color—I use Nebbiolo or Barolo, which has a beautiful color." The chestnuts slightly thicken the sauce, but you can thicken it a tiny amount more with just "a little, little flour."

2½ pounds (1 kg) boned wild boar shoulder

4½ cups (1 lt) red wine

2 stalks celery with leaves, cut in 1-inch (2-cm) pieces

2 carrots, peeled and cut in 1-inch (2-cm) pieces

1 or 2 branches each of rosemary and fresh sage (in any case, not the usual commercial dried sage)

1 whole clove or a tiny pinch of ground clove

black pepper

about 30 chestnuts

excellent, fresh-tasting olive oil

salt

Cut the wild boar into roughly 2-inch (5-cm) cubes, following the grain and division of the muscles as much as possible rather than cutting across them. Marinate the meat for 1 to 2 days in the red wine, celery, carrots, herbs, clove, and a grind of pepper.

Cut an X into the rounded side of each chestnut. Put the chestnuts in boiling water for 8 minutes, and remove the pan from the heat. Take 4 or 5 chestnuts at a time from the hot water, squeeze them lightly to loosen the husk and skin, and peel them, including all the inner skin, using the tip of a sharp knife to help if necessary. Try to keep the nuts whole. If the skin starts to cling as the nuts cool, return them to the hot water and then try again. Smell and, if you're uncertain, taste any suspect chestnut; discard it if it doesn't taste clearly of chestnut.

Remove the meat, vegetables, rosemary and sage, and whole clove from the marinade. Dry the meat, and brown it in the olive oil in a big, deep lidded pan over medium heat. Separately, bring the marinade to a boil, and skim it. Add it to the meat along with the reserved vegetables and seasonings. Lightly salt the liquid, and add a little more wine if needed to immerse the meat. Cook, covered, at a bare bubble for 1½ hours—assuming a truly wild animal; perhaps 1 hour for farmed wild boar. Remove and discard the vegetables and seasonings, carefully skim the fat from the surface, and add the peeled chestnuts. Cook gently for another 1½ to 2 hours, perhaps only 30 minutes for farmed wild boar, or until the meat is tender. *Serves 4.*

DESSERT

BRIOCHE PLUM TART

BRIOCHE IS LESS MESSY AND DIFFICULT TO MAKE than many people think: it is perhaps the form of bread that is easiest for a home cook to master. Novices flailing away in imitation of the French technique for hand-kneading the dough may send sticky bits across the room, but you can perfectly well confine the mess to a bowl, whether a regular mixing bowl or the bowl of a stand mixer or food processor. And generous flavor comes from the eggs and large proportion of butter, and from a fermentation that is less demanding than those for doughs without sugar.

Mine is essentially the recipe set down by Escoffier, including the gradual fermentation over 10 to 12 hours, which produces full flavor. At any point, the dough can be held in the refrigerator for a short while or overnight. The cold slows or halts the yeast, which allows the dough to be prepared in advance of baking. In any event, the dough must be well chilled before shaping or it will be so loose as to be extremely difficult to handle. Before baking, the top is normally brushed with a yolk glaze, whose taste echoes that of the egg in the bread. It shines and darkens the baked surface, although the taste of a too-dark crust distracts from the delicate interior. The darkness is partly a choice, and is also determined by the amount of sugar in the dough and the particular oven. The French generally prefer darker pastry than Americans do. To go on top, there's a range of Old and New World plums to choose from, though Japanese varieties are said to be watery in cooking. The idea is that the plums' rich flavor and acidity stand up to the richness of the brioche.

BRIOCHE DOUGH

2 cups (250 gr) unbleached all-purpose flour

½ teaspoon (2 gr) instant yeast

2 tablespoons sugar

3 tablespoons warm water

3 large eggs at room temperature

continued

To make the brioche dough: *In a large bowl,* mix a large handful of the flour with the yeast, 1 tablespoon of the sugar, the water, and 1 egg. Cover and allow the yeast 30 minutes or more to bubble. Then add the remaining flour and sugar, the salt, and the other 2 eggs, and mix the sticky mixture with your hand in the bowl until the ingredients are fully incorporated. Add the soft butter, and squeeze and stir with a warm hand to fully blend it. *Or in a food processor,* combine a large handful of the flour with the yeast, 1 tablespoon of the sugar, the

½ teaspoon salt

9 tablespoons (125 gr) unsalted butter
at room temperature

1 egg yolk mixed with 1 teaspoon water

1 to 1¼ pounds (500 gr) plums

sugar

1 cup (250 ml) heavy cream

¼ teaspoon vanilla extract

water, and 1 egg; pulse, scrape the sides, and pulse again. Wait 30 minutes or more for the yeast to bubble. Then add the rest of the flour and sugar, the remaining eggs, and the salt, and process for 25 seconds. Add the butter and process to incorporate it fully. A stand mixer with a dough hook also works well; with that, add the butter gradually, in pieces.

Once the dough is mixed, transfer it to a large bowl, and leave it to rise slowly, covered, in a cool place—50° to 70° F (10° to 21° C). Unless hot weather unavoidably accelerates the fermentation, the dough should rise slowly over 10 to 12 hours. Deflate it by pressing down with an open hand after it has increased by 2 to 2½ times, about midway through the rising time. Allow it to increase as much again, deflate again, cover tightly with plastic, and refrigerate.

To assemble the tart: Thoroughly butter an 11- to 12-inch (28- to 30-cm) steel tart mold with a removable bottom. Turn the cold brioche dough out onto a floured counter. Keeping the top and bottom surfaces of the dough well dusted with flour, roll out it just wider than the mold. Fold the dough in quarters onto itself, and transfer it to the mold; open and arrange it, fitting the dough so the edges rise slightly up the sides. Fold the edges in, if necessary, to make a border—a temporarily awkward appearance will be concealed by later rising.

Brush the pastry with the egg-yolk glaze. Don't let it run down between the brioche and the pan or it may glue them together. Halve and pit the plums and arrange them on top, cut side up. Using a sieve, sprinkle sugar over the dough and fruit. Cover the tart with a larger inverted bowl, and leave it in a warm place to increase by about 2½ times. (The plums' juices may be drawn out to combine with the dough just beneath to make a custardy intermediate layer in the baked tart.)

Heat the oven to 375° F (190° C), and bake until the pastry is well browned and starts to shrink from the pan—20 to 25 minutes. Cool briefly before unmolding onto a rack. Serve the tart still warm (I put it in to bake just before the meal begins) with the cream, whipped, flavored with vanilla, and sweetened to taste. *Serves 6 to 8.*

Variation: **CHOCOLATE BRIOCHE TART**

As for the brioche plum tart, butter a mold, line it with the dough, and allow it to rise, *except* roll the dough 2 inches (5 cm) wider than the mold and, when lining the mold, turn in the overhanging border to form a rough, wide enclosure for the chocolate custard. Cover with a very large inverted bowl or drape with plastic film or wax paper.

Break ¼ pound (100 gr) of excellent dark chocolate into pieces and, in a double boiler or bain-marie, set them to melt with ¾ cup (175 ml) of heavy cream, covered and unstirred. When the chocolate is melted, take the pan from the heat and whisk in 2 egg yolks. Cover the pan and set it aside while the brioche completes its rise, increasing by about 2½ times altogether.

When the brioche has risen, heat the oven to 375° F (190° C). Gently brush the broad rim of the pastry with another egg yolk beaten with a little water, and sprinkle granulated sugar over it with the aid of a sieve. Then pour in the chocolate, which will only partly fill the dough, and bake the tart until it starts to shrink from the pan, 20 to 25 minutes. Cool briefly in the pan before unmolding onto a rack. Serve warm to tepid. Whip a cup (225 ml) of heavy cream, flavoring it with ½ teaspoon of vanilla extract and sweetening it to taste. A bowl of raspberries is an ideal accompaniment. *Serves 8.*

UNSWEETENED APPLE PIE WITH MAPLE SAUCE

THIS APPEARS IN *VERMONT MAPLE RECIPES* BY MARY PEARL, which was apparently self-published in 1952. She describes it as "one of the oldest maple recipes." From one perspective, the sauce is marshmallow; from another, almost Italian meringue. Piecrusts in Vermont always used to be made with lard, and as a rule maple syrup producers preferred the lightest grade, which has the mildest flavor. I prefer somewhat darker syrup, like most people today, and I like the taste of butter, rather than lard, in the crust. Tart apples are essential.

2 pounds (1 kg) tart apples, peeled, cored, and sliced

butter or lard for greasing the pie plate

flaky pastry to line a 10-inch (25-cm) tart mold (see page 245)

1 cup (250 ml) maple syrup

2 egg whites at room temperature

a fat pinch of cream of tartar, if you use a noncopper bowl

Heat the oven to 375° F (190° C). Arrange the sliced apples in a greased 10-inch (25-cm) metal or ceramic pie plate, deep enough that the fruit doesn't boil over. Roll out the cold pastry and cover the apples with it, trimming and forming a neat edge, pressing to seal it to the pan, and cutting slits for steam. Bake until the apples are soft and the crust is brown, about 40 minutes.

Over medium-high heat, boil the syrup—which will foam up, so use a larger pan than you may think you need—until it forms a fine thread when poured from a spoon, about 10 minutes. Promptly take the pot from the flame and keep it warm near the stove. Whisk the egg whites until they just form stiff peaks, either in a copper bowl freshly cleaned with lemon juice or vinegar and salt, rinsed, and dried (or in a noncopper bowl, adding the cream of tartar). Then add the syrup in a thin stream while continuing to beat. When the syrup is fully incorporated, the meringue sauce will be thick but flowing. Serve it with the warm pie. *Makes 1 pie and a lot of sauce.*

POUND CAKE

I'M AMBIVALENT ABOUT CAKE. French génoise, a cake with substantial texture meant to withstand being soaked with flavored sugar syrup, seems flawed in concept. A cake ought to be good enough to eat on its own. Much better is the Italian idea of a relatively plain cake flavored with lemon zest, to go with fresh fruit or a glass of sweet wine. In northern Italy, cakes are made with butter, while from the region of Lazio southward, the fat is often olive oil. The taste of good olive oil is scarcely evident in the cake, easily masked by lemon zest. The important difference is in texture: an olive-oil cake is softer and noticeably oilier—more tender and moist. The choice of fat is important to taste, but so is the way the cake is leavened. Modern Italian cakes, like American and even some French, are raised with baking powder, which makes a soft texture, and the cakes don't keep especially well. A few cakes are still raised with yeast. Some others are raised with the fine bubbles of beaten egg whites, which give a texture too close to that of a soufflé. I prefer the leavening effect of whole eggs together with the air beaten into the warm ingredients, such as in an old-fashioned American pound cake.

Many recent recipes for pound cake, however, reject the very idea of it, adding ingredients in whatever proportions they like and relying on powders for leavening. I like the original made of equal weights of flour, sugar, butter, and eggs—a pound each, if I want a large cake or several smaller ones. A real pound cake has character and keeps well; it's moist with a fine substantial crumb. It lends itself to various flavorings. Instead of the lemon zest and dried currants below, for instance, I've also liked the grated zest of several tangerines together with 2 tablespoons of dark rum. To prepare whole cardamom, extract the seeds from the husks, and crush the seeds with a mortar and pestle or with the back of a wooden spoon. The cake goes well with fruit.

1 cup (250 gr) unsalted butter at warm room temperature

½ teaspooon salt

1⅛ cups (250 gr) sugar

1 teaspoon crushed cardamom seed

the finely grated zest, without white pith, of 2 lemons

5 large eggs at warm room temperature

1¾ cups (250 gr) all-purpose flour

⅔ cup (100 gr) dried currants

In a slightly warm bowl, beat the butter and salt with an electric beater. Add the sugar gradually while continuing to beat; the color will lighten. Add the cardamom and zest, and beat 2 to 3 minutes, until you can see that the sugar has begun to dissolve. One at a time, thoroughly beat in the eggs.

Heat the oven to 275° F (135° C). Sift half the flour into the batter, and incorporate it by stirring and smearing with a plastic spatula; then sift, stir, and smear in the rest of the flour. Sprinkle the dried currants over the batter, breaking up clumps, and mix them in. Transfer the batter to a buttered, lightly floured approximately 1½-quart (1.5-lt) mold, such as a rectangular loaf pan or a round one with a central tube. Tap the mold to settle the batter.

Bake the cake until it just starts to pull away from the sides of the pan, 1¼ to 1½ hours, when it will have approximately doubled in size. Cool it in the pan on a rack for 10 minutes, and then unmold it. Allow it to finish cooling, wrap it well in plastic, and store it in the refrigerator, but serve it at room temperature. *Makes one 2-pound (900-gr) cake.*

TORTA DI NOCCIOLE

Hazelnut Cake

UNLIKE MOST VERSIONS OF THE CLASSIC PIEDMONTESE HAZELNUT CAKE, this one is made without flour and is leavened solely by eggs. Usually, the cake also contains a little cocoa powder, which to me distracts from the nut taste. Serve the cake with Zabaione (page 264) made with Moscato or Barolo — the latter should be an old-fashioned, light-colored one or it will turn the sauce an ugly color. Without the sauce, the cake goes well with a glass of sparkling Moscato d'Asti.

1²/₃ cups (200 gr) hazelnuts

¾ cup (150 gr) sugar

a large pinch of salt

5 large eggs, separated

Toast the nuts at 350° F (175° C) for 20 to 25 minutes, the darkness being a matter of taste. Wrap the hot nuts in a kitchen towel, wait 10 minutes, and then rub them vigorously, inside the towel, to remove most of the skins. Grind the skinned nuts with the sugar and salt in a food processor, pulsing, until they are no finer than coarse cornmeal (or use a hand nut grinder and then add the sugar and salt). In a large bowl, combine this mixture thoroughly with the egg yolks.

Heat the oven to 375° F (190° C). Grease and lightly flour a 10- to 11-inch (25-cm) diameter cake pan. Beat the egg whites until they just form stiff peaks. Combine the beaten whites with the nut-and-yolk mixture by thirds, mixing them thoroughly with a plastic spatula. Much of the loft will be lost, but mix gently so that enough air remains to lighten the cake. Fill the prepared pan, and bake until the cake shrinks from the pan all around — about 30 minutes. Cool 10 minutes and unmold onto a rack, keeping the top up. *Serves 4 to 6.*

WALNUT TART

IN RETHINKING THIS RECIPE FOR THIS COOKBOOK, I slightly increased the amount of filling, but the idea is still a thin tart, not too sweet, with a high proportion of crust, the soft crunch of nuts contrasting with the honey-egg binding and the definitely crisp, flaky crust. Walnuts are at their best during the fall harvest. But in North America at the end of the year, many of the walnuts for sale, in or out of the shell, taste as if they were at least a year old — I feel certain they are. Freshly harvested organic walnuts in mottled, unbleached shells are vastly superior. I use a local mixed-wildflower honey — what you might call an everyday honey; dark honey can dominate and delicate honey would be lost. When I'm in a minimalist mood, I leave out the sherry, vanilla, and currants.

dough for one 10- to 11-inch (25- to 28-cm) layer of flaky pastry, chilled (see page 245)

2½ cups (250 gr) shelled walnuts

a large pinch of salt

¾ cup (250 ml) honey, warmed before measuring, if necessary, so it will flow, by setting the whole jar in hot water

1 tablespoon rich sherry, such as Amontillado

1 teaspoon vanilla extract

3 tablespoons (45 gr) unsalted butter, melted

2 large eggs

⅓ cup (45 gr) dried currants

Roll out the cold pastry and fit it to a 10- to 11-inch (25- to 28-cm) shallow steel tart mold with a removable bottom. Cover it with plastic and keep it chilled in the refrigerator. Bake the walnuts at 325° F (165° C) for 10 minutes, wrap them in a kitchen towel, and vigorously rub them, inside the towel, to remove the skins (some will remain).

Raise the oven temperature to 375° F (200° C). Chop the nuts coarsely. Mix thoroughly with the remaining ingredients and spread the mixture over the pastry, which will be only partly filled. Bake until the nut mixture is swollen and well browned, about 20 minutes. Cool for 10 minutes on a rack before unmolding. Best when warm. *Makes one 10- to 11-inch (25- to 28-cm) tart.*

CILIEGIE AL BAROLO

Cherries in Barolo

THE NAME IS EVOCATIVE BUT MISLEADING: good Barolo costs too much for anyone to cook with it. Instead, perfectly good with the cherries is a lesser wine also made from Nebbiolo grapes, such as Nebbiolo d'Alba, Nebbiollo delle Langhe, or Gattinara.

2 pounds (900 gr) fresh sour cherries

1 bottle (750 ml) Nebbiolo wine

1 cup (200 gr) or more sugar

a piece of cinnamon bark, roughly 1 inch (2 to 3 cm) square

about 2 square inches (5 cm square) of orange zest without white pith (in several strips)

Stem the cherries but leave the pits. Bring to a boil the wine, sugar, cinnamon, and orange zest, and add the whole cherries all at once. Cook until tender, about 15 minutes. Taste, and if needed add more sugar (remembering that the cherries will seem less sweet when cool), cooking for another minute to dissolve it. Serve tepid or chilled, warning your guests about the pits. *Serves 8.*

CHOCOLATE MOUSSE

A MOUSSE IS NOT ONE OF THE MOST CHOCOLATEY DESSERTS, because of the foam. That can come from whipped sweet cream, whipped crème fraîche, beaten egg white, or beaten egg yolk. This recipe uses the egg-yolk foam of a *pâte à bombe*—meaning the base for that classic ice cream dessert—which makes the most velvety mousse of all. If you're concerned about the safety of eating raw eggs, make a chocolate soufflé (see next recipe) instead and cook it until it is fully set.

The old gentle way to melt chocolate is in a container over hot water, though chocolatiers now use a microwave oven. But I like easily understood cause and effect, and I still prefer the stove. Beware of driving off fine aromas by heating the chocolate too long or at too high a temperature—it isn't necessary to heat it much, since it normally melts at 86° F (30° C), unless it has to be combined perfectly with something else, when a higher temperature helps. For a perfectly smooth texture here, don't let the cream get warm in whipping and be sure to incorporate the melted chocolate fully with the initial cream.

½ cup (100 gr) sugar

¼ cup (50 ml) water

6 egg yolks

9 ounces (250 gr) dark chocolate (around 70 percent cocoa), chopped

1⅔ cups (400 ml) heavy cream

Cook the sugar and water to the "soft ball" stage (about 240° F or 115° C, when a little of the syrup, dropped into cold water, comes together between the fingers as a pliable ball). Immediately beat the egg yolks by hand or machine, and, while continuing to beat, slowly pour in the sugar syrup. Beat until the mixture is pale and foamy, at least 10 minutes.

Melt the chocolate in a large bowl over hot water, heating it to 122° F (50° C) if you have a thermometer (on your skin that temperature feels uncomfortably close to burning). Whip the cream to soft peaks; then whisk a third of the cream into the bowl of chocolate—taken out of the hot water but still hot—carefully combining the two so as to leave no streaks. Fold in the rest of the cream by halves and then fold in the egg-yolk foam. Fill a serving bowl or 6 individual dishes, smoothing the top. Serve cool but not chilled. *Serves 6.*

CHOCOLATE SOUFFLÉ

A CHOCOLATE SOUFFLÉ CAN TASTE MONOTONOUSLY CHOCOLATEY, unless you take care to give it a luscious texture and add a sauce. The first means ending the cooking before the center is quite set (overcooking dries a soufflé), and the second, here, means offering just rich, pourable cream.

7 ounces (200 gr) dark chocolate (at least 60 percent cocoa), chopped

5 tablespoons (70 gr) unsalted butter

½ cup (125 ml) water

4 egg yolks

1 teaspoon vanilla extract

¾ teaspoon cream of tartar, if you use a noncopper bowl

7 egg whites

¼ cup (50 gr) sugar

1 cup (250 ml) heavy cream

Heat the oven to 400° F (200° C). Melt the chocolate and butter with the water in a double boiler or bain-marie. Off the heat, stir in the egg yolks and vanilla extract, and transfer the chocolate mixture to a large bowl. In a copper bowl, freshly cleaned with lemon juice or vinegar and salt, rinsed and dried (or in a non-copper bowl, adding the cream of tartar), beat the egg whites until they just form stiff peaks. Beat the sugar by quarters into the whites, and then beat the foam for 2 to 3 minutes longer, until it is firm and glossy.

Fold the beaten whites by thirds into the melted chocolate mixture, combining thoroughly to eliminate streaks. Fill a buttered and sugared 2-quart (2-lt) mold, and bake until the soufflé is mostly set but the center is still molten, about 18 minutes — if you're concerned about the safety of eating undercooked egg, wait until the soufflé is fully cooked, perhaps another 5 minutes. (With experience, you can judge the consistency by observing the movement of the soufflé when the mold is shifted.) Take the soufflé from the oven and straight to the table; insert a sharp spoon in the center to make an opening and pour in about a quarter of the cream, which will halt the cooking and partly deflate the soufflé. Pass the rest of the cream at the table. *Serves 4 to 6.*

COFFEE TART

AT LEAST HALF THE SUCCESS OF ANY TART is a crisp, flavorful crust. Usually, I prefer a flaky one. And the only sure path to perfect texture is a lot of practice. The bit of sugar in the dough helps to tie the taste of the crust and filling together. For tenderness, a lower-protein unbleached flour is best, roughly 9 percent protein. If you're afraid of ending up with tough dough, you can always replace a tablespoon of the water with the same amount of light rum, though that pushes the texture toward sandy. Mix the dough minimally to avoid creating tough gluten, and be sure to chill the dough completely both before rolling it out and again afterward. If you've used low-protein flour, handled the dough minimally, and kept it very cold, so that gluten and shrinkage are no problem, you can bake the bare dough, the bottom pricked well with a fork to reduce swelling. But even then, overworked dough made with all-purpose flour can develop enough gluten to shrink badly in the oven. With regular all-purpose flour, it's essential, when you bake the pastry blind, to line it with baking parchment gently tucked into the corners and then weighted with dried beans, rice, or metal pie weights—although they prevent the bottom from cooking as fully as the sides. Immediately on taking the hot crust from the oven, pour the custard filling into it, so the custard that touches the pastry instantly cooks, forming a seal that helps to keep the pastry crisp.

FLAKY PASTRY

1½ cups (200 gr) all-purpose flour

1 tablespoon sugar

⅛ teaspoon salt

11 tablespoons (160 gr) cold unsalted butter, cut in ¼-inch (6-mm) dice

5 tablespoons (75 ml) cold water

To make the pastry: *With your hands*, in a large bowl, mix the flour, sugar, and salt. With your fingers, work the butter into the dough until you have a texture like coarse semolina mixed with roughly pea-sized pieces of butter. Sprinkle the water on top, and lightly mix it in with a fork, lifting and turning. *Or in a food processor*, add the flour, salt, and sugar to the bowl of a food processor and pulse to combine. Then add the butter and pulse just until the larger pieces are roughly pea sized. Sprinkle on the water, and then pulse once or twice.

½ cup (100 gr) sugar

2 large eggs

¾ cup (175 ml) very strong coffee, freshly made with freshly roasted beans from a mild roast

1¼ cups (300 ml) heavy cream

On the counter, press the dough into a ball (a pastry scraper is handy for bringing it together). Wrap it in plastic and chill it completely. Roll it out on a lightly floured counter to about 6 by 12 inches (15 by 30 cm) and fold it to make three layers. Chill again, and roll and fold; chill a third time, and roll and fold. Roll the dough to form a 12-to-13-inch (32-to-34-cm) circle, transfer it to the mold, cover it with plastic, and again chill it completely.

To make the tart: Heat the oven to 350° F (175° C). Roll out the pastry and fit it to an 11-inch (28-cm), shallow steel tart mold with a removable bottom. Cover the dough with plastic and chill it completely in the refrigerator. Prick the bottom all over with a fork. Bake the crust "blind," as described in the note above, until it's fully cooked and beginning to turn golden, 20 to 25 minutes, removing the parchment and weights during the last 5 to 10 minutes of baking. Meanwhile, in a small heavy-bottomed metal pan over medium heat, melt the sugar in ¼ cup (50 ml) of water, and cook it, without stirring, to a dark caramel—just past the point where a faint wisp of smoke appears. Take the pan from the heat, add ½ cup (100 ml) of water water—*beware of dangerous spattering!*—and, returning the pan to medium heat, stir to form a smooth sauce. Set the caramel aside. Whisk together the eggs, coffee, and cream in a bowl, and then whisk in the caramel. When the pastry shell is done, take it from the oven, immediately pour the custard mixture into it, and return it to the oven. Continue baking until the custard is just set, about 20 minutes. Remove the tart from the mold and cool on a rack. *Serves 4 to 6.*

Variation: **CHOCOLATE TART**

Like chocolate in general, this goes very well with a glass of Banyuls or Maury wine (sweet red *vins doux naturels* from the South of France). Also good is jasmine tea. I've made the tart most often with Valrhona Guanaja chocolate, adding no sugar beyond that in the chocolate: Guanaja is about 70 percent chocolate, the rest being sugar. But beware that the percentage given for any chocolate is an imperfect measure of its intensity, and according to your taste and the particular brand, you may want to either add some sugar or opt for a higher-percentage bar.

Heat the oven to 350° F (175° C). Roll out the pastry, line the tart mold with it, cover it with plastic, and chill it completely. Bake it blind, as above. Meanwhile, melt 9 ounces (250 gr) of chopped dark chocolate in 2 cups (500 ml) of half-and-half, covered, in the top of a double boiler or in a small pan set in another pan of hot water. Stir to combine the melted chocolate thoroughly with the half-and-half, and take the pan from the heat. In a bowl, beat 2 large eggs with up to ½ cup (100 gr) of sugar, if you feel the chocolate is not sweet enough by itself. Gradually stir in the still-hot chocolate. When the pastry shell is done, take it from the oven, remove the parchment and pie weights if you used them, and pour the chocolate mixture into the hot shell; continue baking until the center is just set—about 20 minutes. Serve tepid. *Serves 4 to 6.*

PEAR TART

A LITTLE COGNAC UNDERLINES THE PEAR TASTE of plain cooked pears. Among common varieties, I prefer Comice or Bartlett (also known as Williams and Bon Chrétien—an old variety that often survives well in the distribution chain and then ripens beautifully on your counter), followed by Bosc (which has more "sand"), and then D'Anjou. Instead of using fresh pears, make the tart with pears poached in red wine (page 260) for a different and also very good effect—in that case, skip the Cognac and vanilla. Or you could use cooked quinces. The cooked pears are hard to slice neatly when you assemble the tart; it's fine to just cut them in half and not into thin slices. I came across the filling—a rich, cakey flan that won't separate and in a hot oven becomes relatively light—somewhere, years ago, and I don't know who to credit.

flaky pastry to line a 10-inch (25-cm) tart mold (see page 245)

4 pears, weighing altogether roughly 2¼ pounds (1 kg)

1 cup (210 gr) sugar

⅜ cup (50 gr) all-purpose flour

3 large eggs

a large pinch of salt

2 tablespoons Cognac or 1 teaspoon vanilla extract

¾ cup (175 gr) unsalted butter, melted

Heat the oven to 400° F (200° C). Line a 10-inch (25-cm) tart mold, or a flan ring set on a baking sheet, with the pastry. Peel the pears, cut them neatly in half, and remove the stems and cores. One at a time, place each half cut-side down, and cut across it with a small, sharp knife to make ⅛-inch (3-mm) slices, keeping the pear shape intact. Transfer each pear half, holding the slices together, to the pastry, so that 7 halves, narrow ends in, radiate from the center. Tip them, so the slices slant outward from the center. (Unless the pears are very small, you will have half a pear left over to eat yourself.)

Whisk the sugar, flour, eggs, salt, and Cognac or vanilla to a smooth batter; whisk in the melted butter. Pour the batter over the pears. Bake for 1 hour (any shorter period risks leaving the bottom crust undercooked). If you have baked the tart in a ring or a mold with a removable bottom, unmold it and cool it on a rack, to keep the bottom crisp. Best served warm. *Serves 6 to 8.*

CRÉMETS D'ANJOU

Fresh Cream Cheeses

ANJOU IS KNOWN FOR ITS MARKET GARDENS and river fish, and yet three of the province's most emblematic foods are full of fat—*rillauds, beurre blanc,* and *crémets.* The last are an airy dessert, originally made with the single ingredient of crème fraîche (ripened cream), whipped full of air and then, like a cheese, drained in a mold with holes, making a form of cream cheese. Nowadays *crémets* are often molded into heart shapes and contain egg white and fresh cheese, though only the latter makes sense. Unless you have outstanding crème fraîche—perfectly clean in taste and delicate in texture—it's better to mix heavy cream with some fresh cow's-milk cheese. It will provide its own acidity, and it may contain at least a remnant of live culture that will work to ripen the cream (which in a perfect world would be sweet, wholesome raw cream from cows on pasture). In North America, plain white fresh cheese (recipe on page 80), though not clearly labeled as such, is often sold in a plastic-wrapped cylinder. *Crémets* are a typical late spring dessert served with red berries.

1 cup (250 gr) fresh cow's- or goat's-milk cheese

1 quart (1 lt) heavy cream

sugar

red berries or other fruit in season

Rinse and wring out enough cheesecloth to line either a single mold with holes (a small plastic colander will do) or small, individual cheese molds with a collective capacity of about 6 cups (1.5 lt). Thin the fresh cheese to a pourable state with some of the cream. Thoroughly mix 2 cups (500 ml) of the cream with the thinned cheese, and whisk the combination by hand until it is airy—firmer than the usual whipped cream but not at all buttery. Fill the lined mold or molds with this, set them in a pan or dish, and let them drain at room temperature for 2 to 4 hours. After that, refrigerate them, on the chance that the culture from the cheese may not be active and therefore won't protect the *crémet* from spoilage at room temperature. Unmold a large *crémet* into a bowl or individual ones onto a deep platter. Pour the rest of the heavy cream over the top, and sprinkle on sugar to taste. Accompany with fruit. *Serves 8.*

CRÈME CARAMEL RENVERSÉE

Upside-Down Caramel Custard

THE VELVETY TEXTURE OF WELL-MADE CRÈME CARAMEL comes from careful cooking that leaves the custard completely free of bubbles. It is set by gentle heat, and the custard is taken from the oven at the moment the center has crossed over from thickened to set. It may go without saying that a good custard is free of flour, an old crutch that prevents the liquid from separating in case of overcooking. The finest flavor comes from farmyard eggs, which also make a firmer custard. If you don't have them — I'm assuming farm eggs in this recipe — an extra egg makes the custard easier to unmold. You can use just egg yolks — 9 for this quantity of milk — and heavy cream in place of milk, but those give a richer, almost cakey texture, and at the end of a meal the lightness of whole eggs and milk is more appealing. Where I was once drawn to Tahitian vanilla (*Vanilla tahitensis*), in most uses I have long since come to prefer the Bourbon species (*V. planifolia*). Most important with a vanilla bean are the obvious signs of quality: an appearance that isn't dry and shriveled but fat and glossy — moist. A glossy bean has stronger flavor. No one likes burnt caramel, but I like a dark one that stands up to the strong flavor of saffron, which goes well in custard. I've used a temperature as low as 275° F (135° C), but some ovens are slow, and 350° F (175° C) won't harm the custard if you watch carefully and remove it as soon as it's done.

1 vanilla bean

4 dozen saffron threads, *optional*

3 cups (700 ml) whole milk

3 large eggs

1 cup (200 gr) sugar

mild-flavored cooking oil

Over a medium flame, heat the vanilla bean and the saffron in the milk until it begins to bubble. Take the pan from the heat, cover it, and leave it to steep. Stir the eggs with a spoon — avoid the foam created by a whisk — and combine them with ¼ cup (50 gr) of the sugar. Cook the remaining sugar with ¼ cup (50 ml) of water over medium heat, without stirring, until it forms a dark caramel — just to the point where a faint wisp of smoke appears. Immediately add another ¼ cup (50 ml) of water — *beware of dangerous spattering!* — and stir the caramel over the heat just until smooth. Again acting immediately, coat the bottoms of 8 custard cups, about ¾ cup (175 ml) capacity, with the hot caramel, tipping and rotating each so the caramel comes partway up the sides and is about the same thickness all over. When the caramel is firm, lightly coat the exposed sides with oil.

Heat the oven to 350° F (175° C). Remove the vanilla bean from the milk, and stir the milk into the eggs, combining the two well with a spoon. Strain this mixture, and pour it into the cups. Place these in a roasting pan, and add boiling water to come about two-thirds of the way up the sides of the cups; drape them with a sheet of aluminum foil. Place the full pan in the oven, and poach the custards until they are just set, 35 to 45 minutes, depending on the oven and cups. With experience, you can tell whether the custard is set by jostling a cup; otherwise, insert a knife point in the middle and see if it comes out clean.

Cool the custards. Chill them if you won't serve them soon, but they taste best cool to tepid. Before serving, unmold the custards, very gently so as not to break the surface, pressing down with your thumb around the edge of the custard in each cup to loosen the sides. Put a dessert plate over the cup and invert the plate and cup together. If the custard is reluctant, hold the two securely together with both hands, and give them a little downward shake to start the movement. *Makes 8.*

LEMON-HONEY FLAN

HONEY COMPLEMENTS LEMON. I USE A LIGHT-FLAVORED HONEY for this flan, but you may prefer a strong floral honey, such as lavender or lime tree (also called linden, *tilleul* in French, *tiglio* in Italian—better examples come from Europe than North America), or even one of the strong, dark honeys, such as thyme or heather. A flan, in France, is an open tart, but the word can also have the specific meaning of custard tart, closer to the Spanish meaning of a sweet egg custard. In the French countryside, a custard-filled flan was once common—one of the many baked goods, now largely disappeared, flavored with orange-flower water. Because the acidity of lemon juice tends to make the custard break, use heavy cream rather than milk for this flan. (To avoid any danger of separation, a lemon tart is more often filled with lemon curd—lemon juice and zest, eggs, sugar, and butter brought momentarily to a boil to create an emulsion, which gives a different taste.) For me, a sandy-textured crust and a flaky one are equally good here. And because the crust of a custard tart quickly softens, it's best when still warm.

dough for a single 11-inch (28-cm) tart crust, chilled (either sandy textured or flaky, such as the one on page 245)

zest of 1 medium to large lemon, peeled or grated, without bitter white pith

2 cups (500 ml) heavy cream

⅓ cup (100 gr) honey

3 egg yolks plus 2 whole eggs

⅓ cup (75 ml) freshly squeezed juice from the lemon

a pinch of salt

Heat the oven to 350° F (175° C). Butter an 11-inch (28-cm) tart mold with a removable bottom, for easy unmolding, or use a simple flan ring set on a baking sheet. Roll out and fit the dough to the mold or ring, cover it with plastic, and chill it completely in the refrigerator. Bake the pastry "blind" (see page 245), until it is cooked through completely.

While the crust is baking, bring the lemon zest and cream to a simmer in a small pan, then take it from the heat. In a bowl, stir the honey with the 3 egg yolks, then stir in the whole eggs. Stir in the cream and lemon zest, whose warmth will melt any remaining honey crystals. Stir in the lemon juice and salt. Skim to remove any air bubbles.

Pour the custard mixture through a strainer into the hot baked tart shell, filling it up to ⅛ inch (3 mm) from the top of the pastry. Holding the tart carefully level, return it to the oven, still at 350° F (175° C). Bake until the custard is just set (it jiggles slightly when jarred but is no longer liquid, except perhaps a small circle in the very center) — about 30 minutes. Unmold the tart or remove the ring, and cool it on a rack. *Serves 8.*

LITTLE CORN CAKES

CORNMEAL SWEETS APPEAR IN, AMONG OTHER PLACES, the Basque country of France and Spain and the Piedmont and Veneto of Italy; in the latter region, a few pastries are made from cooked polenta. Using freshly ground cornmeal from an old milling variety makes a big difference in flavor. If the cakes in this recipe are made in advance and not dusted with sugar, they can later be made crisp again in a medium oven and then sugared. This way they are literally *biscotti,* "twice cooked," which is of course the Italian word for "cookies."

1 cup (125 gr) stone-ground yellow cornmeal

½ cup (65 gr) white flour

a pinch of salt

¼ cup (50 gr) sugar

5 tablespoons (70 gr) unsalted butter, melted

½ cup (125 ml) water

2 large eggs, separated

cream of tartar, if you use a noncopper bowl

confectioners' sugar

Heat the oven to 400° F (200° C). In a large bowl, mix the cornmeal, flour, salt, and sugar, then stir in the melted butter, water, and egg yolks. In a separate, copper bowl freshly cleaned with lemon juice or vinegar and salt, rinsed and dried (or in a noncopper bowl, adding a fat pinch of cream of tartar), whisk the egg whites until they just form stiff peaks. Fold them by thirds into the cornmeal mixture. Space quarter-cupfuls (50-ml scoops) of the batter well apart on a buttered baking sheet; with the back of a spoon, spread each so it's about 2 by 5 inches (5 by 12 cm). Bake until the edges turn brown, about 12 minutes. Remove the cakes to a rack to cool, then, using a fine strainer if you have one, dust them with confectioners' sugar. *Makes about 12 little cakes.*

MELON ICE

THE MOST REFRESHING ICE, AND THE EASIEST TO EAT, is slushy firm. I like a texture that is not just slightly loose but also grainy—icy—coupled with not too much sweetness, the kind of ice often called a granita. Less sugar and icier texture happen to go together. Softer texture as well as finer crystals occur when more things interrupt the water crystals, especially sugar but also fruit pulp, sometimes alcohol (and in ice cream, butterfat, of course, and sometimes egg yolk). Besides, efficient churning breaks up the crystals and can introduce more or less air. But in any frozen dessert it's mostly sugar that prevents the water from turning into into a solid block; too much sugar prevents freezing altogether. (An ice, having no fat to keep it soft, typically contains far more sugar than ice cream does.) Yet enough sugar to create a soft texture makes the taste too sweet. For a slight sweetness and a soft texture, you either have to serve the ice as soon it hardens to that in-between state or hold it in the freezer until roughly an hour before you're ready, then take it out, allow it to somewhat soften, and mix it to break up the crystals. If you don't have a machine, electric or hand-cranked, then a large glass or metal bowl and the freezer compartment of your refrigerator will do, and in fact they produce the coarse texture I like. Try to make ices no more than a few hours in advance; they taste best eaten right away.

Choose a particularly aromatic ripe melon, not a watermelon but one of the *Cucumis melo*, which includes varieties of muskmelon, cantaloupe, and honeydew. Some sugar is called for, because cold suppresses sweetness, and a little added acidity is needed to give dimension. A clean, fresh-tasting white wine blends better with melon than lemon juice does. You can make a similar cucumber ice, which, depending on your taste, can also be a dessert. (Just-picked, young cucumbers, not yet seedy, taste best for any purpose. Peel them, halve them lengthwise, scrape out and discard the seeds unless they're merely embryonic, and purée the flesh; combine equal parts purée and plain water—no sugar at all.) Almost any fruit is most aromatic and sweetest at the blossom end, and the flesh at the center of a melon is riper than that near the rind. In making melon ice, any precise recipe is defied by all the variables, including the fruit's sweetness and strength of flavor, both of which are affected by, for instance, how much water the vine may have pumped into the fruit after a recent rain.

¼ cup (50 gr) sugar

1⅝ cups (400 ml) water

a fully ripe melon weighing at least
3½ pounds (1.5 kg)

½ cup (125 ml) or more fresh, light,
cold white or rosé wine

Boil the sugar and water together, stirring to dissolve the sugar. Set this syrup aside to cool, and then chill it completely in the refrigerator.

Cut the melon in half, discard the seeds, and with the sharp edge of a spoon scrape out thin pieces, concentrating on the center and blossom end, until you have 2 compressed cups (a 500-ml measure) of flesh. Purée the flesh in a blender or food processor. Combine the purée with the chilled sugar syrup and wine, and chill them deeply in the refrigerator, at least 1 hour, followed by 5 to 10 minutes in the freezer.

Churn the mixture in a machine or put it in a shallow bowl in the freezer, breaking up the ice crystals thoroughly every 20 minutes with a fork, until the liquid has turned into a firm slush of fine crystals. If you don't serve the ice immediately, put it in the freezer, where it will continue to harden, and then before serving partly thaw it, breaking it up and mixing it to a firm slush. Serve in chilled bowls. *Makes about 1 quart (1 lt).*

ROSE ICE

FOR THIS, YOU NEED HIGHLY SCENTED ROSES—lots and lots of them, I'm afraid. Many different varieties qualify, such as the ancient *Rosa gallica* and its offspring the damask rose (itself centuries old), which have a perfumer's focused aroma, or a rose with floral spice, such as the part-rugosa Thérèse Bugnet or the hybrid rugosa David Thompson. (I have a large bed of the last.) Be certain to pick the flowers early in the morning before the sun warms them and from branches held well off the ground, so they haven't been splashed with dirt. Choose only flowers that are partly opened, in approximately tulip shape. Pull off the petals, and discard the bases. If you have no bed of roses to deplete, there are delicious rose syrups from which you can surely make an excellent if much more expensive rose ice. (A superb organic syrup from *gallica* roses comes from Azienda Agricola Magliano in Tavarnelle Val di Pesa, Tuscany; it's sometimes available in the United States at www.purelyorganic.com but not as I write, so I can't experiment and offer proportions.)

¾ cup (150 gr) sugar

3 cups (700 ml) boiling water

enough highly scented roses, grown without toxic chemicals, to yield 2 lightly compressed cups (a 500-ml measure) of petals

¼ cup (60 ml) lemon juice

Boil the sugar and water until the sugar dissolves, and take the pan from the heat. Wait 2 minutes, and then stir the petals into the hot liquid. Cover and leave to cool. The color will be a mere dull bluish red. Add the lemon juice, whose acidity will act on the anthocyanin pigments in the petals to create a powerful neon pink. Strain the petals from the syrup, pressing to extract all the liquid; put the syrup into a glass jar and chill the mixture completely in the refrigerator, about 1 hour, followed by 5 to 10 minutes in the freezer. Freeze as for Melon Ice (page 255). *Makes a little less than 1 quart (1 lt).*

COFFEE ICE

THE SUCCESS OF THIS ICE NATURALLY DEPENDS ON THE BEANS, the roast, and the brewing, and it's hard to make any comment on those without entering deep into the vast, complicated territory of coffee, from which it's difficult to make a quick retreat. Nonetheless, I'll say that you should choose a lighter roast, which will retain more of the acidity and more of the fruit and floral aromas typical of the highest-quality beans. With coffee, the shorter the time from brewer to mouth, the more aroma in the drink. A coffee ice aims to capture the just-brewed flavor, and yet chilling brewed coffee in the refrigerator kills much of the aroma, while actual cold brewing is out, because it's inherently flawed: cold water fails to draw out the beans' full aroma and acidity (just as dark roasting drives them off). It's best to start with iced coffee made by the Japanese method (popularized in the United States by Counter Culture of North Carolina) in which the brewed coffee falls from the filter directly onto a measured quantity of ice, which instantly chills it and saves maximum aroma. The ice finishes melting at about the moment the brewing is complete and contributes a precise amount of liquid. (The quantities below make 3⅛ cups, or 750 ml, of brewed coffee, the extra water being absorbed by the grounds.) Using a filter avoids the sensation of fine particles on the tongue; furthermore, cloudy liquids are harder to taste because the particles physically get in the way of your taste buds. Coffee supplies its own acidity, so there's no need to add any.

1 whole vanilla bean

⅞ cup (80 gr) coffee beans, freshly ground (to yield about ⅞ cup of grounds)

a scant ½ cup (90 gr) sugar

3 cups (350 gr) ice cubes

2¼ cups (530 ml) boiling water

Use a cone-shaped filter coffeemaker such as Melitta or Chemex, or the automatic Technivorm. Place the vanilla bean in the paper filter. Mix the ground coffee with the sugar, and add that to the filter. Place the ice in the glass pot below. Pour the water into the coffeemaker to brew the coffee. Retrieve the vanilla bean from the hot grounds; rinse and save it for future use. Further chill the brew for 5 minutes in the freezer. Freeze as for Melon Ice (page 255). *Makes about 3½ cups (800 ml).*

HONEY ICE CREAM

IN MAKING ICE CREAM, HONEY ISN'T COOKED, so it retains all its fine flavor — assuming the beekeeper or honey processor didn't heat it to begin with, in the course of eliminating crystals that would lead to granulation in the jar, as harmless as that is. (Even conscientious beekeepers do warm their honey a little, so it will flow easily into jars.) But the cold mutes flavor too, so, for instance, orange-blossom honey makes an elegant ice cream whose precise flavor is hard to identify. You might think the solution is to add more honey, but you can't go higher than about one part honey to six of heavy cream by volume, or the ice cream won't harden. My solution is to use the strongest-flavored honeys, such as lavender honey, lime tree honey (*Tilia platyphylla* or relatives; look for *"tilleul"* on French labels, *"tiglio"* on Italian), Greek thyme honey, or dark European forest honey, which has flavors of malt, nuts, and dried fruits. (Forest honey comes not from nectar but from honeydew, which is secreted by aphids and other insects living, typically, on fir trees; the bees gather the honeydew like nectar.) A satisfyingly smooth ice cream requires a machine, hand-powered or electric, and the less expensive sort that requires you to prefreeze the bowl in your freezer is perfectly adequate. The minimal combination of honey and heavy cream tends to be smooth anyway. I don't make this as a custard-based ice cream, which also leads to smoothness, because the egg flavor is a distraction. With heavy cream, a potential problem is that some machines churn bits of butter into the mix. To minimize that, start with as cold a mixture as possible. After the ice cream is churned, put it into a regular freezer to harden fully; the faster that happens, the smoother the result.

3½ cups (800 ml) heavy cream

½ cup (125 ml) strong-flavored honey

Warm about ½ cup (125 ml) of the cream no hotter than your finger can easily stand. Add the honey and stir to combine the two completely. Then stir in the rest of the cream, and chill the mixture deeply in the refrigerator, for about 1 hour, ending with 5 to 10 minutes in the freezer. Stir again, because the honey will have begun to settle, and freeze the mixture according to the instructions for your machine. Once the mixture is thick enough that churning requires considerably more effort — from your arm or from the electric motor — transfer the ice cream to another, covered container and into a regular freezer to complete the hardening. *Makes about 1 quart (1 lt).*

PEARS POACHED IN RED WINE

THE SWEET-ACID BALANCE OF THIS COMBINATION DEPENDS on the particular pears and wine. Unlike most other fruits, most varieties of pears can be picked firm (though not immature), because they ripen off the tree at room temperature. They're ready when their shoulders yield to moderate pressure. For poaching, I like Comice (too ripe, though, and these become too soft when cooked) and Bartlett (the same as Williams and Bon Chrétien). I buy extra pears, letting them ripen for a day or two as needed, and then I choose the best ones for poaching.

2 cups (750 ml) water

about 1½ bottles (750 ml each) nontannic red wine

⅞ cup (180 gr) sugar

1 vanilla bean

1 bay leaf

10 black peppercorns

2 whole cloves or 3 allspice berries

a small piece of cinnamon bark, about 1 inch (2.5 cm) square

a small piece of orange zest, about 1 inch (2.5 cm) square

6 ripe pears

Combine all the ingredients but the pears in a nonreactive pot that is tall rather than wide, and bring the liquid briefly to a boil, stirring to dissolve the sugar.

Peel the pears, leaving the stems, and then core them from the bottom using a melon baller or a small sharp spoon. Simmer the pears slowly in the liquid, adding water if needed to cover, until they are cooked through (a narrow blade should meet no resistance)—30 minutes to 1 hour, depending on the pears' variety and ripeness. Cool the pears, covered, in the syrup.

Remove the pears with a wooden spoon, which is less likely than a metal one to cut into them, and place them on a serving dish. Set each pear upright, taking a thin slice off the bottom if necessary to stabilize it. Remove the spices and orange zest from the liquid, and boil until it is reduced by about two-thirds to a slightly thick syrup—at that point it will boil over if not stirred down. Cool the syrup to room temperature, and just before serving spoon it over the pears to give them a light, ephemeral glaze. *Serves 6.*

PETITS POTS DE CRÈME AU CHOCOLAT

Chocolate Custards

PETITS POTS DE CRÈME PRESENT GOOD CHOCOLATE in a particularly luscious form. Whether you prefer 60 percent, 70 percent, or a higher percentage chocolate is a matter of taste, and the number doesn't necessarily indicate the intensity of chocolate flavor, because it combines both the flavor component and the cocoa butter (the rest being almost all sugar). Some brands, especially Belgian ones, contain significantly more cocoa butter than others. I add no extra vanilla, on the theory that good chocolate already contains the right amount.

1 cup (250 ml) light cream

3½ ounces (100 gr) dark chocolate, at least 60 percent, coarsely chopped

¼ cup (50 gr) sugar

3 egg yolks

Heat the oven to 350° F (175° C). In a small pan on the stove, heat the cream almost to a simmer. Off the heat, add the chocolate to the hot cream, wait 5 minutes, and stir the two together. In a bowl, stir the sugar into the egg yolks, then stir those into the chocolate mixture. Strain into 6 small ceramic cups (no more than ½ cup or 125 ml). Place these in a small oven pan, pour boiling water into the pan up to the height of the custard inside the cups, cover the cups lightly with a sheet of aluminum foil, and poach them in the oven until the custard is barely set, about 20 minutes. Serve tepid. *Serves 6.*

PRUNES IN RED WINE FOR ROQUEFORT

TO BE MORE OR LESS REGIONALLY CONSISTENT, THE PRUNES for this cold-weather combination would come from Agen, which, like the village of Roquefort, is located in the South of France. In late fall, serve the prunes and cheese with a bowl of newly harvested walnuts to crack. I'm not a fan of most of the sweet things that are served today with cheese; it's not that the combinations are necessarily bad but that most of them—especially chutneys with their complicated flavors of fruit, dried fruit, and spice, and tastes of sweet-and-sour and even salt—compete head-on with the cheese. But a few sweet items work very well with cheese. Apart from these prunes, the Basque complement of cherry preserves matches firm Pyrenees ewe's-milk cheese, just as quince goes well with a wider number of firm cheeses. Any cheese has more flavor at cellar temperature than it does cold. When I serve Roquefort, I like a generous wedge (and no other cheese), about 1½ pounds (750 gr) for 6 or 8 people, expecting that some of the cheese and perhaps prunes will be left over. Fresh bread is essential, ideally a tan sourdough loaf (not toast, and never, ever the crisp buttered toast grimly offered today in some restaurants). It's hopeless to try to match this pair with wine; better to pause and return to your glass afterward.

2 dozen prunes

2 cups (250 ml) nontannic red wine

1 tablespoon sugar

Soak the prunes overnight in the wine. Pour off the wine into a nonreactive pan, and reduce it over medium-high heat by half. Add the prunes and sugar, and simmer for 2 to 3 minutes. Serve tepid with cheese and fresh bread. *Serves 6 to 8.*

STEWED RHUBARB WITH HONEY

ALONG WITH ASPARAGUS, MORELS, AND A FEW OTHER ITEMS, rhubarb is one of the ritual foods of spring. The old-farm rhubarb plants I've known in northern New England are green stemmed and much more acidic than the modern red-stemmed varieties, which are also more flavorful. When cooking rhubarb, pay careful attention and take it from the heat before the pieces melt entirely into sauce. There's no noticeable loss in flavor, but the texture is less interesting. Because rhubarb's acidity varies, you have to sweeten it to taste. Here, so as not to diminish the flavor of fine honey with heat, add it only when the rhubarb is nearly cool. The honey shouldn't be strong; to stick to the seasonal theme, it could be a spring honey.

2 pounds (1 kilo) rhubarb stalks, washed and trimmed of bases and leaves

½ cup (100 gr) sugar

light-flavored honey

Cut the rhubarb into pieces of a convenient size for eating, and sprinkle the sugar over them to draw out moisture so the rhubarb won't burn as the cooking starts. Wait at least 45 minutes, then cook the rhubarb slowly, uncovered, starting with low heat and then switching to medium, and stirring once or twice, until the pieces of stalk are soft but not quite falling apart, perhaps 10 minutes. Cool the rhubarb until it is merely warm to the touch. Sweeten to taste with honey, starting with ¼ cup (85 gr). *Serves 6 to 8.*

ZABAIONE

Egg-Wine Foam

TO THE 16TH-CENTURY ITALIAN CHEF Bartolomeo Scappi, *"zabaglione"* was an egg yolk–wine mixture cooked over water to the consistency of "a thick broth" — no foam; it was made with Malmsey (Malvasia) "or some other sweet white wine." Marsala became the preferred wine only in the 20th century, before it fell out of fashion, probably because most Marsala is not very good. A little of it, however, is excellent, such as that from Marco De Bartoli, and many other wines can be used, including very good, old, sweet wine. It's not at all needed, but you can find a copper bowl with a long potlike handle made just for whisking zabaione, or sabayon (the French name came from the Italian two centuries ago). Zabaione can be served warm or cool, on its own or as a warm sauce to complement fresh fruit, such as strawberries or other berries.

4 egg yolks

¼ cup (50 gr) sugar

¼ cup (60 ml) dry Marsala or other white wine

Choose a large metal bowl (if unlined copper, clean it well with vinegar or lemon juice and salt, rinse and dry it) that will sit inside a large pot without resting on the bottom. Fill that large pot with enough water to partly immerse the bowl, and heat the water to a simmer. Put the egg yolks and sugar into the bowl, and whisk until the sugar has mostly dissolved and the mixture has turned pale yellow. Add the wine, and continue to whisk as the zabaione thickens and inflates, more than doubling in volume over a period of 5 to 10 minutes. When spooned out, the zabaione should mound and yet still slowly flow (overcooked, it will begin to deflate). Pour the warm zabaione into individual cups or glasses or into a pitcher for serving warm at the table. Serve immediately, or cool the individual cups to room temperature. With these proportions, the foam will begin to separate after about 2 hours. *Serves 4.*

INDEX

EDWARD BEHR is the chief writer, sometime photographer, and publisher of *The Art of Eating*, the widely acclaimed magazine about food and wine. He is also the author of *The Artful Eater: A Gourmet Investigates the Ingredients of Great Food*. He lives in Vermont.

JAMES MACGUIRE, a New Yorker by birth, is a master of classical French cooking as well as a master bread-baker. He was the chef-owner of the restaurant Le Passe-Partout in Montreal, where he lives; he teaches and consults in the United States and Canada.

GEORGE BATES, an accomplished illustrator, drew inspiration for this collection from his store of vintage cookbooks. He lives in Brooklyn, where most evenings he can be found whipping up some deliciousness for his wife and Boston Terrier, Yardley, who patiently waits by the cutting boards.